MICHEL DEVILLE & BRENDAN O'FARRELL

Brothers in the Kitchen

A Celebration of Friendship and Fine Food

*There is nothing more satisfying than sharing a fine meal with
family and friends, where conversation flows even more liberally than
wine and the bonds we share are strengthened by the experience. Fast food
on the fly, with barely time to say hello, is just not as
enjoyable or memorable and never will be.*

*Great meals need not be excessively elaborate or difficult to prepare.
In these pages, we share what we have learned in our two
lifetimes of cooking and entertaining. We hope that they
will contribute to your own culinary joys.*

Brothers in the Kitchen

DreamCooks.net
140 Lakeside Avenue
Seattle, Washington 98122
www.dreamcooks.net

Compendium, Inc.
600 N. 36th St., Suite 400
Seattle, WA 98103
www.compendiuminc.com

Art Direction and Design by Ani O'Farrell with Ron Snowden

Cover and Food Photography by Christopher Conrad
Conrad & Company
333 2nd Avenue West
Seattle, Washington 98119
www.conradfoto.com

Project Management and Graphic Services by Walter Bell
Trademark Graphic Services
8213 Greenwood Avenue N.
Seattle, Washington 98103
www.trademarkgs.net

Library of Congress Cataloging-in-Publication Data
Deville, Michel, and O'Farrell, Brendan
     Brothers in the Kitchen – A Celebration of Friendship and Fine
     Food/Michel Deville and Brendan O'Farrell
     p. cm
Includes index
ISBN: 0-9779807-0-7
1. Cookery, International
I. O'Farrell, Brendan II. La Table de Michel (Restaurant)

First printing, 2006

Printed in Hong Kong

Dedication

To my darling wife, Ani, my partner in life and love, and to Michel, my mentor in the kitchen and dear friend, for almost all of my adult life.

Without Ani's avid support and artistic talents this book would not have been possible. She has been our collaborator, conscience and gentle critic, every step of the way, from original concept through recipe testing, design, photography and printing.

Michel and I are more than friends and think of each other as brothers. With such clearly French and Irish names we are not entirely sure of the genealogy but we know we are brothers in our hearts, as well as in the kitchen.

The village of Les Baux de Provence

Statue of Molière, French playwright, we assume contemplating a fine evening meal

- CONTENTS -

- Anecdotes & Stories -

The castle ruins at Les Baux de Provence

Foreword

As a long-time publisher and an enthusiastic home cook, I have seen hundreds of cookbooks. Every year many new cookbooks are released, but only a few really catch my eye and fewer still ever get to my kitchen. However, from the first time I saw the manuscript, *Brothers in the Kitchen* really stood out.

Michel Deville and Brendan O'Farrell understand that most people simply do not have unlimited hours to devote to their cooking. The premise of this book is that great meals can be prepared in a reasonable amount of time, and that many of the best dishes are actually quite simple to make. Equally important this book offers far more than recipes. It is filled with other interesting and useful information that I am sure you will enjoy. In a way, the book is a 'collage' of cooking tips, instructions and stories, plus recipes for delicious dishes from an international perspective that can only be gained by living and cooking around the globe.

The authors' attention to detail, in recipe specifications, as well as in testing and refining recipes for the home cook will help to assure successful results. The wine suggestions, with each recipe are a bit of "icing on the cake." The 'guest recipes' are from internationally acclaimed chefs and restaurateurs. Their contributions are testimony to the regard they have for the authors and this book.

One thing that I think makes this book quite special is the personal relationship of Michel and Brendan. Their close friendship and shared passion for food, wine and entertaining comes through very clearly. Our motto, at Compendium Publishing, is "Live Inspired." This book exudes inspiration, celebration and friendship.

If you have a love of good food and find true excitement in cooking to entertain family and friends, this book should inspire you to greater culinary accomplishments, for many years to come.

Dan Zadra
Publisher and Editor
Compendium, Inc.

In front of La Table de Michel restaurant before the evening guests arrive

Friendship and Fine Food

Michel Deville and I met by chance in 1969. He and three of his colleagues were walking past my house in Seattle and asked for directions to a local park. Instead of just pointing the way, I walked them to the park and stayed to chat. Michel explained that they had all come to work at new French restaurant, The Mirabeau, where he was to be the executive chef. That chance meeting was the beginning of a lifelong friendship.

With respect to Neil Simon and his award-winning Broadway play, I suppose that in some ways Michel and I are a bit of an 'odd couple'. Michel is a master chef who has spent his career life in restaurants and the hospitality industry. He is truly an artist, with a God-given, instinctive talent for cooking. My own career has been in the technical worlds of finance and corporate management.

But our similarities far outweigh our differences. We are both passionate about our work and our hobbies, and we are both perfectionists. We share a love of food and cooking, although in that arena, Michel is the master and I am still his student. We have both traveled the world in our work, living and/or working in Asia, Europe and North America, always seeking out the best of local cuisine to add to our own culinary repertoires.

Michel was born and raised in Provence, in the South of France, where a bounty of produce, meat and game is famous around the world and where sea creatures from the Mediterranean and the Atlantic arrive freshly caught every day. Michel began his training as a chef in Avignon at age 14 and it became instantly apparent that he was born to cook. His career progressed rapidly, moving quickly up the kitchen hierarchy to become a fully qualified chef at age 20.

At age 22, Michel left France and went to London, where he became a *chef de partie* in the kitchens of the world famous Savoy Hotel under the guidance of the Chef Monsieur La Planche, a legend of the culinary arts. He then moved to become Sous-chef at the Knightsbridge Sporting Club, with Chef Jean Banchet. With Jean and four other French chef colleagues, Michel moved to America, where all worked at the Playboy Club & Resort at Lake Geneva. Later, Jean opened the renowned Le Français Restaurant, in Wheeling, Illinois. *Bon Appétit* magazine proclaimed Le Français the "Best Restaurant in America" and Chef Jean the "Best Chef in America."

My own early exposure to food and cooking, on the other hand, was far from gourmet. As a child in British Columbia and Seattle, most home cooking emphasized meat and potatoes, with fish thrown in on Fridays to satisfy the local parish priest. No matter the ingredients, they were invariably cooked beyond recognition. Herbs and spices consisted of salt and pepper, with hot mustard for Sunday roast beef, always on the table and rarely included in the preparation. Luckily, my own mother was an exception to the local norms, an accomplished cook and baker and the head cook in a school dining room. She guided me in my earliest cooking endeavors. A friend's Italian mother introduced me to Italian cooking, teaching me a few of her own dishes. In college, I frequently ate at a neighborhood restaurant, which featured a mix of Italian and broader 'continental' dishes. Over time, I became acquainted with the chef and soon spent time in the kitchen, learning to cook a few more dishes that I could make at home. These experiences began a lifelong passion for good food, cooking and entertaining.

Chef Michel Deville (c. 1970)

The Mirabeau was Seattle's first award-winning French restaurant and its first real taste of classic French cuisine. Located on the 46th floor of Seattle's tallest building, the restaurant enjoyed a sweeping view of the city that included Mt. Rainier rising into the southern sky, Puget Sound and the Olympics to the west, and sometimes, on a clear night, the northern lights dancing on the horizon. The venue was spectacular and the food was even more so. With Michel directing the kitchen, The Mirabeau quickly became the place to dine in Seattle and the Pacific Northwest. I often went there and always stopped by the kitchen to see Michel. We soon became fast friends. Michel acquired in me a personal Northwest tour guide and I found the ultimate personal cooking tutor.

Learning at the Elbow of a Master Chef

On Saturdays, when The Mirabeau was open only for dinner, I would join Michel in the morning as he prepared for the evening meal. At first, I just watched and listened, somewhat in awe. Gradually, Michel encouraged me to try things, patiently showing me again when I hesitated or faltered. With each lesson, my meager skills began to improve. Over time, as I came to feel more comfortable and relaxed, the benefits of his expert tutoring really began to show.

My first impression was, "he makes it look so easy but why, when I try it, is it so difficult?" John McEnroe made serving tennis balls and placing them, almost every time, at the corners of the service court, look easy. He was a world top ranked tennis professional who had practiced serving for an hour or more each day for years. So too it is with top chefs like Michel. He has been practicing for many hours, every day, since he started his training, at age 14. And, like great athletes or other kinds of artists, he is blessed with tremendous natural talent.

When I first spent time in Michel's kitchen, at The Mirabeau, it wasn't the first time I had been in a restaurant kitchen or the first time I had been given a lesson by a professional chef. But there was something different; something that, at first, I just could not put my finger on. And then it came to me. When Michel did anything in the kitchen, chopping an onion, cutting steaks from a whole tenderloin or making a sauce, it just seemed completely natural and absolutely effortless. And everything seemed to turn out perfectly, every time. It was a bit intimidating, to say the least, even though Michel showed tremendous patience with his new 'apprentice'. I once commented to a mutual friend, "It is like taking painting lessons from Vincent Van Gogh, except that Michel has both ears and is not nearly as mad."

Something that made a tremendous difference, for me, was Michel's approach to teaching. First, he would carefully show me how something should be done. Second, he would watch as I tried to replicate what he had done, providing a bit of coaching, as needed. And third, after I had practiced, by myself, a few times, Michel would observe, taste the result, and praise or critique the outcome.

He also helped me to understand that you do not have to be a naturally talented, professional chef, in order to learn to make excellent meals of which you can be very proud. But you do have to work at it and lessons will definitely help, as long as the chef you are learning from follows Michel's 'show, coach, practice and check' approach to teaching. After more than 35 years, I am is still learning from Michel every time we are together in a kitchen, which is now at least several days each month.

Michel taught me the fine points of preparation and, perhaps much more importantly, his special chef's knowledge of cooking techniques and which ingredients worked well together, as well as those that did not. He coached me in the selection of food products and showed me cooking by the senses: sight, smell, touch, and taste.

A Growing Bond

In our time together away from the kitchen, our friendship continued to deepen. Whether dining at someone else's restaurant, walking in the hills or going fishing, we shared our hopes and dreams and often laughed until our sides hurt. Sometimes, when he had a day off, Michel would cook with me, in my own home kitchen. Those were wonderful times. Other friends I invited for those dinners were amazed, first at the surprising collaboration between the French 'celebrity' chef and their enthusiastic amateur cooking pal and, second, by the delicious meals they were able to enjoy.

Michel eventually moved on from The Mirabeau but we stayed in close touch. Wherever Michel was, I would visit and, in time, as teacher and pupil we became cooking compatriots. In 1975, Michel opened his first restaurant, Chez Michel, in a Seattle suburb. After three years, Michel sold Chez Michel and moved on, again, to become executive chef for a leading hotel company.

In 1979, he returned to Seattle, where he opened Deville's on Broadway, a bistro-style French restaurant

Michel in the Chez Michel dining room (c. 1976)

La Table de Michel restaurant in Saint Rémy de Provence, France

that became an immediate success. After six years, however, Michel sold that restaurant also and moved to England, as head chef at the White Elephant Club, the chosen gathering place for many film and theater celebrities. He moved from there to become Executive Chef and Director of Food & Beverage, for London's Richmond Gate Hotel Group.

After six years, he opened another new restaurant, Chez Maria, in scenic Richmond upon Thames. As luck would have it, I had been spending part of every month in

Michel carving tableside at the Richmond Gate (c. 1988)

London on business and our kitchen collaboration was able to continue. However, after 10 years, the Chez Maria property was sold for development and that chapter of Michel's life came to a close.

My own work took me across the country and around the world. My travels enabled me to experience an array of new cuisines, which I brought home to my home kitchens, in America and Europe. Whenever Michel and I were together, I would share the new dishes I had learned or developed and he would help me refine them.

In 2001, Michel returned to Avignon, where his career began, to become executive chef and Director of Food & Beverage at the Hôtel du Palais des Papes and the Lutrin Restaurant. The family of his old mentor, Denis Gayte, owns the hotel and Denis' grandson, Bruno, manages it. Every few weeks, I would travel to Avignon to spend time in the kitchen with Michel and he would show me that area of Provence, as only a native can.

Some Dreams Do Come True

In the earliest years of our friendship, we talked about having a restaurant together. But life and our two very different careers intervened in such a way that, until recently, it was no more than idle conversation. In early 2005, Michel and I finally opened La Table de Michel Restaurant together, in the village of Saint-Rémy de Provence, near Avignon in the South of France.

In 1982, Michel published a small cookbook for his restaurant patrons, which included just ten classic French dishes, all chosen for the simplicity of their preparation. Over the years, we also often talked about writing a cookbook together that would expand on Michel's original concept, adding from our experiences together and bringing in dishes from other cuisines that we both love. But that too was only conversation, until now. Opening the restaurant in Provence turned out to be the catalyst for finally getting started with the book.

Creating the Cookbook

Although this book is written in the first person, it is the product of close collaboration between the two of us and my wife, Ani. English is my first language and I have written many articles, papers and other books, as part of my normal work. So Michel

and I agreed that we would plan everything together but I would be responsible for the writing. He would review and edit and we would each cook all the dishes to be sure the recipes actually worked.

We then had friends who are avid home cooks with varying knowledge, experience and skills, test every recipe as first written. They each made notes of anything they found unclear and let us know when they thought we had missed the boat on our specification of seasonings or quantities. We also had chef friends, who have authored successful cookbooks, review our drafts and make suggestions, as well as debate the merits of some of our initial text.

What We Have Included and Why

This book features some of our favorite dishes and celebrates our friendship, our shared love of food and wine, and our years of cooking and entertaining together. We wanted every dish to be easy to make, so we have only included recipes that meet that criterion. Since I am primarily a home cook, with limited time, most of the meals I make take no more than a couple of hours for total preparation and attended cooking.

In my earliest years of cooking and entertaining, I often agonized over what wine to serve with a particular dish or course. In the days when I cooked from recipes, I remember using cookbooks that suggested specific wines, with winemaker, vineyard and vintage. Invariably, when I wanted to find one of these wines, they were sold out. In time, I came to appreciate that many different wines could be successfully paired with almost all dishes. So, we have included wine suggestions, for each starter and main dish, based on styles of wine rather than specific selections.

Over the years, there have been certain restaurants and chefs who Michel and I have known and whose culinary talents we have particularly admired. We have included a few of those chefs' 'signature recipes', along with information about them and the restaurants where we discovered the particular dishes.

Naturally, our recipes are influenced by the places where Michel and I grew up and have lived. Michel was raised and began his cooking career in Provence and I discovered Provençal cooking when I began to travel there on vacations. I grew up in the Pacific Northwest, which is also where Michel first became a celebrated chef. We have both lived and worked in the British Isles, which accounts for why we have included 'Guest Chef' recipes, stories and photographs from England and Ireland. Provence was under Roman and Italian rule for centuries and there are significant French and Italian influences in our own cooking and as a result, in this cookbook. For the recipes that originated in France, we start with the name of the dish in French and provide the English language description directly underneath.

This is also not a cookbook for the diet obsessed. You have come to the wrong cookbook if you want to avoid all butter and cheese or richness. We do, however, believe strongly in healthy eating but our emphasis is on simplicity and flavor, not calorie counting. In truth, none of the recipes included here will cause instantaneous obesity. We know that for some people, healthy eating does mean avoiding almost all sugar, fat or carbohydrates. But for most, eating in moderation does allow a bit of occasional indulgence and since our focus is on entertaining, we hope you will find that our dishes are appropriate for that purpose.

In developing this book, we have focused on dishes we particularly enjoy for which all ingredients should be readily available at your local supermarket or specialty food shop. We have intentionally avoided more complex preparations and harder to find ingredients.

When cooking in a restaurant, we are always 'entertaining', so our recipes reflect that reality. This cookbook, therefore, is aimed primarily at entertaining friends, family or other guests in your own home. It is not an every-day, meals-on-the-fly cookbook and it is not intended to be although many of our recipes are completely suitable for every-day family meals.

Appendices to the book include: additional information about wine; detailed tables for converting American measures to metric measures and vice-versa; and references for food and wine information resources, kitchen tools and equipment, food producers, and food producer organizations.

Producing this book has truly been a labor of love. As I said earlier, Michel and I had talked about doing this for years and actually doing it has been an absolute joy for both of us. When Ani and I were living in Dublin, with our children, Michel would visit us. On one occasion, we cooked together for a home dinner party for friends. Over dessert, we told our guests about the early dreams we had had of opening a restaurant together and writing a cookbook. One of our guests, with her lilting Irish accent, said, "Ah well, you really should because you two are definitely dream cooks." The name stuck and we have laughed about it ever since. Finally, those youthful dreams are a reality.

We hope that you will enjoy preparing, sampling and serving these dishes, as much as we always do. We wish you happy cooking and successful entertaining.

Bon appetit!

Getting Started

Love of good food, a bit of desire, and a couple of hours at most, are all that is needed to prepare great meals that your family, friends and guests are guaranteed to remember. Great dishes can be surprisingly easy to create but before you turn on the stove, you need to have some basic ingredients and tools on hand.

Preparing dishes with friend and work colleague, Anthony Major

THE MOST IMPORTANT INGREDIENT

The most important ingredient, in all cooking, is the cook! Without someone who wants to cook, nothing else matters. Note that we said, *"wants to cook,"* not *"likes to"* or *"has to."* *"Wants to cook,"* for us, has a silent, parenthetical *"well"* appended to it. Some people eat to live and others live to eat. Some people cook, simply to eat, while for others cooking is a joy. It is both a craft and an art. An artist has his canvas, paints and brush; a chef has his pots, knives, flames, ovens, and food ingredients. So, the most important ingredient in cooking is someone who wants to create well prepared and artfully presented meals.

Often, I meet people who say to us that they *"would love to be able to cook but are hopeless in the kitchen."* No one is born knowing how to cook, just

as no one is born knowing how to produce magnificent artworks or how to successfully perform cardiac surgery. When I talk more with these people I usually find that they have had little practice and often have been discouraged by one or two less than stellar cooking performances. In the latter case, they have avoided any possibility of improvement by staying out of the kitchen except to go to the refrigerator.

Wanting to cook well is the starting point. Learning to cook well takes time and practice. Like any other skill or expertise, cooking well requires cooking often, at least until a solid foundation, level of ease with preparation, timing and accomplishment has been achieved. So, if you do want to cook well, accept that lots of practice and some disappointments along the way are just part of the journey from novice to

accomplished chef. As cooks, we really do learn from our mistakes. So accept those, as well, with good cheer and determination.

PLANNING YOUR MENUS

A menu is a complete meal, usually consisting of three or more courses, although there are certainly times when a complete meal may be only one course, such as soup with bread and cheese. In planning menus, for the restaurant, we pay attention to what ingredients are likely to be available over the next couple of months. Other than special occasion menus, the restaurant menus remain the same for 8 to 10 weeks but allow for 'specials' that change each day, depending on what we find at the market.

Planning home menus is different. They are almost always meant for only one meal so, in a way, everything is a 'daily special'. But the same principles also apply. Start out with an idea of what you are going to make but be prepared to modify it with what you discover at the market. If you planned a Caesar Salad (page 37) with shrimp but discover that there is no fresh shrimp available that day, you will need a Plan B. Fresh crabmeat that is available is a perfect substitute. Voilà, problem solved!

In planning home entertaining menus, take care to select courses that complement each other. A spicy soup or starter may not work well with a delicately flavored fish as the main dish. Think about your guests. Will they have large or small appetites? Will some want cocktails, before dinner, in addition to wine? How many are you serving and what implications may that have on your choice of dishes? Also think about portion sizes. If you are serving four or more courses, instead of three, portion sizes should be proportionately smaller. Before you go to the market, check your cupboards and refrigerator to confirm supplies of any necessary staples you will need like eggs, butter, onions, flour or rice. And be sure to remember the small touches, like herbs, greens or decorative small fruits and 'baby' vegetables to add accents to your dishes.

Ideas for full three- and four-course dinners are provided at the end of the book. Each menu has been chosen with balance and complementary dishes in mind.

QUALITY FOODS

The second most important ingredient in great cooking is quality raw food material. Achieving great meals becomes much easier with quality food. Of course, poor preparation can turn the best ingredients into an unpalatable meal. And, sometimes, a talented cook can turn ordinary or even mediocre ingredients into a decent meal.

Note that the word used here is "quality." I did not say "expensive." Great meals can be created using quite inexpensive foodstuffs. Many of the recipes contained in this book call for ingredients that are not expensive and none should be hard to find. Hearty soups and stews, such as *Soupe au Pistou* (page 59) or *Boeuf en Daube à la Provençale* (page 89), are made with less expensive cuts of meat, bones and scraps and other inexpensive ingredients. Some recipes do call for relatively more costly ingredients but many do not.

How does one know the quality of the foods he or she is buying in this age of mass production? Most foods are derived from animals, including sea creatures, and vegetables; formerly living creatures and inanimate but live growing things. They are, therefore, highly variable and innately complex. In recent years, the term "organic" has come to be used to indicate varying degrees of a lack of chemicals or pesticides used in growing both animal products and produce. In fact, however, regardless of growing methods, almost all food is organic. That is, in the dictionary definition

Shopping for vegetables, on a Saturday morning, at 'Turnips', Borough Market, London

of the word, *"Of, relating to, or derived from living organisms: organic matter."*

Given the innate complexity and variability of foodstuffs, how do we know if the foods we are buying are, in fact, quality? In many cases we can judge quality, at least in part, by sight, touch, smell and taste. Green vegetables and salad greens should be crisp and bright. With fresh produce, look for shape, color, texture and fresh smell, and avoid vegetables that show any bruising or discoloration. Colors should be pronounced. If melons are very soft to the touch, they are probably over-ripe. With melons, apples, pears, peaches, apricots and similar fruits, look for even slight bruises and avoid any that have such blemishes. Berries should be firm but not hard and vividly colored. Always check the bottoms of berry containers for any signs of developing mold.

When selecting poultry products, be sure that those you choose are cold to the touch, look at color and texture, and be sure to smell the package. Color should be consistent. If the edges are dry or even slightly discolored, leave it. Fresh poultry will smell clean. And, in the United States, only buy poultry products that are 'Grade A'. When choosing fish and seafood, shop with your eyes, fingers and nose. Fresh fish does

not smell 'fishy'. It has a fresh, mild smell. Skins of fresh finfish should have a shiny, almost metallic appearance. The eyes of a whole fish should be bright, clear and full, and slightly bulging. Check the inside of the gills, which should be a vivid red color. If the gill color is faded or there are hints of slime on the inside of the gills, pass on that fish. Avoid shell fish with broken or damaged shells and be sure that the shells of clams, mussels, and oysters are tightly closed. An open shell is a sure sign of a dead animal inside, which is likely to be spoiled. With crab, prawns, lobster and crayfish, look for damage to shells and be sure to smell fresh crustaceans. A mild sea smell is normal but a 'fishy' smell or any hint of ammonia indicates that the animal's flesh is beginning to decompose.

Meat, however, is more difficult. Our friend, Andrew Sharp, pictured here, says, "buy the man." Andrew's family and ancestors have been in the beef and sheep business, in the North of England, for more than 400 years. Andrew finishes beef, veal, mutton and lamb products, sourced from a co-operative of small farmers, in Cumbria, in the Northwest of England. From Tuesday to Saturday he has a stall at Borough Market in London. Andrew knows how every creature has been raised, fed and cared for. The co-operative has its own stringent rules for the care, feeding and killing of animals, which go beyond governmental requirements. We know that the meat we buy from Andrew is absolutely top-quality.

When Andrew says "buy the man", he means know the people from who you buy your food. We have more than a commercial or retail relationship with all of our suppliers. I have been buying from Pure Food Fish in Seattle's Pike Place Market for more than 40 years. It was Michel's source for fish and seafood in his Seattle restaurants. The owner, Sol Amon, supplied fish to my mother, when she ran the school kitchen. It's the relationship that makes the great difference in the quality of the fish and seafood I serve family or guests. When Sol recommends one fish over another, I know that I can count on his expertise and honesty.

In England, Ireland, and France, we have dealt with the same butchers and poultry or game producers and food stores for many years. In many cases, we source foods directly from the producers and, although that may not be possible for everyone, the same principles apply. Deal with people you trust. Stick with them and get to know them personally. They will value your loyal patronage and help assure that you are getting true quality. If they do not, you will soon know and you can move on to find ones who will. I have found that this works just as well with local supermarkets as with specialty food stores.

COOKING WITH GAS

It is true that cooking on a gas range makes it easier to control your heat and timing. Electric stove burners take longer to rise to a given heat and much longer to come down to any reduced level of heat. That is an inconvenience but not a fatal flaw. I do prefer to cook with gas, as practically all restaurants do, but with a little extra patience and a few tricks, great meals can also be created on an electric stovetop. In fact Michel's friend Anton Mosimann, the world renowned chef and proprietor of Mosimann's in London, recently told a group of visiting hospitality executives that he had switched his kitchens to electric induction cooking, which he considers superior to gas. When we asked Chef Anton about this, he said:

"When Mosimann's opened, 17 years ago, the kitchen was 90% gas and 10% electric. Five years ago we took the decision to introduce electric induction cooking which saved us approximately 50% in costs and

Andrew Sharp

today we continue to reap the benefits. Contrary to those who claim 'gas is the only way', the advantages of cooking with electric are numerous. Not only is it financially beneficial but it also makes a more comfortable environment for our chefs to work in as it produces less heat in the kitchen. Further, as the surfaces are flat they are easier to clean and maintain."

One simple trick with home electric ranges, for things that need to boil and then immediately simmer, is to use two burners; one at high heat and the other lower. Boil on the first and simmer on the second.

COOKING WITH WINE

Many of our recipes and sauces call for wine as an ingredient in the preparation. In most cases, at home, where just a little bit of wine is required, I use the same wine I am going to serve with the dish. In recipes calling for more wine, such as *Boeuf en Daube à la Provençale* (page 89) or *Coq au Vin* (page 103), be sure to use a wine that you would also be happy to drink.

If you are going to cook with a wine that has been opened for more than a week or two, be sure to taste it to confirm that it has not spoiled. Spoiled wine can ruin the taste of a dish. You will know when a wine is spoiled by tasting it. It may not have turned to vinegar but the taste will be unpleasant enough that you should recognize it instantly.

KITCHEN STAPLES

Just as offices need paper, pens, envelopes, and other basic consumables, a well-stocked kitchen needs a few basic foodstuffs, always on hand. The list is actually quite short and these things, like paper and pens, tend to have very long shelf lives so there is little danger of spoilage if properly stored. We are talking about very basic ingredients that are needed for many dishes, like flour, cornstarch, pasta, rice, salt, pepper and sugar. Basic foods that have longer shelf lives, such as onions, garlic, potatoes, and eggs also make sense to have on hand unless you only cook occasionally.

Herbs and spices, used well, can be the difference between ordinary and extraordinary dishes. Fresh herbs are almost always desirable but dry herbs, if they are not too old, can be a fine substitute and are always readily available. Dry herbs and spices should be replaced once a year to ensure the best quality and flavor. We grow fresh herbs in the garden or planters at home and always have them on hand.

Fresh herbs are, of course, seasonal but many of the most common herbs can be obtained fresh at most times of the year. The ones used most frequently in our recipes include basil, bay leaves, cilantro, fennel, mint, oregano, parsley, rosemary, tarragon and thyme. There are dozens of varieties of other herbs that can make your dishes really stand out and introduce wonderful additional hints of flavor.

In past centuries, men sailed the world in search of spices. Today, we need only go to a local supermarket to find a vast array of spices to enhance flavors in our dishes. Having a selection of spices on hand enables you to be prepared to create a variety of flavors. Over the years, I have found two spice brands that I can

always rely on for freshness and quality, Spice Islands® and Vanns®. Spice Islands products are found in many supermarkets in the Western U. S. and Vanns products are found more commonly in the Eastern and Southern U. S. Both offer a wide array of different spices.

Pre-mixed spices and flavoring blends can also be useful. Vanns, with its Southeastern roots, is our source for Creole Seasoning and Gumbo Filé (Sassafras) Powder, which we use in our New Orleans Style Gumbo (page 67). Vanns' products are all natural and do not contain any sugar, salt, fillers, MSG or preservatives and they package and ship products within 90 days of harvesting, which guarantees freshness.

Two other favorites are Spice Islands® Beau Monde seasoning and Szechuan Seasoning, both from the Spice Islands Trading Company. Spice Islands® Beau Monde seasoning is an all-purpose seasoning containing salt, dextrose, onion, and celery seed. Its purpose is to subtly enhance the natural flavor of ingredients without creating a specific taste. Spice Islands® Szechuan Seasoning is a blend of oriental spices that, used sparingly, adds a bit of zest to meat, poultry and fish dishes without becoming too spicy. It also adds an interesting taste to Asian salad dressings.

There is an absolutely wondrous array of vinegars and oils available on the market. Think of quality olive oil as the first absolute essential oil for any kitchen, but other oils are also important. We like different

Ani at a local supermarket, with list in hand

French, Greek and Italian olive oils, and California is now producing excellent ones. Catherine and Jean-Benoit Hughes, in Les Baux de Provence, produce one particular favorite, Castelas, on 100 acres of olive groves, located just 6 miles from our restaurant. At a recent international competition held in Paris, it was rated as one of the ten best olive oils in the world and has won many other awards. It is now available at many specialty gourmet food stores in North America.

Olive oil and vinegar selection at DeLaurenti's Specialty Food and Wine, Seattle

Other oils are also important and you may wish to have supplies of vegetable oil, seed oils and nut oils on hand. Sesame oil is an important ingredient in many Asian dishes and nut oils, such as peanut, almond, hazelnut, and walnut oils can add to the taste of many dishes.

A variety of vinegars are also good to have on hand. My 'staple' vinegars include balsamic, cider, raspberry, red wine, and unseasoned rice wine. Balsamic vinegar, from Modena, Italy, is the original but other regions, including California, are also producing excellent varieties. It is also important to remember

that different vinegars, within a particular category of vinegar, are very different from one another. Red wine vinegars range from very light to very dark. Balsamic vinegar comes in a variety of flavors not to mention a variety of prices. You need to taste different vinegars, just as you need to taste different wines and olive oils, in order to know the ranges of tastes. One balsamic vinegar may go very well in an Italian salad dressing but not nearly as well if it is used in cooking.

You may also want to keep several fruit sauces (blackberry and raspberry, as well as red and/or black currant) on hand, and brandy, Armagnac, cognac, liqueurs and rum for use in cooking.

POTS, PANS & TOOLS

These are the tools of the chef's trade. The right equipment can make a significant difference to your cooking and the ease with which you prepare wonderful dishes. That is not to say that great meals cannot be made with less than ideal equipment; it is just that the right equipment makes everything easier. In recent years, professional grade kitchen equipment, tools, pots, and pans are being made for the home kitchen.

There are many kitchen tools used for specific purposes. Although you can use a saucepan in a skillet of water as a substitute, an actual double boiler is purpose-made and, for certain sauces, frostings, and desserts, makes it much easier to achieve the desired result. A wok or stir fry pan makes stir frying much easier than using an ordinary skillet. Different sized skillets make cooking dishes of different sizes and volumes much easier.

Good knives are a chef's most essential preparation tools and there are a number of very high-quality knives available on the market. Better knives hold their edges longer and will last longer, even with constant use. Always keeping your knives sharp makes preparation and serving easier. I like 6" and 8" cook's knives for most preparation chores but for filleting fish, boning a leg of lamb, slicing bread or cheese, carving a roast or making decorative cuts, I use specialty knives made for each purpose.

The feel of a knife in your hand will probably lead you to using one knife, more often than others. You may find that larger cook's knives make dicing and slicing vegetables go faster, as you can cut a greater number of pieces at the same time.

One item of kitchen equipment I would never be without is a mandoline, which makes everyday slicing

chores easier. It duplicates some of the functions of food processors but is very handy to have, especially when your food processor is being dedicated to other cooking chores. In fact, for its functions, I usually choose the mandoline over the processor, simply for ease of set-up, use, and clean up.

TIMING IS EVERYTHING

Many experienced chefs will tell you that timing is often the most difficult aspect of fine cooking. Knowing what can be prepared in advance and what must be 'cooked to order' is the first issue in timing. Cooking different foods to the right degree of 'doneness' is the second. And, finally, assuring that all hot parts of a single course are actually served hot is another challenge for many home cooks.

There are some very important, fundamental differences between cooking in a restaurant and cooking to entertain at home. Cooking in a restaurant is just cooking. When cooking to entertain at home, the cook is usually cooking and entertaining, as well as eating with his or her guests, all in the same timeframe. That places additional burdens upon the home cook-host in relation to timing of dishes and courses, as well as balancing time to be with guests with time to be sure the meal is right. Of course, the home cook-host has one other very distinct advantage over chefs in a restaurant. They have only one set menu to prepare.

Timing is the variable ingredient in cooking that foils many novice cooks as well as some experienced ones. Mastering timing in the kitchen, to some considerable extent, comes from practice but other factors are also important. Planning is the key. Before you start preparing a meal be sure that everything you need is at hand. **The best way to do this is by reading all your recipes, including ingredients and cooking method, before you even think about starting.** This includes foods, as well as equipment and tools. Be sure you know where all your equipment, tools, and ingredients are, and be sure that everything is readily accessible. Taking time to look for a colander when the pasta is already done is sure to result in overcooked pasta. There is nothing worse than realizing you are missing a key ingredient or tool in the middle of preparing a meal.

Although timing is important it doesn't have to be perfect to the second or even the minute. Most small errors in timing will not ruin your cooking so relax and focus on your dishes with attention to, but not paranoia about, timing. Timing can also be variable, depending on factors like the thickness of ingredients and stove or oven temperature fidelity.

ADVANCE PREPARATION

Many ingredients and some complete dishes can be successfully prepared ahead of time. All stocks and many sauces can be prepared in advance and kept refrigerated or frozen until you are ready to use them. Salad ingredients, vegetables and potatoes can be washed, peeled, chopped, cut or torn at least an hour or two before assembly or cooking. Store peeled or cut potatoes in cold water to prevent discoloration. Cut vegetables can be stored for several hours in a refrigerator, preferably in airtight containers or plastic Zip-Lock™ bags.

Almost all soups can be made in advance and, in some cases, one or two days before you plan to serve them. Many soups benefit from advance preparation and their flavor is enhanced by the storage process, which can either be simmering or refrigeration, depending on the specific soup and ingredients. Some dishes (see Seared Ahi Tuna, page 77, and Crème Brûlée, page 172) absolutely require advance preparation and most meals will benefit from as much advance preparation as possible.

PRESENTATION

The way you arrange food on a plate can contribute significantly to the overall impression of the main meal. In the culinary world, this is called "plating" your dishes. Each main and side dish is placed neatly on the plate but not touching or overlapping the rim.

In most cases, the main dish is at the front of the plate, slightly to the side but not touching the rim, with side dishes next to it. Sauces are poured over and around both main dish and starch side dishes, and sometimes also over the vegetable side dishes. Sauces may also be poured first with food placed on top.

The most appealing placements will depend on the specific combination of foods and the shapes of the dishes or bowls you are using. If you are plating main dishes individually, place a steak or chicken breast at the front of the plate facing a guest and slightly to one side. Arrange longer, thin vegetables in the same direction as each other on the plate, alongside the meat. Serve a starch dish alongside the vegetables and just behind the meat dish. Serve rice using a mold or ramekin to make a neat, attractive serving. A sprig or two of herbs and a bit of color will also enhance the appearance of a dish. And don't forget to wipe drips of sauce or food from the rim of the plate with a clean cloth or paper towel.

The same principles apply when you are serving a family style meal on serving platters and in serving bowls. Garnish and accent is just as important for the appearance of food served family style as it is for individual plates. Great taste and attractive presentation, together, will assure success.

A FINAL WORD

Whenever you are entertaining at home or just cooking a casual meal, we hope that the information provided here, as well as our recipes, will help your cooking experiences be more successful and enjoyable. Remember that consistent success in the kitchen requires practice. Also remember the "6 Ps": Prior Proper Planning Prevents Poor Performance, and that practice makes perfect, in time. So, take the time, learn from your successes and your mistakes and, above all, enjoy yourself.

Happy Cooking and Bon Appétit!

Sol Amon, Pure Food Fish at Seattle's Pike Place Market with some of the morning catch.

Matching Wines with Foods

*"Which wine should I serve with this dish?" "What wine would
you recommend?" How many times have we heard these questions?
As the most experienced sommeliers will tell you there are so many wines
produced in the world that the choices can seem almost overwhelming.
The sheer variety of wines is just as vast as the variety of foods.*

Many wine shops as well as distributors have wine specialists to guide and answer specific questions. The sommelier in a restaurant has a more complex role. How many times have you gone out for dinner with a party of four who all order the same thing? Not many, I'm sure. Therefore, the sommelier's challenge is to find one bottle that complements all the orders or recommend two bottles that accomplish that purpose.

Most serious wine shops will typically stock between 1,000 and 4,000 different wines, at any one time. Most specialty wine shops can find a particular wine you are looking for but if they cannot find the exact one, a knowledgeable wine merchant will get one that is very similar in taste and character.

Michel and I have both tasted and enjoyed literally thousands of different wines in our lives. We taste new releases to decide which wines we will cellar for later use and which ones to include on the current restaurant wine list. We choose wines for our own home cellars, some of which we will drink very soon and others we will lay down for many years, until they reach their peaks.

We are most familiar with American and French wines and we have some knowledge of Australian, Chilean, German, New Zealand, South African, Spanish and Swiss wines.

Every year we visit the wine regions in France and America and go to wineries we have known for many years and discover others that are new or just new to us. In selecting wines for a particular meal or dish at home we begin with those we know best and usually those we already have on hand.

Wine selection is primarily a matter of personal taste. If you enjoy a particular wine with a particular dish then it is the right one!

If your experience and knowledge of wine is limited, what can you do to be certain that a wine you select will go nicely with a particular dish and, more importantly, that your guests will like it? Wine likes and dislikes are so personal that you can never know that every guest will like all of the wines that you choose.

There are, however, some things you can do to increase the chances that your selections will please most, if not always all, of your guests and yourself. First, find a knowledgeable wine merchant who you can trust. Second, taste wines with particular dishes and make a few notes about the wines. Learn what styles of wine you like best with certain foods and note those with which you and your guests are less than impressed. Over time, you will develop an understanding of which styles of wine are most successful for you.

Remember that wines do not need to be expensive to be enjoyable. There are very nice wines all over the world that you can obtain at reasonable prices that will complement your dishes and leave your guests smiling. If they are happy, you should be as well.

Matching wines with foods seems to be a problem for many people. Both Michel and I are inclined toward dry and medium dry wines. Our tastes for sweeter wines lean toward dessert wines and fortified wines, such as ports or sherries. The most common advice is, "Red wine goes with meat and white wine goes with fish." There is some truth in that statement so it is a reasonable starting point but the real truth is somewhat more complicated. And, as I said before, the most important criteria are what you and your guests like best and only you can discover that. You will find that some wines complement particular dishes more than others. You will know it almost instantly when you find a pairing you really like.

Red wines contain tannins so when served with some fish, they can take on a bit of a metallic taste. Red wines that are light in tannins, like lighter red Burgundies, merlot and pinot noir can be very nice with some fish, such as salmon or trout and also with fish that has more dense flesh such as monkfish. Lighter, dry and somewhat acidic white wines go best with most

Brendan opening wine for guests at home

more delicate fish. Chablis, Montrachet, Meursault, Mâcon villages, Sancerre and lighter, less oakey new world chardonnays are preferred matches with most fish dishes.

One thing you may wish to avoid is serving or drinking any dry wines with desserts and sweet dishes. Wines served with dessert should be at least as sweet as the dessert itself, which is why late harvest Rieslings go well with fruit tarts. Before serving dessert, remove the wines from the table that you have served with the main course and then allow your guests a few minutes to finish any wines remaining in their glasses.

Serve more robust red wines with more robust and flavorful red meat dishes. Full-bodied claret, American cabernet sauvignon, or petit sirah all go well with steaks, such as Filet au Poivre (page 87). Medium-to-full-bodied red Burgundies or pinot noir go nicely with game dishes. With roast poultry, try oakey, more full-bodied American chardonnays, red Burgundies, merlot or pinot noir. There are also some Provence reds that go extremely well with both game and roast poultry. With lighter chicken dishes, such as Sautéed Chicken Breasts (page 102), lighter, dry white wines go best and always use the wine you are serving, in the preparation. Preferred choices would be Montrachet, Mâcon Villages, and Meursault.

Acidic foods, such as tomatoes and vinaigrette salad dressings go well with fairly dry, acidic white wines. But for dishes with richer or heavier tomato-based sauces, red wines will often work better. Egg dishes or dishes containing a lot of eggs (omelettes, Frittatas and quiches) seem to work best with balanced white wines, with moderate acid and medium texture.

I like serving Italian red wines with Italian dishes such as *Porc Rôti Bellagio* (page 93), Veal Parmigiana (page 94) and Veal Marsala (page 95). With these dishes, Barolo, Brunello, Tiganello or a nice Chianti never seem to go wrong. A general rule of thumb is that wines from a particular area often go well with dishes common to the same area. As wines and foods from an area or region evolve, they tend, more often than not, to complement each other.

Rosés are enjoying a rise in popularity, although many people say they have never tasted rosés that they have liked. When I ask them about wines they prefer I am often able to find a rosé that they discover they

actually do like. Rosés are made in many wine-growing regions and their tastes and styles vary significantly, from light and dry to rich and fruity. Some rosés are heavier and quite dry, sometimes with a long aftertaste. American rosés tend to be a bit heavier and sweeter but, recently, are changing to the demands for lighter, drier styles of rosé.

Provence rosés are personal favorite and I tend to drink or serve them during warmer weather, with salads and lighter dishes, such as poultry and fish. Dry, crisp, mildly acidic and lightly fruity rosés go well with many fish and seafood dishes. Such wines are a perfect accompaniment to dishes such as Dungeness Crab Cakes (page 79).

I think that medium-bodied, dry Provence reds often go really well with traditional Provence dishes such as *Soupe au Pistou* (page 59) and *Boeuf en Daube à la Provençale* (page 89). American zinfandels and petit sirah can also go very well with these sorts of dishes. Remember that in many wine regions, wines evolve and change over time. California wine makers who only made very rich, oakey chardonnays ten years ago are now making much lighter, drier, and more complex chardonnays. Joseph Drouhin is now making a distinctly Burgundy-style chardonnay in Oregon's Willamette Valley and some vintages have won rave reviews.

Once again, however, personal tastes should be the first criteria in your selections. If you have a guest who "only likes white wine," go ahead and serve them a full-bodied oaken California chardonnay or, for that matter, whatever white wine they prefer. For those who "only like reds," try to avoid the obvious problems we have cited but do serve them red wine with their grilled sea bass if that is what they want.

There are classic pairings of certain foods and wines that have proven to be enjoyed by a majority of people, over time. Prime examples are: Bordeaux or cabernet sauvignon, with roast lamb or beef; Chablis or chardonnay, with sole and similar fish dishes; and sweet dessert wines, such as sauternes or muscats with sweet fruit and cream desserts, such as crêpes and fruit or crème brûlée.

Stocks & Sauces

Stocks and sauces are the chef's foundation for creating truly memorable dishes. Since many sauces are made from stock, we include both in this introduction. Of course, many soups also begin with stock but those are saved for a later chapter.

STOCKS

Nothing can quite take the place of homemade stocks. Although pre-made stocks are available commercially and in most supermarkets, they never fully measure up to the real thing. Stocks are the base ingredient and foundation for many soups, sauces and gravies. All can be prepared in advance and frozen for later use. Stocks take very little actual preparation time (generally less than a half-hour in total) and are definitely worth the effort. The bulk of time is in cooking and your stove will do most of that work without your attention.

Always use cold water and only enough to just barely cover the ingredients. Stocks need to simmer but not boil. Stirring stocks, while they are cooking, does nothing but cause fats to combine with the liquid, making it more difficult to strain impurities from your stock. Cooking at the correct temperatures and

cooking times are both important. If you forget to remove your stock from the heat at the right time or cook it too vigorously, you will risk losing too much liquid and ruining the stock. Adding more water late in the simmering process to 'rescue' your stock, is not recommended. And remember, before you use your stock or freeze it for later use, allow it to cool to room temperature and be sure to skim off the fat that rises to the top.

Three notes of caution regarding stocks are important. First, proper preparation and timely storage of all stocks is essential. Refrigerate or freeze stocks as soon as they are cooled to room temperature. Second, frozen stocks will keep about 2 to 3 months and should be discarded after that time. Finally, stocks should never be thawed and re-frozen as this risks contamination.

Veal (or Beef) Stock

Veal stock begins with scraps of veal, always including bones, and some meat and fat, along with an assortment of vegetables. Beef parts may be substituted for veal parts. Makes about 3 quarts (2.9 liters).

3	lbs (1.4 kg) veal or beef bones and trimmings
2	large carrots, cut into 3-inch lengths
1	large onion, quartered
1	celery stalk, chopped
2	tomatoes, chopped
1	bay leaf

The carrots, onions and tomatoes do not need to be peeled. The skins enhance the flavor of the stock and will be discarded, along with all other hard ingredients.

Preheat the oven to 400° F (200° C). Place the veal/beef trimmings and bones in a large roasting pan. Bake for approximately 1 to 1½ hours, stirring occasionally, until the bones are nicely browned. Remove the pan from the oven, transfer the bones and scrap to a large stockpot and place the roasting pan on the stove over medium-high heat. Add 3 cups (720 ml) water and stir to capture juices from the bottom of the pan. Pour the liquid into the stockpot and add the carrots, onions, celery, tomatoes and the bay leaf. Add just enough cold water to cover the 'hard' ingredients. Simmer uncovered to allow steam to escape for about 3 to 4 hours, until the liquid reduces by one-quarter, skimming off foam about every half-hour as the stock simmers.

Remove from heat. Remove the larger ingredients with a straining ladle or kitchen tongs then strain the stock through a fine sieve, discarding the solids. Allow the stock to cool to room temperature and skim off any fat that rises to the surface. If you are using the stock right away, be sure to keep it hot at about 160° F (70° C), without boiling. If you are freezing the stock, place it in plastic containers with airtight lids and freeze immediately.

Poultry Stock

My favorite poultry stocks are made using the carcasses from roast poultry. Any time I roast poultry, I always use the carcasses for stock. If you are not roasting any poultry yourself, fresh carcasses can often be obtained from local markets or butchers. The preparation for poultry stock is similar to that for veal/beef stock. Makes about 2 quarts (1.9 liters).

2	whole chicken carcasses cut in pieces
2	carrots, cut into 3-inch lengths
1	large onion, quartered
1	celery stock, chopped
1	bay leaf

Place the poultry carcasses, carrots, onions, celery and bay leaf in a large stockpot. As for veal stock, just cover these ingredients with cold water. Simmer, uncovered for about 3 to 4 hours, until the liquid reduces by one-quarter. Again, be careful to assure that the stock does not boil but simmers. Remove from the heat and follow the same process as for veal stock, from this point.

Fish Stock

Fish stocks serve as a base for fish soups and for sauces used in fish dishes. The preparation is similar to that for veal or poultry stock but the ingredients vary and cooking time is shorter. Generally, we make smaller quantities of fish stock and use them on the day they are made, although freezing is also an option, particularly for use in fish soups or stews. Makes about 2 quarts (1.9 liters).

Fish stock is fundamentally lighter and more delicate than either beef or poultry stock. Its flavor tends to be less pronounced and, therefore, will depend more on other ingredients, when used in sauces or soups. Fish stock, however, does enhance the flavor of either and adds a definite extra flair to such dishes.

Fish Stock, continued

3	lbs (1.4 kg) white fish trimmings, including heads, skins and bones
2	tablespoons olive oil
2	carrots, cut into 3-inch lengths
1	large shallot, chopped
2	celery stalks, cut into 3-inch lengths
1	cup (240 ml) dry white wine
1	bay leaf

Heat the oil in a large stockpot over medium-high heat, add the fish trimmings, and cook for approximately 3 to 4 minutes, stirring frequently. Add the carrots, shallots, celery, white wine and the bay leaf. Then add enough cold water so that the liquid just barely covers the 'hard' ingredients, bring to a boil, reduce the heat and simmer uncovered for approximately 40 to 45 minutes. As with other stocks, be careful to assure that the stock does not boil but just simmers.

Remove from the heat and follow the same process as for veal or poultry stock, from this point.

Shells and scraps from lobsters, prawns, crayfish and other crustaceans, as well as shells and scrap from other shellfish can also provide the base ingredients for terrific seafood stocks.

Vegetable Stock

Simply eliminate the bones, carcasses and meat from either the veal or poultry stock recipes and then increase the volume of vegetables to replace the meat or poultry ingredients.

The choice of vegetables is a matter of personal preference. For vegetable stock, we always include carrots, celery, and onions or shallots. You can add other vegetables as well, based on what you have on hand.

SAUCES

Most professional chefs will tell you that, although there are dozens of different sauces, most are created from only a very few basic recipes. The rest are just variations made by substituting or adding to the basic ingredients. These basic or 'mother' sauces are brown sauce, béchamel, hollandaise, and tomato. From these four, you can make dozens of other sauces by simply varying the ingredients.

Sauces are the finishing touch for many dishes and can make the difference between ordinary and extraordinary dining experiences. Some people seem to believe that sauces automatically mean heavier dishes and calorie-laden foods. Sauces simply enhance foods and need not be either heavy or calorie intensive.

Sauces should complement a dish and never overpower or hide the flavors of the dish's ingredients. Many sauces or gravies begin with a stock as the base, which is why we have combined these topics in a single chapter. For other sauces, the base ingredient is simply the juice or liquid obtained by cooking, such as meat juice from a roast beef or the juices obtained in frying poultry. Finally, some sauces, such as béchamel and hollandaise, are made to order with neither stock nor base liquids from cooking.

Brown Sauce

Brown sauce or gravy is made from thickened veal or beef stock, to which one can add various herbs and spices that complement the dish with which it is to be served. Brown sauce keeps well, if refrigerated, for several days. Yields 2 cups.

2	cups (480 ml) veal or beef stock
2	tablespoons (15 g) cornstarch
2	tablespoons cold water
	Salt and freshly ground black pepper

Heat the stock over medium heat in a saucepan, without boiling. In a small bowl, mix the cornstarch with the cold water until completely smooth. Slowly stir the thickening mixture into the stock, and continue stirring, until the stock thickens to a rich, creamy consistency. Season to taste with salt and pepper. Reduce heat to low and keep hot, until ready to serve.

Variations

MUSHROOM SAUCE – Add 1 cup of sliced, sautéed mushrooms. Be sure to sauté the mushrooms separately, before adding them and their juices to your sauce, to enhance the mushroom flavor.

POIVRADE SAUCE – Add 2 tablespoons (40g) red currant preserves, ½ teaspoon Provence herbs, ½ teaspoon cracked black pepper and 2 tablespoons (30 ml) whipping cream. Poivrade sauce goes well with game and roast poultry dishes.

Sauces top to bottom:
Mornay Sauce
Brown Sauce
Béchamel sauce

Béchamel Sauce

Béchamel sauce is the basic white sauce that is most often used with poultry, or fish and shellfish. Various herbs and spices can be used to achieve different flavors and accents in the sauce. Béchamel sauce will keep well, if refrigerated, for several days. Yields 2 cups.

¼ cup (60 g) unsalted butter
¼ cup (30 g) cup all-purpose flour
2 cups (240 ml) milk
   Salt and ground white pepper to taste
I small bay leaf

Melt the butter in a medium saucepan over low heat. When the butter begins to bubble, add the flour, stirring continuously until the butter and flour are well combined and bubbling. Continue stirring and cook the mixture, over low heat, for another minute or so, or until the mixture just begins to change to a golden color. Remove the saucepan quickly from the heat and set aside to cool down. This mixture is called a *roux*. You may immerse the saucepan in a bowl filled with cold water to hurry the process of cooling down.

In another saucepan, heat the milk seasoned with the salt, pepper and bay leaf over medium-low heat. Let it simmer for a few minutes, just below the boiling point.

Place the first saucepan with the *roux* on medium-high heat, and pour in the hot milk all at once whisking the milk and *roux* together until fully combined. Reduce the heat to low and simmer for 3 to 5 minutes stirring continuously, until the sauce is thickened and smooth. Remove the bay leaf.

Variations

SPICES – Some chefs add a pinch nutmeg to the milk in the béchamel preparation. A pinch or two of cayenne pepper will add a bit of spiciness to your béchamel.

VELOUTÉ – Use chicken or fish stock, in place of the milk. The type of stock used should match the main dish. If the sauce is to be used with chicken, use poultry stock, or use fish stock for fish dishes.

CAJUN CREAM SAUCE – Add Cajun seasoning to the milk in the béchamel preparation.

Mornay Sauce

Mornay sauce is a derivative of béchamel sauce that goes well with fish and other seafood. Once you have mastered the béchamel, making this sauce is a snap.

2 cups (480 ml) Béchamel Sauce
½ cup (60 g) grated Gruyère or Jarlsberg cheese
   Salt and freshly ground black pepper

First make the béchamel and then stir in the grated cheese, until it is fully melted and blended in. Add salt and pepper, to taste.

Béchamel sauce is a white sauce and therefore requires a 'white' or 'blond' roux. To achieve this, remove your pan with the flour and butter mixture from the heat before it has a chance to take on color and darken as it cooks. The color defines the kind of roux; for example, brown sauces require a 'dark' roux.

Another useful rule to remember is that one moistens a hot roux with cold milk, or vice versa, a cold roux with a hot liquid, and that you pour the hot liquid all at once into the roux. Also, it is always helpful to have extra liquid on hand in case your sauce gets too thick and you wish to thin it.

Note that the roux and final sauce must both be made with care. Too high heat or not enough timely stirring will result in a lumpy, overcooked sauce.

Hollandaise Sauce

Hollandaise sauce is a rich egg-based sauce, usually flavored with lemon or vinegar, and butter. Hollandaise is typically served over vegetables or fish and egg dishes. It is also the base for several other sauces. Note that hollandaise should be prepared immediately before serving, and does not keep or reheat well. Makes 2 cups.

6	large egg yolks
¼	cup (60 ml) fresh lemon juice, warmed
¼	cup (60ml) boiling water
I	cup (240 g) unsalted butter, melted
½	teaspoon cayenne
I	teaspoon salt

In a double boiler, fill the bottom pot with water, only up to the level that the top pot's bottom will not touch the water. Heat the water over medium-low heat, until it is just below the boiling point. Do not let the water boil.

Put the egg yolks in the top pot and whisk vigorously, until the egg yolks begin to thicken. Add one tablespoon of boiling water, continuing to whisk until the egg and water mixture thickens. Repeat with one tablespoon of water at a time. Stir in the lemon juice. Remove the double boiler from heat and slowly pour in the melted butter, while whisking vigorously and continuously.

Add salt and cayenne, and continue whisking the mixture until it thickens to the approximate consistency of cake batter. Serve immediately.

Other Hollandaise Variations

There are a multitude of other hollandaise derivatives. You may enjoy these four, each of which is an easy addition to the basic hollandaise recipe.

CHORON SAUCE – Add ½ cup finely chopped tomatoes to béarnaise sauce. For broiled and grilled meats, and roasts.

MOUSSELINE SAUCE – Add ½ cup of whipped cream to your hollandaise. For fish and vegetables.

MOUTARDE SAUCE – Add Dijon mustard, to taste.

WITH CAPERS – Add 2 tablespoons (25 g) minced capers. For fish dishes.

Béarnaise Sauce

This is one of the most common variations of hollandaise, served with broiled and grilled meat dishes. To make béarnaise sauce, simply follow the hollandaise recipe and add a reduction of white wine, white wine vinegar, finely chopped shallots and tarragon. To make the reduction, use:

I	minced shallot
¼	cup (60 ml) dry white wine
¼	cup (60 ml) white wine vinegar
¼	teaspoon freshly ground black pepper
¼	teaspoon finely chopped fresh tarragon

Place all ingredients in a saucepan, over low heat and simmer until no liquid remains. Add the remaining solids to your sauce.

Note
The greatest problem cooks have with hollandaise is that the ingredients separate, when the sauce becomes too hot or too cold. If your sauce does start to separate, try adding a tablespoon of cold water and continue whisking vigorously.

Egg based sauces do not hold well, so be sure to time your preparation to serve immediately.

Provençal Tomato Sauce

We generally prefer homemade tomato sauce to pre-made varieties although, if you are short of time, you can certainly use those. Makes about 2 quarts (1.9 liters).

5	lbs (2.3 kg) ripe tomatoes
4	tablespoons (60 ml) olive oil
2	large finely chopped onions
½	cup (5 g) chopped fresh basil
4	minced garlic cloves
2	tablespoons Provence herbs
¾	cup (180 ml) full-bodied red wine
1	teaspoon granulated sugar
	Salt and freshly ground black pepper

Blanch the tomatoes in boiling water to loosen the skins and then cool them immediately, in cold water. Remove the skins and seeds, dice the tomatoes and set aside.

In a large stockpot or saucepan over medium-high heat sauté the onions in the olive oil, until they begin to brown. Reduce heat to low, add the basil, garlic and herbs, cover the pot, and cook for 10 minutes. Add the red wine, turn the heat up to medium and simmer, until the wine is reduced by half. Stir in the diced tomatoes and simmer, over medium heat, for 15 to 20 minutes, until the sauce reduces a bit and thickens. Use on the same day or refrigerate for use within a few days. Tomato sauce can also be frozen for much later use.

Sauces top to bottom:
Béarnaise Sauce
Tomato Sauce
Hollandaise sauce

SALADS

Caesar Salad   37

Salad Mara   39
(Fresh Summer Salad with Shrimp)

Spinach Salad with Warm Bacon Dressing   40

Hearts of Romaine with Avocado Dressing   41

Salade Provençale   43
(Mixed Greens, Roast Peppers, Tomatoes and Onions)

Avocado, Cucumber & Chèvre Salad   44

Tri-Colore Salad   45
(Avocado, Tomato and Mozzarella)

Penang Salad   47
(Malaysian Salad with Sesame Soy Dressing)

DRESSINGS

Dijon Vinaigrette   49

Classic Italian   49

Creamy Stilton   50

Creamy Buttermilk & Herb   50

Malaysian Sesame Soy   51

Salads

Salads can be the introduction to a meal, as starters, or can be the main dish by themselves. The difference is primarily a question of quantity and, in some cases, ingredients. A small salad, served as a starter, can set the tone for an entire meal and have your guests eager to see what comes after.

When salad is just one course in a multi-course meal, the salad you serve should complement your other courses. Lighter, less heavily flavored salads will complement lighter main courses such as fish dishes. For more flavorful meat and game dishes, richly flavored salads and dressings will also work. A main dish salad, with fresh bread can make a great light meal.

Most North Americans eat their salads as the first course of a meal. In many other countries, however, salads are served after a main course. I particularly favor the latter approach when serving four or more courses. Regardless of when you serve your salad, the key to successful salads is using fresh ingredients. Crisp, fresh lettuce washed and spun dry, to remove excess water, will make your salad tastier. Of course, not all salads contain lettuce. The salads we have included are just a few of our favorites but, of course, we like many other salads and you may have your own favorites.

Salad dressings should complement your salads and not overwhelm their ingredients. Good dressings enhance the overall flavor of a salad. Best of all, really delicious dressings are easy to make.

Dressings made from fresh ingredients do not contain preservatives, and although some keep well in the refrigerator, most have shorter 'shelf lives' than bottled dressings. So, it is important to consider shelf life when deciding on the quantities you are going to make.

Hail Caesar

Caesar salad is truly a classic. It was first created by Caesar Cardini, an Italian chef who lived in Mexico, and is named after the chef, not the Roman Emperor of the same name. Classic Caesar salads are very popular in America and can be found in restaurants all across the country.

The original recipe from Señor Cardini, with or without anchovy fillets, is very much to our liking. However, many people are not particularly fond of the taste of anchovies. Because of this, we usually make them optional or simply leave them out.

Adding other ingredients to a Caesar salad is also popular with many people. For either main dish or starter Caesar salads, you can use bay shrimp, crabmeat, or crumbled bacon and leave the anchovies out of both the dressing and the salad.

Croutons are an important ingredient in any truly memorable Caesar salad. Although you can use pre-made croutons, I prefer to make my own on the day they will be eaten. Simply dry slices of French bread, in the oven, until they are dry but still a bit soft. Remove the bread slices from the oven and let them cool. Discard the crusts and cut the slices into ½-inch cubes. Place them in a skillet, over medium-high heat, with a little olive oil and a few finely chopped herbs, and brown them, coating the croutons with oil and herbs. To give your croutons a hint of garlic flavor, simply add a clove of very finely chopped garlic to the pan with the olive oil.

Caesar Salad

A large Caesar Salad, with bread on the side, can make a full meal by itself.
I usually serve a smaller Caesar Salad as a starter or after a main course. Serves 8.

2	large heads romaine lettuce, chopped large, stalks discarded
3	cups French bread croutons (page 36)
2	cups (340 g) bay shrimp
½	cup (50 g) shaved Parmesan cheese

DRESSING

2	cups (480 ml) olive oil
¾	cup (75 g) finely grated Parmesan cheese
¼	cup (60 ml) fresh lemon juice
3	large egg yolks, at room temperature*
4	large garlic cloves, finely chopped
2	teaspoons (10 ml) Worcestershire sauce
2	teaspoons dry mustard
2	teaspoons salt
2	teaspoons freshly ground black pepper

* *Although the risk is statistically small, raw eggs can contain salmonella bacteria; so exercise caution when using recipes containing raw eggs.*

Note *that having the egg yolks at room temperature for about 10 to 15 minutes before you blend them in the dressing makes it easier to combine them smoothly with the other dressing ingredients.*

For the dressing, in a food processor or blender, whip the olive oil, Parmesan cheese, lemon juice, egg yolks, garlic, Worcestershire sauce, mustard, salt and pepper, until well blended.

In a large salad bowl, toss the romaine pieces with the dressing, croutons, and shrimp. To serve, arrange portions on large salad plates or shallow bowls and top with shaved Parmesan.

If you want to make the original, simply add two finely chopped anchovy fillets to the dressing and one or two whole anchovy fillets, as a garnish, on top of each serving.

 With its tangy dressing, Caesar salad can stand up to a wide range of wines but I usually choose a lighter chardonnay, Semillon blanc or Riesling. Lighter red wines, such as Beaujolais, also complement a Caesar salad.

Saint-Rémy de Provence

A lake in the hills above Saint-Rémy, originally built as a reservoir by the Romans in the 4th century

The village of Saint-Rémy de Provence is located 11 miles (18 kilometers) south of Avignon and approximately one hour by car, northwest of Marseilles. Such notables as Nostradamus and Vincent Van Gogh lived in Saint-Rémy. It is also the site of Glanum, one of the best preserved examples of Roman architecture in Provence, and of course, the location of our restaurant, La Table de Michel.

The scenery in the countryside around Saint-Rémy is breathtaking, with tree-lined roads dating back to the time of Napoleon, majestic stone hills from which the fortifications of ancient castles and walled cities were cut, and pristine forests lining the hillsides. The area is a paradise for food and wine lovers, as well as those who like hill walking and mountain biking.

Within a few miles of Saint-Rémy, you can find ancient walled cities, such as Avignon, with the walls largely in the same condition as when they were originally constructed in the Middle Ages. Beautiful Provence textiles and pottery are still made in the same way as they were crafted hundreds of years ago with intricate, brightly colored floral and geometric designs.

Salade Mara
Fresh Summer Salad with Shrimp

*This is a very simple but delicious salad that Michel served at his Seattle
restaurant, Deville's on Broadway, during the spring and summer months.
It is light and refreshing, without any lettuce or other leafy greens. Serves 6.*

3	celery stalks, diced
3	cups (300 g) sliced mushrooms
3	tomatoes, diced
2	cups (340 g) bay shrimp
2	avocadoes, diced
2	cups (20 g) small parsley sprigs
2	carrots, julienned

DRESSING

1	cup olive oil
¼	cup (60 ml) fresh lemon juice
1	tablespoon (15 g) mayonnaise
1	garlic clove, finely chopped
	Salt and freshly ground black pepper

For the dressing, mix the olive oil, lemon juice, mayonnaise, and garlic in a blender until
smooth. Season to taste with salt and pepper.

In a large salad bowl, toss all of the ingredients together with the dressing and serve on
individual plates or bowls. A bed of cucumbers, as shown, or a large lettuce leaf on the plate,
will help this salad stand out when you serve it.

*A light, fruity Rosé is the perfect complement to this salad. Lighter, dry Rieslings and Burgundy-style
chardonnays are also nice. Provence rosé wines are particularly nice with this salad during the warmer
times of the year.*

Spinach Salad with Warm Bacon Dressing

This salad is one that I first learned from Bruno Patassini, Maître d' at Victor's restaurant, atop the St. Francis Hotel in San Francisco. Its warm, sweet, slightly aromatic dressing, accompanied by the fresh spinach leaves has a particularly appealing taste. This salad makes a great starter with heavier and more robustly flavored meat or poultry main dishes. Serves 6.

8	thick bacon slices
2	tablespoons (30 ml) cider vinegar
I	tablespoon (15 ml) soy sauce
I	tablespoon water
I	teaspoon sugar
¼	cup (60 ml) olive oil
	Salt and freshly ground black pepper
¾	lb (360 g) spinach, washed, dried and torn into pieces
2	avocadoes, peeled, pitted, and diced

Note *that the hot dressing wilts the spinach leaves a little without actually cooking them, which contributes to the unique taste of this salad.*

Cook the bacon in a large skillet over medium heat, turning frequently until almost crisp. Turn off the heat and transfer the bacon to paper towels to drain and cool. Break the bacon into small pieces. Reserve 3 to 4 tablespoons of bacon drippings in the skillet and remove any extra with a spoon.

Add the vinegar, soy sauce, and water to the skillet, stirring continuously, until the mixture boils. Sprinkle the sugar across the mixture so that it does not stick together. Cook over medium heat, stirring continuously, until the sugar melts, and stir in the olive oil. Reduce heat to very low, add salt and pepper to taste, and cover.

In a large salad bowl, toss the spinach with half of the bacon pieces. Quickly stir the dressing in the skillet and pour it over the spinach. Toss again. Arrange on salad plates or shallow bowls and top with the remaining bacon, diced avocado, and a sprinkling of freshly ground black pepper. Serve immediately.

A range of either red or white wines can accompany this salad. I prefer a Burgundy-style chardonnay or Beaune, an American west coast merlot or, in summer, a Provence rosé.

Hearts of Romaine with Avocado Dressing

This is a very fresh salad that makes an excellent starter with almost any main dish and works just as well following a main dish before dessert. It is one that Michel often served at his Seattle restaurants. Serves 6.

3	heads romaine lettuce
2	cups (340 g) bay shrimp
3	dozen cherry tomatoes, halved
¾	cup (110 g) sunflower seeds

AVOCADO DRESSING

1	avocado, peeled and diced
1¼	(300 ml) cups olive oil
½	cup (120 ml) red wine vinegar
1	large egg*
1	garlic clove, minced
	Salt and freshly ground black pepper

* Although the risk is statistically small, raw eggs can contain salmonella bacteria; so exercise caution when using recipes containing raw eggs.

For the dressing, purée the avocado, olive oil, vinegar, egg, and garlic in a blender until smooth. Season to taste with salt and pepper.

To prepare the salad, remove and discard the outer leaves from each romaine head, down to the heart (the lighter green leaves) and separate the leaves.

Arrange the leaves on a chilled salad plate with bay shrimp and cherry tomatoes. Pour dressing over each salad, sprinkle with sunflower seeds and serve.

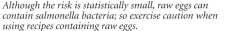 *With the rich avocado flavor, an oakier American or Australian chardonnay will go nicely with this salad.*

Gardens and Vineyards of Provence

The hilltop fortress at Les Baux de Provence looms on the horizon not far from Avignon and Saint-Rémy de Provence. This natural rock formation rises above the valley below to a height of more than 2,000 feet (700 meters). The ruins of Les Baux de Provence have been turned into a very special tourist village, with shops, restaurants and what is left of the old castle fortress. On a clear day from the top of the castle, you can see the surrounding countryside for miles, and to the south, all the way to the Mediterranean.

Everywhere you look there are fields of produce, olive groves, and vineyards organized in symmetrical rows. Provence is, quite literally, the garden of France. When it comes to growing foodstuffs, Provence is to France as California is to America.

The bounty of fresh produce grown in Provence is simply overwhelming and, with its perfect climate and rich soils, the flavors of Provence fruits and vegetables are amazing. Another factor contributing to this phenomenon is that the local farming methods have not given way to mass production. Farmers still till the soil and tend their crops as their grandfathers did, except that they now use modern tractors and machinery.

Herbs grow wild all across Provence and, together with other natural ingredients in the soil, their subtle flavors are present in grapes and other produce. When wine connoisseurs discuss wines they taste, they will often refer to things like "hints of rosemary or black currants" in the wines. These flavors come from the soil in which the grape vines grow. In summer, Provence melons have incredible sweetness and flavor, often with a very faint evidence of herbs.

Salade Provençale
Mixed Greens, Roast Peppers, Tomatoes and Onions

This is a very typical starter or luncheon salad served in Provence restaurants. This salad works well as a starter served with more fully flavored meat, game or poultry dishes. Lightly roasted bell peppers give it a very unique extra taste that complements the fresh greens and sets off the olives, onions and tomatoes with slightly contrasting flavors. Serves 6.

1	red bell pepper, cored, seeded and quartered
1	green pepper, cored, seeded and quartered
2	tablespoons (30 ml) olive oil
	Salt and freshly ground black pepper
½	head green lettuce, washed and torn into pieces
½	head red leafed lettuce, washed and torn into pieces
3	large ripe tomatoes cut into eighths
½	sweet onion, thinly sliced
24	black olives (not canned), pitted
1	cup (240 ml) Dijon Vinaigrette (page 49)

Preheat the oven to 400° F (200° C). Coat the bell peppers with the olive oil, and sprinkle with salt and pepper. In a small roasting pan, roast the peppers, until they are softened but still a bit crisp, about 5 to 6 minutes. Let cool and cut into ½-inch slices.

In a large bowl, toss all of the ingredients together, except for the dressing. Season to taste with salt and pepper. Just before serving, toss, again, this time with the dressing.

Light-to-medium-bodied red wines, such as red Burgundies, a lighter Provence red or an American pinot noir are preferred choices with this salad.

Avocado, Cucumber and Chèvre Salad

No salad is easier to make than this one. The total preparation time is about five minutes. It is light and flavorful, and goes well as a salad course or starter for either lunch or dinner. We sometimes serve this salad on top of a large romaine or iceberg lettuce leaf, or sliced tomatoes, which adds a decorative touch. Serves 6.

3	ripe avocados, peeled, pitted and sliced
2	large cucumbers, peeled, halved lengthwise, seeded and cut into ¼-inch slices
12	ounces (360 g) Chèvre
	Salt and freshly ground black pepper
½	cup (120 ml) Dijon Vinaigrette (page 49)
	Paprika or freshly ground black pepper, for accent

Variations

Almost any soft, white cheese can be substituted for Chèvre. The Chèvre adds a bit of tartness that complements the smooth flavor of the avocados and crisp cucumbers.

Cut the Chèvre into small pieces and set aside to warm to room temperature. Arrange the slices of avocado and cucumber on the plates and season with salt and pepper. Add the cheese and drizzle the dressing over the salads.

Lightly sprinkle paprika or black pepper around the perimeter of the plate to complete the presentation.

Chèvre is a soft white goat cheese from France. It can be found in most specialty cheese shops and many supermarkets. Excellent domestic goat cheese varieties are also available in many areas of North America.

 Either lighter red or somewhat bolder white wines go best with this salad. My own first choice would generally be a Beaune or Châteauneuf-du-Pape, or a lighter American pinot noir.

Tri-Colore Salad

'Tri-Colore' is Italian for 'three colors'. In this salad, green avocado, red tomatoes, and white mozzarella represent the three colors of the Italian flag. This no-lettuce salad is the perfect prelude to Veal Parmigiana (page 94) or Veal Marsala (page 95), or any pasta main dish. Serves 6.

3	large ripe avocados, peeled, pitted and cut lengthwise into ¼-inch slices
3	large ripe tomatoes, cored and cut into ¼ inch slices
	Salt to taste
1½	lb (450 g) fresh buffalo mozzarella balls, cut into ¼-inch slices
¼	cup (60 ml) Classic Italian dressing (page 49)
18	pitted black olives (not canned)
	Paprika or black pepper

Season the avocado and tomato slices to taste with salt. Arrange the avocado, tomato, and mozzarella slices around salad plates, alternating and overlapping them. Sprinkle lightly with the Italian dressing. Garnish with olives and a sprig of fresh oregano or alfalfa sprouts. Sprinkle paprika or black pepper around the perimeter of the plate, for a decorative accent, and serve.

Variations

Some people prefer using only balsamic vinegar, which gives a sharper flavor to this salad than Italian dressing. You might try both to see which you prefer.

You can substitute sliced cucumbers for the avocados, although the flavor will not be as pronounced.

Lighter, dry, fruity wines will complement this dish, although lighter reds, if you prefer, can also work well. A light, fruity Italian white, such as Gavi di Gavi, a Saint Aubin from France, or a Semillon Blanc from America are all good choices.

Fresh produce at a local supermarket

Penang Salad
Malaysian Salad with Sesame Soy Dressing

This salad with its sesame, ginger and soy dressing has a distinct Asian flavor. It is inspired by a salad I originally tasted in Penang, Malaysia, on a business trip in the mid-1980s. Penang is a food lover's paradise, with its diverse local cultures, hawker stalls, and restaurants featuring a combination of Chinese, Malay, and Thai cuisines. This salad goes very well as a starter with spicier main dishes. Serves 6.

1	large head green leaf lettuce, torn into pieces
1	stalk bok choy, washed and cut into ½-inch pieces
1	small red onion, thinly sliced
1	cucumber, peeled, quartered lengthwise and cut into ½-inch slices
¾	cup (170 g) canned mandarin orange sections
¼	lb (120 g) bean sprouts
½	cup (110 g) canned water chestnuts, thinly sliced
2	garlic cloves, thinly sliced
1	cup (240 ml) Malaysian Sesame Soy dressing (page 51)
	Freshly ground black pepper

Combine the lettuce, bok choy, onion, cucumber, mandarin orange, bean sprouts, water chestnuts, and garlic in a large bowl and toss to mix. Cover and refrigerate until ready to serve, for up to 3 hours. Just before serving, add the dressing and toss to coat. Arrange the salad on plates and top with a sprinkling of pepper.

Note that bok choy may not be readily available in all markets. Celery makes a good substitute for bok choy. Enoki mushrooms, if available, make a nice complementary garnish on the top of this salad.

Variations

Add ½ cup (85 g) each bay shrimp and crabmeat to the ingredients, to make a main course salad that becomes a sort of Asian 'Shrimp Louie'.

A Semillon Blanc or medium-dry Riesling will go best with this salad.

Salad Dressings

Freshly made salad dressings are often the difference between ordinary and really delicious salads. The right dressing enhances the overall flavor of a salad without hiding the tastes of other ingredients.

Quality vinegars, oils and other ingredients make for more flavorful dressings than other choices. There are literally thousands of olive oils and vinegars produced throughout the world. The better quality vinegars and oils do tend to be a bit more expensive but, since the quantities used in dressings are small, the extra investment is generally worth it. Some gourmet shops will have oils available for tasting. Try a few and see which ones you prefer.

We have a bias towards making our own salad dressings and we like simplicity, so our choices tend in that direction. The perfect Vinaigrette needs little more than quality olive oil, vinegar, and a touch of seasonings, a starting point from which countless variations can be made.

Dressings pictured, top to bottom:
Dijon Vinaigrette
Classic Italian
Creamy Stilton

Dijon Vinaigrette

This is a traditional French dressing that lends itself well to a number of variations. The key ingredient is Dijon mustard and the pepper and mustard, together, give it a bit of zing. This dressing goes very well with fairly simple green or mixed leaf salads. This dressing can be stored in the refrigerator for up to 2 weeks. Makes about 1½ cups.

¼ cup (60 ml) red wine vinegar

2 tablespoons (30 ml) cold water

¼ teaspoon salt

¼ teaspoon freshly ground black pepper

1 tablespoon (15 g) Dijon mustard

1 cup (240 ml) olive oil

In a small bowl, whisk together the vinegar, water, salt, pepper and mustard, until smooth. Add the olive oil whisk thoroughly, before pouring on your salad.

Classic Italian Dressing

Italian chefs and cooks alike are serious about their salads. A simple olive oil and vinegar dressing with salt, pepper and Italian herbs can be the perfect accompaniment to a memorable green salad. This dressing will last in the refrigerator for 2 to 3 weeks. Makes about 1¼ cups.

6   tablespoons (90 ml) balsamic vinegar

1   tablespoon (15 ml) cold water

4   sun-dried tomatoes, minced

2-3 garlic cloves, minced

1   teaspoon dry oregano, crushed

1   teaspoon dry thyme, crushed

    Salt and freshly ground black pepper

¾   cup (180 ml) olive oil

In a bowl, whisk together the vinegar, water, sun-dried tomatoes, garlic, oregano, thyme, salt and pepper, until well blended. Add the olive oil and whisk thoroughly. Serve immediately or store in the refrigerator in a tightly covered container.

Variations

For a lighter version of this dressing, use red wine vinegar instead of balsamic. To spice up this dressing, add ¼ teaspoon cayenne pepper.

Creamy Stilton

Blue cheese dressings are a perennial favorite. I prefer a creamy preparation, as it is somewhat subtler than many blue cheese dressings made only with cheese, oil and vinegar. There are a multitude of blue cheeses available and this recipe works well with most of them. This dressing, made with cream, will only keep for a day or two in the refrigerator. Makes about 1¼ cups.

6	ounces (180 g) Stilton, or other blue cheese, crumbled
2	tablespoons (30 ml) white wine vinegar
¼	teaspoon freshly ground black pepper
2	tablespoons (30 ml) heavy cream or crème fraîche
4	tablespoons (30 ml) olive oil

In a food processor or blender, whip the Stilton, vinegar and pepper, together until smooth. Add the cream and olive oil, and pulse, until the dressing is creamy smooth.

Creamy Buttermilk and Herb Dressing

This is our favorite buttermilk dressing; it goes well with almost any salad greens. The flavor is slightly tangy, without being too strong. This dressing will keep for up to three days if covered tightly and refrigerated. Makes about 1 cup.

2	tablespoons (30 ml) fresh lime juice
1	tablespoon (15 ml) olive oil
2	garlic cloves, chopped
1	tablespoon (30 g) chopped fresh parsley
1	teaspoon (10 g) chopped fresh thyme
1	teaspoon (10 g) chopped fresh chives
½	cup (120 ml) buttermilk
¼	cup (60 g) sour cream or crème fraîche
	Salt and freshly ground black pepper

In a blender or mini food processor, mix the lime juice, olive oil, garlic and herbs until well blended. Add the buttermilk and sour cream, and mix at medium-high speed until well blended. Season to taste with salt and pepper, and serve.

Malaysian Sesame Soy Dressing

This dressing is adapted from one I first encountered in Malaysia, in the coastal city of Penang. It is a very flavorful dressing that will go well with many salads. This dressing will keep well for up to two weeks, if refrigerated. Makes about 1 cup.

2	tablespoons (30 ml) rice wine vinegar
3	tablespoons (45 ml) soy sauce
2	garlic cloves, finely chopped
½	teaspoon finely grated fresh ginger
I	tablespoon chopped fresh cilantro leaves,
½	teaspoon Szechuan Seasoning
¼	teaspoon freshly ground black pepper
½	cup (120 ml) olive oil
2	tablespoons (30 ml) toasted sesame oil
I	tablespoon (15 ml) honey

In a blender or mini food processor, mix the vinegar, soy sauce, garlic, ginger, cilantro, Szechuan Seasoning, and the pepper until well blended. Add the olive oil, sesame oil and honey, mixing at medium-high speed until all ingredients are smoothly blended. Serve or store in the refrigerator.

Dressings pictured, top to bottom:
Creamy Buttermilk and Herb
Malaysian Sesame Soy

SOUPS

Chicken, Rice and Butternut Squash Soup 54

Soupe Marché 55
(Cream of Turnip and Vegetable Soup)

Seafood Bisque with Cognac and Cream 57

Soupe au Pistou 59
(Bean and Vegetable Soup with Garlic and Basil)

Mulligatawny Soup 61

Leek and Potato Soup with Bacon 62

Northwest Corn and Crab Chowder 63

Mansion Tortilla Soup 65
Chef Dean Fearing, The Mansion on Turtle Creek, Dallas

New Orleans Style Gumbo 67

Beef Barley Soup 69

Soups

*Nothing is quite as satisfying as a hearty soup on a cold winter day.
As you will see, most of the soups we have included here definitely
meet the criteria for 'hearty'. Lighter soups, such as consommé, gazpacho,
or broth, can make truly wonderful starters and, in our opinion, all of
these do as well, when they are served in smaller quantities.*

Stocks, as detailed earlier, are the first ingredients for all of these soups. The quality of your stocks will have a direct influence on the taste and success of soups made from them. So, make sure that you have stocks on hand before you embark on turning them into delicious soups. Soups are very easy to make but do require a little attention while they are cooking. Just check every so often to see how ingredients, such as vegetables, rice, noodles or beans are cooking, and taste as you go. When tasting during cooking, you can add salt and pepper or other spices to adjust the flavor of your soup.

An entire meal can consist of only a small salad, large bowl of soup and some fresh bread just out of the oven from the local *boulangerie* (bakery). Michel and I usually serve wines that we select specifically to complement the particular soup and salad.

Soups lend themselves well to experimentation with different ingredients. Different vegetables, grains, rice, and other starches can be used in place of those specified in a recipe. First try these soup recipes, as specified, and then use your own taste and imagination to create new variations that you enjoy more.

Chicken, Rice and Butternut Squash Soup

Although the medicinal healing powers of chicken soup may be subject to debate, there is no question that this soup will be appreciated at any table, either as the start to a multi-course meal or as a main course. Note that you can also use leftover chicken meat, in which case you do not need to sauté it. Serves 8.

1	butternut squash (about 2.2 lbs/1 kg), halved and seeded
3	tablespoons (45 g) unsalted butter
2	shallots, thinly sliced
1	large garlic clove, thinly sliced
1	tablespoon (15 ml) olive oil
1	lb (450 g) diced chicken meat
1	tablespoon (15 g) finely chopped fresh thyme
½	teaspoon mild yellow curry powder
2	quarts (1.9 liters) poultry stock (page 28)
	Salt and freshly ground black pepper
1½	cups (350 g) cooked rice

Bake the squash in a 400° F (200° C) oven, with 1 tablespoon of butter in each cavity, until the squash is fully tender (about 30 to 45 minutes). Let cool and remove the skin. Purée the squash in a food processor. Sauté the shallots and garlic in the olive oil and remaining 1 tablespoon of butter over medium-high heat, until just translucent. Add the chicken pieces, thyme and curry powder, and continue sautéing, stirring frequently, until the meat is browned.

Place the chicken sauté mix, poultry stock and puréed squash in a large stockpot, over medium-high heat and bring to a rolling boil, for 2 to 3 minutes. Reduce to low heat, cover and simmer for 1 hour; do not let the soup boil. Add salt and pepper, to taste. Add the cooked rice, cover and simmer for an additional 10 minutes. Remove from the heat, let stand for 5 minutes, stirring occasionally, and serve.

 Full-bodied white wines, such as California or Australian chardonnays will go well with this soup, as will somewhat lighter red wines, such as Burgundies, pinots or merlots.

Soupe Marché
Cream of Turnip and Vegetable Soup

Soupe Marché means 'soup from the market' and any fresh vegetables, in season, can be used. This is a recipe that Michel contributed to the Dining in Seattle II *cookbook. It is ideal as a small first course in a multiple course meal. The flavor is light, creamy and sophisticated. Serves 6.*

2	large tomatoes
5	tablespoons (75 g) unsalted butter
2	leeks (about 3/4 lb), white and pale green parts, chopped
¾	lb (300 g) chopped onions
6	cups (1.4 liters) poultry stock (page 28)
¼	cup dry white wine
4	carrots, diced
1	lb (450 g) turnips, peeled and diced
3	potatoes, peeled and diced
	Salt and freshly ground black pepper
12	mushrooms
2	cups (480 ml) whipping cream
	Fresh basil or parsley leaves, for garnish

Blanch the tomatoes in boiling water, peel, remove seeds and dice. Melt 4 tablespoons of the butter in a large stockpot over medium heat and sauté the leeks and onions until translucent. Add the poultry stock, wine, carrots, turnips, potatoes, and tomatoes. Cook for 40 minutes over medium heat, stirring occasionally. Add the mushrooms and cook for 10 more minutes.

In a food processor or blender, purée the soup and then return it to the pot. Stir in 1¾ cups of the whipping cream and remaining butter, cooking long enough for the cream to warm. Season to taste with salt and pepper, ladle into bowls, and garnish with a swirl of cream, fresh basil or parsley and paprika.

Medium-bodied Provence red wines go very well with this soup but Burgundy-style reds and American pinot noirs are equally good choices..

The Staff of Life

Dupont's Bakery, Borough Market, London

Freshly baked bread adds an extra touch to any meal but is almost a requirement with soup. Today, we have access to a wide selection of wonderful breads, from light golden baguettes to Indian Naan and tasty loaves of Italian Focaccia laced with herbs. The choices are endless.

My favorite breads are an eclectic collection that I have discovered in my travels over the years. Soft Armenian braided bread sticks are made with yogurt and sesame or poppy seeds and are just delicious. Lahvosh, sometimes called 'Armenian cracker bread', is a flat bread with origins dating back to biblical times. When the Bible refers to 'breaking bread', lahvosh is probably the bread that was broken. Ciabatta is moist Italian bread made with olive oil. It gets its name from its shape and translates to "old shoe or slipper," which doesn't sound nearly as appetizing. When I was young, my mother often made Irish soda bread. It is still something I have at breakfast when I visit Ireland. It is probably just my imagination but sourdough bread never seems to taste quite as good anywhere but in San Francisco. Cinnamon bread or rolls, affectionately known in the Northwest as "sticky buns," are always a treat at breakfast. For me, pita bread warmed in the oven until it puffs up is a must with Greek or Lebanese food. I am addicted to cheese so cheese breads and rolls have a special place in my heart. I also love corn bread and found the best I have ever tasted at a dinner in the Amana Colonies in Iowa. Some bread has a religious connection. I discovered challah at a Jewish friend's wedding. Challah is traditional on the Sabbath and also for Jewish religious holidays and celebrations such as Passover feasts and bar mitzvahs. Coarse whole grain peasant breads are wonderful and, when served together with soups, can be a filling meal.

In France, fresh breads are baked twice each day and most locals make morning and afternoon trips to the boulangerie for breads they will eat at home. The French are not very interested in day-old bakery goods so any bread left unsold at the end of a day is often used for other purposes, such as breadcrumbs.

Seafood Bisque with Cognac and Cream

Fish soups and stews make wonderful starters or main courses. Cioppino from San Francisco and Bouillabaisse from Marseilles are two renowned favorites. This is a sophisticated soup usually served as a starter. Firm fleshed fish, such as salmon, monkfish, swordfish, and tuna work best in this soup. Serves 8.

6	cups (1.5 liters) fish stock (page 28)
4	tablespoons (60 g) unsalted butter
1	stalk celery, thinly sliced
1	carrot, thinly sliced
2	leeks, white and pale green parts thinly sliced
1	onion, finely chopped
1¼	cups (300 ml) heavy cream or crème fraîche
2	lbs (900 g) prawns, shelled and deveined
1	lb (450 g) fish fillets, cut into 1-inch chunks
	Salt and freshly ground black pepper
	Cayenne pepper
½	cup (120 ml) Armagnac, cognac or other brandy
1	cup (100 g) freshly grated Parmesan cheese
24	lightly toasted baguette slices
24	mussels in the shell (optional)

Heat the fish stock in a large saucepan. In 2 tablespoons of butter, sauté the celery, carrot, leeks and onion in a large stockpot over medium-high, stirring frequently until the onions are translucent. Add the fish stock all at once, reduce heat and simmer for 15 to 20 minutes until the vegetables are tender, stirring occasionally. Continue simmering and add the cream, stirring frequently, until reduced by one-quarter. Purée the soup in a food processor or blender and return to the stockpot, keeping hot over very low heat.

In a skillet, melt the remaining butter over medium heat, and sauté the prawns and fish chunks for about 3 to 4 minutes, until the prawns turn bright orange. Add to the soup and season to taste with salt, black pepper and cayenne pepper. Warm the cognac in a small saucepan over low heat and carefully light it with a long match, then pour it very gently on top of the soup while the cognac is still burning. Once the flames have subsided, ladle the soup into individual bowls, sprinkle with Parmesan and serve with toasted slices of French bread.

Optional Mussels
Steam the mussels in their shells, with a tablespoon of butter in a pot with water, season them with salt and freshly ground black pepper, and add three mussels to each serving.

A medium-dry, somewhat oakey or lighter chardonnay, such as a Chablis or Meursault, will go best with this very rich soup.

Saint-Rémy and Nostradamus

Back street leading to Nostradamus' house

Michel de Nostradame, more commonly known as Nostradamus, was born on December 14, 1503, in Saint-Rémy de Provence. He was a seer and a time traveler living in two realities. He was also adept in astrology and astronomy and, along with his clairvoyance, he used science to interpret the visions he received in the secrecy of his study. He was often referred to as the Prophet of Doom because of the visions he had involving death and war. His followers say he predicted the French Revolution, the birth and rise to power of Hitler, and the assassination of John F. Kennedy. His writings have enthralled generations of readers. The house he lived in while penning most of his 'quatrains', dates from the 16th century and is still standing in the village and visited by tens of thousands of tourists each year.

Soupe au Pistou
Bean and Vegetable Soup with Garlic and Basil

This is a very traditional Provence soup, served in homes and restaurants across the South of France. It is equally successful as either a starter or main course. Serves 8 to 12.

½	lb (230 g) dry red beans, soaked overnight
½	lb (230 g) dry white beans, soaked overnight
I	tablespoon (15 ml) olive oil
I	large onion, finely chopped
3	quarts (2.9 liters) veal or beef stock (page 28)
2	large ripe tomatoes, peeled and chopped
I	tablespoon Provence herbs
½	lb (230 g) dry, small macaroni
2	potatoes, peeled and diced
4	carrots, diced
4	zucchini (courgettes), diced
I	cup (150 g) green peas
	Salt and freshly ground black pepper
I	cup (100 g) freshly grated Parmesan cheese
8	sprigs fresh basil leaves

THE PISTOU

2	cups (80 g) chopped, fresh basil
3	garlic cloves, chopped
3 to 4	tablespoons (45 to 60 ml) olive oil

To prepare the pistou, purée the basil and garlic in a food processor. With the machine running, slowly add the olive oil, continuing until the mixture becomes pasty. Season to taste with salt and pepper and set aside.

To prepare the soup, drain the beans and set aside. Heat the olive oil in a saucepan and sauté the onion until browned. Place the stock, red and white beans, tomatoes, sautéed onions, and Provence herbs in a large stockpot. Bring to a rolling boil, for 3 minutes. Reduce heat and simmer, for 1½ hours. Add the macaroni, potatoes, carrots, zucchini and green peas and continue to simmer for 30 minutes or until the beans and vegetables are tender. Remove from heat and season to taste with salt and pepper. Serve in individual bowls, with a dollop of pistou, a sprinkling of Parmesan and a sprig of fresh basil.

This soup *is one that can be served a day or two after it has been made with great results. To store the soup in the refrigerator, let it cool and cover tightly. To reheat, simply pour into a pot and heat to serving temperature, without boiling.*

Soupe au Pistou is very robustly flavored and goes best with a chunkier full-bodied red wine. An American or Australian cabernet or syrah goes nicely but your personal taste should ultimately dictate the selection.

Colonial Influences

In the 18th century, the British Empire encompassed vast areas of the world from North America and the West Indies, to Hong Kong, Singapore, Australia, South Africa, most of East Africa, Egypt, the Sudan, and the Middle East. It was said that, "the sun never sets on the British Empire," which was, at one time, quite literally true.

Traditional English cuisine is not always highly regarded. That notion, however, may be a bit unfair since, at one time, England was a culinary center of Europe. British colonists often introduced dishes they brought back from the colonies when they returned home to England. In later years, as the Empire began to shrink and the colonies gained varying forms of independence, many former British colonial subjects immigrated to England. Today, British cuisine has been transformed and the influence of immigrant cultures and former colonies are evident across the British Isles. Not long ago, the British press reported that the single most popular dish served in England was Chicken Tikka Masala, an Indian red curry dish. Chinese restaurants and take-away shops exist in every village in England, Scotland, and Wales, and Donner Kebab shops are nearly as common. There are far more Indian restaurants in England than French or Italian ones.

But Britain is not the only former colonial power whose local cuisine has been influenced dramatically by its colonial history.

Indonesia was a Dutch colony for more than 200 years and today there are many wonderful Indonesian restaurants and Indonesian dishes are cooked in many Dutch homes. A definite two-way effect on food is evident in France and the current and former French colonies. In Quebec, Polynesia, Louisiana, West Africa, North Africa and Indochina, the French influence on local cuisines is obvious. But the French, like the English and Dutch, also brought the foreign dishes home to France. Today, restaurants in Paris, Nice, Toulouse, Lyon, and Marseilles offer side dishes of couscous and sauces that clearly have oriental inspiration.

Mulligatawny Soup

Mulligatawny is the Anglicized version of the Tamil (a southern Indian Dravidian language) words for "pepper water" or "pepper broth." Its primary seasoning is mild, yellow Madras curry powder. People who say that they do not like Indian food or curries simply love this soup. Serves 8.

4	tablespoons (60 g) unsalted butter
3	lbs (1½ kg) cubed chicken pieces
1	cup (230 g) chicken giblets, chopped (optional)
1	large onion, chopped
3	large garlic cloves, finely chopped
3	leeks, white and pale green parts, sliced
4	celery stalks, cut into ½-inch slices
3	quarts (2.8 liters) poultry stock (page 28)
1	cup (200 g) uncooked basmati rice
2	tablespoons (30 g) yellow curry powder
1	tablespoon (15 g) grated fresh ginger
¼	teaspoon cumin seeds
8	whole cloves
¼	teaspoon cayenne
2	apples, peeled, cored and diced
1	cup (240 g) small green peas
1	cup (240 ml) heavy cream or crème fraîche
1	cup (230 g) plain yogurt
2	tablespoons (30 ml) fresh lemon juice

	Salt and freshly ground black pepper
¼	cup (10 g) chopped fresh parsley
¼	cup (30 g) flaked almonds, toasted
½	cup (50 g) shredded coconut

Variations

Add sliced carrots as an optional ingredient at the same time as the poultry stock, for flavor and color.

Heat half the butter in a large skillet over medium-high heat and sauté the chicken pieces, giblets, onions, and garlic until the chicken just begins to brown. At the same time, in another skillet, sauté the leeks and celery in the remaining butter.

Put the poultry stock in a large stockpot, add the rice and bring to a rolling boil, for 1 minute. Reduce heat to simmer and add the curry, ginger, cumin, cloves, cayenne and all of the sautéed ingredients. Simmer for 20 minutes over medium-low heat and then add the apples and peas, simmering for another 10 minutes. Stir in the cream, yogurt and lemon juice, and add curry powder, salt and pepper to taste. Pour into cups or bowls, garnish with parsley and almonds and serve. Serve the shredded coconut on the side, so that your guests can add it to suit their own tastes.

This soup, with its spicy flavor, is one that may be best with beer, rather than wine. India Pale Ale or a European lager would be my choices. If you are serving wine, I would suggest a medium-bodied red.

Leek and Potato Soup with Bacon

Inspired by the French classic of baby leek and potato soup, this is always a hit with guests at the restaurant and at home. It works well as either a starter or a main course. If used as a starter, it makes a nice prelude to a main course with full flavors, such as a red meat or game dish. Serves 6.

4 to 5 medium leeks, about 1½ lbs (690 g)

8 thick smoked bacon slices, diced

3 tablespoons (45 g) unsalted butter

1 large onion, chopped

1½ lb (690 g) waxy potatoes, peeled and diced

2 quarts (1.9 liters) poultry stock (page 28)
or vegetable stock (page 29)

Salt and freshly ground black pepper

Sour cream or crème fraîche, for garnish

Note *that leeks vary greatly in size and supermarkets will trim them very differently before displaying them. You will need to judge the right quantity to buy on a case-by-case basis.*

To prepare the leeks, chop off and discard the root ends, the top dark green parts and any discolored outer leaves. Halve the white and tender pale green parts lengthwise, then cut into ¼-inch slices. Wash the slices thoroughly in cold water to get rid of any trapped sand or soil, and drain in a colander. You should have about 4 cups of cut leeks after trimming and cleaning.

Fry the bacon over medium heat in a large skillet until it begins to brown. Remove the bacon from the skillet and set aside in a bowl lined with paper towels. In a large saucepan or heavy stockpot, melt the butter over medium heat until it bubbles. Add the onion and leeks, and sauté for 3 to 4 minutes, until the leeks soften.

Add the potatoes, bacon, and the stock. Bring to a boil, for 1 minute, then reduce heat, cover and simmer gently over low heat, stirring occasionally for 20 minutes, or until potatoes are cooked through, without becoming too soft. Season with salt and pepper to taste and serve with a dollop of sour cream or crème fraîche.

 With the bacon providing a more robust flavor, any full-bodied white wine or medium-bodied red wine will go well with this soup. In whites, I would choose a west coast chardonnay and in reds, a lighter Meritage from California, or a merlot.

Northwest Corn and Crab Chowder

This is one of the soups typically found in the Pacific Northwest that both Michel and I really like. It is quite easy to make and the combination of vegetables, corn and crab creates a special taste. Serves 6.

4	tablespoons (60 g) unsalted butter, softened
2	tablespoons (15 g) all-purpose flour
3	ears fresh sweet corn or 1½ cups (225 g) frozen kernels
⅓	cup (75 g) thick bacon slices, diced
2	large shallots, finely chopped
2	garlic cloves, finely chopped
1	teaspoon finely chopped fresh thyme
1	teaspoon finely chopped fresh parsley
1	teaspoon finely chopped fresh rosemary
1	carrot, diced
2	celery stalks, finely diced
1	small white or yellow onion, chopped
2	medium red or white potatoes, peeled and diced
6	cups (1.5 liters) fish stock (page 28) or vegetable stock (page 29)
1½	cups (360 ml) heavy cream or crème fraîche
½	red or orange bell pepper, cored, seeded and, finely diced
¾	lb (360 g) Dungeness crabmeat
	Salt and freshly ground black pepper
	Fresh basil or parsley leaves, for garnish

Mix 2 tablespoon of the butter with the flour, until well blended and set aside. If fresh, shuck the corn, cut the kernels from the cobs, and set aside.

In a large stockpot over medium-high heat, sauté the bacon, shallots, garlic, and herbs in 2 tablespoons butter until the shallots are translucent and just barely beginning to brown. Add the carrot, celery, onions, and potatoes, continuing to sauté for 2 to 3 minutes, until they begin to soften.

Add the stock, bring to a boil, and whisk in the butter and flour mixture, a little at a time. Reduce the heat and simmer for 5 to 7 minutes, whisking frequently, until the soup thickens slightly. Add the cream, stirring continuously. Stir in the corn kernels, bell pepper, and crabmeat. Reduce heat to low, season with salt and pepper to taste, and simmer, without boiling, until corn is cooked through. Ladle the soup into bowls, garnish with fresh basil or parsley, and serve.

A crisp, medium-dry Burgundy-style white wine goes really well with this soup, as it complements the crab and vegetable flavors. I would select Mâcon Villages, a semillon blanc or a lighter American chardonnay.

Guest Chef DEAN FEARING

The Dean of The Mansion

Dean Fearing is the renowned and highly creative chef at The Mansion on Turtle Creek in Dallas, Texas. He is one of a small number of American chefs who have capitalized on combining local cuisine with other regional influences and ingredients to create truly unique and sensational dishes. Dean was at the forefront of developing the new Southwest cuisine genre when he became The Mansion's executive chef in 1985.

Influenced by extensive worldwide travel, Dean infuses his Southwest culinary creations with concepts and techniques from Italian, Thai, Southern, Cajun, and Mexican cuisines. Such notables as Her Majesty The Queen of England and President George W. Bush have expressed delight upon tasting the Southwest cuisine served at The Mansion.

I first met Dean in London at the Lanesborough Hotel on Hyde Park Corner, when he spent a week as a guest chef, introducing his unique international fusion dishes. During his visit, I had the opportunity to introduce Dean and his wife to Lebanese food at our favorite Lebanese restaurant in London, Al Sultan, located at Shepherd's Market, in Mayfair.

Dean has won numerous awards, including the 1994 James Beard Perrier-Jouet Restaurant Award for Best Chef: Southwest. He creates new dishes each week, most of which begin with seasonal native ingredients complemented by an intriguing array of flavors from around the world. The result is both exotic and harmonious.

Classically trained at the Culinary Institute of America, Dean began his career at Maisonette in Cincinnati, followed by The Pyramid Room at The Fairmont Hotel in Dallas. When The Mansion on Turtle Creek opened in 1980, Dean came to the restaurant as executive sous-chef, a position from which he later resigned to become chef and part owner of the wildly successful Agnew's restaurant in Dallas. There, his daring experiments with indigenous Southwest ingredients drew the attention of Craig Claiborne, food editor at the New York Times, sparking the beginning of his rise to international prominence. Shortly thereafter, Dean "returned home" to The Mansion on Turtle Creek as executive chef.

A decade and countless culinary awards later, Dean is clearly in his element. He continues to develop Southwest cuisine, using all varieties of Texas-grown chili peppers, jicama, epazote, other native herbs, tomatillos, and avocados, and wild game, birds and venison, which the Texas hill country supplies.

The Mansion Restaurant

Mansion Tortilla Soup
Dean Fearing, Executive Chef, The Mansion on Turtle Creek

Mansion Tortilla Soup is one of Dean's signature dishes. This hearty soup, which is suitable on warm spring days as well as cold winter nights, has been on the menu since The Mansion on Turtle Creek opened. It is an easy to make dish that we come back to time and time again. Serves 8.

1	tablespoon olive oil
1	large onion, chopped
3	tablespoons (45 ml) corn oil
4	corn tortillas, coarsely chopped
6	garlic cloves, finely chopped
1	tablespoon chopped fresh epazote* or cilantro
2¼	cups (540 ml) fresh tomato purée
1	tablespoon cumin powder
2	teaspoons chili powder
2	bay leaves
2	quarts (1.9 liters) poultry stock (page 28)
	Salt and cayenne pepper
1	cooked chicken breast, cut into thin strips
1	cup (100 g) grated medium cheddar
1	avocado, peeled, pitted, and diced
3	corn tortillas, cut into thin strips and fried in oil until crisp

Heat the olive oil, over medium-high heat, sauté the onions until they are translucent. Add 1½ cups water, boil until onions are soft and mushy, and then purée in a blender or food processor and set aside.

Heat the corn oil in a large saucepan over medium heat. Sauté the chopped tortillas with garlic and epazote until the tortillas are soft. Add the tomato and onion purées and bring to a boil. Stir in the cumin, chili powder and bay leaves, and then add the chicken stock. Bring to a boil, again, and then reduce the heat to simmer. Add salt and cayenne pepper to taste and cook, stirring occasionally, for 30 minutes. Skim any fat from the surface, if necessary. Strain the soup and pour it into warm soup bowls. Garnish each bowl with equal portions of chicken breast, cheese, avocado, and crisp tortilla strips and serve.

* Epazote is an herb well known to Mexican and Caribbean cooking, and is an essential ingredient in Mexican black bean recipes. Also known as pigweed or Mexican tea, it is a pungent herb, and much like cilantro, one must acquire a taste for it.

With the spicy taste of this soup, a full-bodied red wine or a more oakey chardonnay works best. We particularly enjoy it with a California petite sirah or zinfandel. An oakey, buttery chardonnay from California or Australia can also go nicely. Cold beer is also a fine alternative.

Creole & Cajun Food

Malcolm Hébert was born and raised in Louisiana. At one time he was the food and wine editor at the San Jose Mercury News and wrote about Louisiana, Cajun, and Creole cuisine. I met Malcolm at a luncheon where he spoke on Cajun food. His articles were published in many food and wine magazines and Malcolm kindly sent me a copy of one he had written. That day piqued my interest and I began to experiment with Cajun and Creole dishes, for the first time. Here is Malcolm's article.

"The best way to know the cooking of New Orleans is to be raised there. My mother and father, who were born nearby, were proud of their heritage. Every year my parents drove "south" to visit my relatives, to feast on crabs, crawfish, gumbos, bisques, grits, preserved figs, salt pork, black-eyed peas, smothered chicken, oysters, shrimp, redfish, speckled trout, pain perdu, etc. From three years old until today, my greatest food memories were of the cooking of Louisiana.

I consider myself fortunate to have Creole parents raised in Cajun country so that I have been privileged to sample both cuisines. Obviously, both the Creole and Cajuns take food as seriously as they take anything on earth, and more so than the Chinese. The latter greet people with "Have you eaten well today?" In contrast, Creoles and Cajuns not only want to know what you have eaten, but what are you planning to eat for the remainder of the day as well as for tomorrow. Then they will tell you what they have eaten, will eat today, and what's on the menu for tomorrow.

Creoles and Cajuns live to eat. Their very existence is food, more food and still more food. They are not greedy and certainly not selfish. They will gladly share a meal with you, offering the choicest morsels for your pleasure. They have adopted the Spanish "my house is your house" philosophy and are happy to make sure your stomach is full.

What is the difference between Creole and Cajun cooking? Most Louisiana chroniclers claim the answer is simple. Many Creoles were rich planters and their kitchens aspired to grande cuisine. Their recipes came from France or Spain, as did their chefs. By using classic French techniques with local foodstuffs, they created a whole new cuisine, Creole cooking.

On the other hand, the Acadians, pronounced <uh-CADE-ee-uns>, later contracted to Cajun, were a tough people that were used to living under strenuous conditions. They tended to serve strong country food prepared from local ingredients. It was pungent, peppery and practical, as it was all cooked in a single pot. Thus Cajun cuisine was born.

While both cuisines are distinct, there are cross-references between the two. Rice is a staple of both and Creole and Cajun chefs usually start a dish by making a roux of oil and flour. In addition, there are many common ingredients such as crab, river shrimp, lake shrimp, oysters, crawfish, freshwater and saltwater fish, plus squirrels, wild turkeys, ducks, frogs, turtles, pork, homemade sausages, beans of all kinds, tomatoes, okra, yams, pecans, oranges, and wines, liqueurs and brandy.

There is one rule that both the Creoles and Cajuns agreed upon and that is that there is no one rule and no one recipe when it comes to matters of food. There are hundreds of different recipes for gumbo, jambalaya, turtle soup and they are all right because no one is wrong. Privately, they know that everything they cook is original, because their kitchens are kitchens of "ad lib." They are experimenting, creating, changing, and always trying to make it taste better."

New Orleans Style Gumbo

Gumbo is the signature Cajun stew and has delighted millions of visitors to Southern Louisiana. It is a hearty dish with a unique texture from the okra and the flavor from the filé powder. This is a fairly simple gumbo recipe that is quite easy to make. Serves 6.

¾ cup (180 ml) olive or vegetable oil

¼ cup (60 g) unsalted butter

1½ lbs (690 g) boneless chicken breasts and thighs,
     cut into bite-sized pieces

1 lb (900 g) Andouille or other smoked sausage,
     cut into ½-inch pieces

1 tablespoon Cajun seasoning
     Salt and freshly ground black pepper

2 tablespoons (15 g) all-purpose flour

2 large onions, finely chopped

4 garlic cloves, minced

2 bell peppers, cored, seeded and finely chopped

2 celery stalks, finely chopped

2 quarts (1.9 liters) poultry stock (page 28)

1 lb (450 g) fresh okra, ends trimmed,
     cut into ½ inch pieces

2 bay leaves

1 teaspoon dry thyme

½ cup (20 g) chopped fresh parsley

12 green onion tops, finely chopped

6 cups (1 kg) cooked white rice
     Filé powder, for serving
     Tabasco sauce, for serving

Filé powder, *sometimes called gumbo filé, is made from ground sassafras leaves. It will thicken a gumbo and add a distinctive kick of flavor. Filé powder should only be added just before serving. If allowed to boil, filé powder will cause a liquid to become stringy and unappetizing.*

Heat 2 tablespoons of the oil and 1 tablespoon of the butter in a large skillet over medium heat. Add the chicken, sausage, and Cajun seasoning with salt and pepper to taste. Cook, stirring occasionally, until cooked through, about 8 to 10 minutes. Remove from heat and set aside.

Heat the remaining butter and oil in a large, heavy stockpot over medium-low heat until it bubbles. Slowly add the flour, stirring constantly until the flour is well mixed with the oil and butter, forming a roux.

When the roux becomes a rich golden brown, add the onion, garlic, bell peppers, and celery, stirring continuously, for about 4 minutes. Add the poultry stock 1 cup at a time, mixing well to avoid lumps. Bring to a boil, and then reduce heat enough to maintain a gentle boil, allowing liquids to thicken slightly. Finally, stir in the okra, bay leaves, thyme, chicken, and sausage. Reduce heat to low, and simmer for 15 to 20 minutes, or until okra is cooked, stirring occasionally. Add the parsley and green onions and continue simmering for 4 to 5 minutes. To serve, mound one cup of warm rice in a shallow bowl and ladle gumbo over it. Sprinkle with filé powder, if desired, or allow each guest to add as much or as little as they like to their own gumbo. Provide Tabasco sauce as another option.

Many people prefer cold beer with gumbo, and I would not disagree, but if you prefer wine, I would suggest a lighter, medium dry white wine or a medium-bodied fruity red.

Kitchen Teamwork

Teaming up at home in London, with the irrepressible Stan Berde

Whether there are only two chefs or an entire team, coordinating work in a restaurant is essential to producing quality meals. Each chef has a role, in preparation and cooking or assembling dishes, and each is dependent on the other or others. As in all cooking, timing is everything. A restaurant kitchen is like a variable assembly line where specific tasks are unknown until the moment that an order is received. From that moment the kitchen team must work together like an orchestra, each person performing his or her role.

Teamwork in home cooking is much easier than in a restaurant. You have the advantage of knowing what dishes will be 'ordered' because it has already been decided. If one person is making the main dish while another is making side dishes, timing still needs to be coordinated so that the entire main course is ready to serve at the right time.

I love cooking at home with family and friends. I make a list of what we are going to make and the order in which each dish needs to be prepared. Then I collaborate with my cooking compatriots to divide up the preparation and cooking chores. It really helps to get us in sync and to be sure we have everything covered. Sometimes one person is responsible for prep and another for cooking. Other times we allocate responsibilities for complete dishes. This sort of coordination has two advantages. First, it minimizes the chances that we will miss something and, second, it allows for more time with guests.

Beef Barley Soup

This soup is simply a classic. Made well, it is a rich, filling soup that, with a bit of bread on the side and, perhaps a small salad, makes a complete meal. Serves 8.

1	cup (230 g) barley, pre-soaked in cold water for 2 to 3 hours
1	large onion, chopped
2	garlic cloves, finely chopped
2	tablespoons (20 ml) olive oil
1	lb (450 g) beef stew meat, cut into 1-inch cubes
2	tablespoons finely chopped fresh thyme
2	quarts (1.9 liters) beef stock (page 28)
8	large carrots, halved lengthwise and cut into ½-inch slices
1	bay leaf
	Salt and freshly ground black pepper

Drain the pre-soaked barley and set aside. In a skillet, sauté the onion and garlic in the olive oil over medium-high heat, until just translucent. Add the beef cubes and thyme, and continue sautéing, stirring frequently, until the meat is browned.

Place the beef sauté mix, beef stock, barley, carrots, and bay leaf in a large stockpot over medium-high heat and bring to a rolling boil, for 2 to 3 minutes. Reduce the heat to low, cover and simmer for 1½ hours, until the barley is soft and tender. Season to taste with salt and pepper. Remove from heat and let stand for 5 minutes, stirring occasionally, and serve.

You can keep this soup over very low heat for several hours before serving. It is also just as good refrigerated and reheated, 1 to 2 days later.

Almost any medium-to-full-bodied red wine will go well with this soup. An American cabernet sauvignon or a cabernet-merlot blend would be my own preference.

STARTERS

Avocado Mousse with Shrimp, Cucumber and Lemon   72

Boulettes de Porc avec Cacahuètes   73
(Pork Meatballs, with Peanuts and Cilantro)

Coquilles St. Jacques au Basilic   75
(Sautéed Sea Scallops with Basil, Garlic and Pine Nuts)

Seared Ahi Tuna with Soy and Sesame Sauce   77
Chef Matt Burns, The Don Restaurant, London

Dungeness Crab Cakes   79

Salmon and Asparagus Terrine   80

Chicken Liver and Mushroom Pâté   81

Starters

Starters, more commonly called appetizers in America, should pique your taste buds and leave you anxious to move on to the next course, but not too quickly. In larger quantities, some starters can work equally well as main dishes and vice-versa. Smaller portions of dishes like Salmon in Puff Pastry (page 119), Filet de Sole avec Crevettes Roses (page 121) and Jumbo Prawns Flambéed with Pernod (page 115) will also produce wonderful starters.

Fish or seafood starters work well as a prelude to meat, poultry and seafood main dishes. Meat or poultry based starters work best with more robustly flavored meat or game main dishes. Chicken Liver and Mushroom Pâté (page 81) is one poultry starter that goes well with seafood main dishes.

Although there are no hard and fast rules for choosing starters and main dishes, the following guidelines, which I first learned from Michel, have always helped my decisions.

Starters should be relatively small portions, enough to satisfy but not so much as to detract from subsequent courses. The objective is to please your guests without overfeeding them. A good rule of thumb in planning menus is to make starters that are less than half the size of your main dish portions.

The starters you serve should complement and neither detract from, nor overwhelm, the main dish that follows. A very spicy or robustly flavored starter should generally not be served with a lighter, more delicate main dish unless the flavors are complementary. If the starter is spicy, be sure that your main dish has enough zing to be compatible with it.

Sometimes two or three starters can make a satisfying meal. In some cultures, entire meals often consist only of small starter portions of several different dishes. In Spain or Portugal, *tapas* are often served without any larger main dish. In the Middle East, whole meals called *mezas* consist of a variety of small dishes. In Japanese cuisine, *kai seki ryori* is a gourmet feast made up of very small, ornate dishes that are served in seashells and tiny porcelain plates or shallow bowls.

Avocado Mousse with Shrimp, Cucumber and Lemon

This light and flavorful mousse makes for an excellent starter with almost any main dish, and, as it is served cold, can be made well in advance and stored in the refrigerator. I usually prepare it before starting other dishes, on the day I plan to serve it, and add the garnish just before serving. Serves 8.

4	whole avocados, peeled, pitted and chopped
¼	cup sour cream or crème fraîche
¼	cup (60 ml) fresh lemon juice
¼	cup (10 g) fresh parsley, finely chopped
2	cups (340 g) bay shrimp (reserve 8 for garnish)
½	red or orange bell pepper, finely diced
½	cucumber, peeled and diced
	Salt and freshly ground black pepper
	Cayenne pepper

GARNISH

	Paprika
4	cherry tomatoes, halved
1	avocado, peeled, pitted and cut into 8 wedges
	Bay shrimp
	Dill or parsley sprigs

In a food processor, combine the avocados, sour cream, lemon juice, and chopped parsley, until well blended. Transfer to a medium bowl and fold in the shrimp, bell pepper and cucumber, with salt, pepper and cayenne to taste.

Place the mixture in small glass bowls or glass cups. Cover with plastic wrap and store in the refrigerator at least 1 hour before serving. To serve, sprinkle paprika very lightly on the top, and garnish each with an avocado wedge, a whole bay shrimp, a cherry tomato half, and a dill or parsley sprig.

 A lighter rosé, Champagne, or a sparkling rosé is the perfect accompaniment to this dish. A light, fruity wine like a Riesling or semillon blanc would also work well.

Boulettes de Porc avec Cacahuètes
Pork Meatballs with Peanuts and Cilantro

Delicious as a starter, these flavorful pork boulettes can also be a great success as hors d'oeuvres for a cocktail party or reception. The dish originates from southwest France, near Toulouse. This recipe is modified from the original by the addition of soy sauce, sesame oil, and oriental dipping sauce. Serves 8.

1	lb (950 g) ground lean pork
½	lb (470 g) ground veal
1	cup (230 g) finely chopped unsalted peanuts
2	large eggs, beaten
1	tablespoon (15 ml) soy sauce
1	teaspoon (5 ml) sesame oil
1	teaspoon (5 ml) clear honey
¼	cup finely chopped cilantro
¼	cup (10 g) finely chopped parsley
1	tablespoon finely chopped fresh rosemary
2	cups Teriyaki or Thai peanut dipping sauce
	Whole cilantro leaves, for garnish

Preheat the oven to 400° F (200° C). Line a baking pan or dish with foil.

In a large bowl, mix the pork, veal, peanuts, eggs, soy sauce, sesame oil, honey, cilantro, parsley, and rosemary, together with your hands, until all of the ingredients are well mixed. Form 24 1-inch balls and place in the baking pan, with a bit of space between the balls.

Bake for about 20 to 25 minutes, until the meat is just cooked through and lightly browned. Be careful not allow the *boulettes* to cook too long or they will become dry.

Remove from the oven and arrange the *boulettes* on individual plates (3 each for starters) or a serving platter for hors d'oeuvres. Garnish with whole cilantro leaves and serve with dipping sauce.

Note that you can find ready made dipping sauces in your supermarket's ethnic foods section.

Note *that boulettes can be prepared a day in advance and left uncooked. Cover and store them in the refrigerator. When you are ready to serve them, proceed with the final baking instructions.*

A lighter, medium-dry fruity red wine will go well with this starter, as will cold beer. For white wine, I would choose an Alsace Riesling.

Scallops

Scallop shells displayed on ice

Scallops are known for their beautiful and distinctive shells, which have been the subject of many works of art dating back to ancient Greece and Rome. Buildings in ancient Pompeii, unearthed in the rubble of Mount Vesuvius, were decorated with scallop-shell ornaments.

There are two common types of scallops; larger sea scallops and smaller bay scallops. As their names indicate, sea scallops are found in the ocean or sea and bay scallops in bays and estuaries. Sea scallops are typically about 1½ inches in diameter, while their smaller cousin, the bay scallop, is usually about one third that size. Several hundred different species of scallops are found worldwide in shallow, shoreline areas and most seas.

Scallops are special for their delicious taste and the many ways they can be prepared. They do need to be cooked carefully as they can easily toughen, losing their flavor and texture. They should be removed from the heat as soon as they lose their translucence and turn opaque. When cooked properly, scallops are sweet and tender but still firm.

Versatility for cooking is one particularly appealing aspect of scallops. They can be prepared in many ways including grilling, broiling, sautéing, or stir-frying. They work equally well very simply prepared by themselves, such as in Coquille St. Jacques au Basilic, on the facing page, or as one of several ingredients in a larger dish such as Paella Seattle (page 129).

Coquilles St. Jacques au Basilic
Sautéed Sea Scallops with Basil, Garlic and Pine Nuts

This starter works well with any main course and only takes minutes to prepare. Best of all, it is just delicious and always gets lots of praise from guests. As with all seafood, freshness is key to a successful dish. Fresh, large sea scallops will work best. Serves 8.

½   cup (20 g) chopped fresh basil
4   garlic cloves, finely chopped
¼   cup (40 g) chopped pine nuts
2   tablespoons (30 ml) olive oil
2   tablespoons unsalted (30 g) butter
24   large sea scallops
     Salt and freshly ground black pepper
8   lettuce leaves, washed and dried
12   cherry tomatoes, halved
½   cup (75 g) toasted pine nuts, for garnish
8   rosemary sprigs, for garnish
     Paprika or freshly ground black pepper, for accent

In a food processor or blender, blend the basil, garlic, chopped pine nuts, olive oil and 1 tablespoon of the butter into a smooth paste and set aside.

Cut each of the scallops in half, horizontally. Sandwich a layer of the paste, about ⅛-inch thick, between the two halves of each scallop. Melt the remaining oil and butter in a large skillet over medium-high heat, until the butter bubbles. Season with salt and pepper and sauté the scallops until golden brown (about 2 to 3 minutes on each side).

To serve, place a lettuce leaf on each plate and arrange 3 scallops and 3 cherry tomato halves on each leaf. Scatter a few pine nuts over the scallops, sprinkle paprika or black pepper around the edge of the plate for accent, and serve.

A dry, light white wine will complement this dish. I would recommend a white Burgundy or lighter American chardonnay, as more oakey, buttery chardonnays will detract from the dish's natural flavors.

The Spirit of The Don

Guest Chef MATT BURNS

The Don is one of my favorite restaurants, in London. Many of the staff are French and the menus, created by Chef Matthew Burns, show a decidedly French influence. The food is consistently excellent and the wine list is extensive, with expert Sommeliers on hand to assist with selections.

The Don is located at 20 St. Swithins Lane, in the 'City of London', at a site with much history. It takes its name from the Sandeman Don, a symbol of excellence in the world of ports and sherries, and the occupant of the premises, from 1798, when George Sandeman from Perthshire Scotland, took over the site as the cellar for his port, sherry, and wine company. Ports, sherries, and Madeiras were bottled here until 1969. The black-caped figure of The Don, with his flat black sombrero, graces the labels of Sandeman ports and sherries to this day.

Chef Matthew Burns, originally from Bury, Lancashire, grew up on a race horse and rare breed dairy farm, and says, "that meant shooting hare, rabbits and pigeon, so we had an interest in food and preparation from a young age." Matt started work at 16 at The Ritz, in London as apprentice and went on to work with the Roux Brothers for 6 years at Le Gavroche, then Interlude and La Tante Clare. Matthew creates original dishes based on his classical training but inspired by other international cuisines and his own imagination.

I have been making seared tuna dishes for more than 25 years and have seldom tasted one in a restaurant that I liked as well as my own. Then one night at The Don, I tried Matthew's seared tuna. It was simply the best I had ever tasted. He was kind enough to share his recipe, which is shown on the facing page, and that is the only way I have done it since.

With an elegantly open upstairs restaurant and a downstairs bistro housed in the original cellars, The Don offers a choice of more formal or more relaxed dining. Booking well in advance is recommended for either, as both are usually filled for every lunch and dinner.

The bistro is a true wine cellar with thick vaulted brick walls and an arched ceiling, recapturing precisely the atmosphere of a working port and sherry house, in past centuries. At one end, there is a small bar that is perfect for enjoying a cocktail or aperitif, before sitting down to your table, and it features an extensive selection of single malt whiskies.

Service is friendly, without being overly familiar. The staff is alert to each guest's every needs and special requests are almost always accommodated with a smile.

London, England

Seared Ahi Tuna with Soy and Sesame Sauce
Matthew Burns, The Don Restaurant, London

Purchase one whole tuna fillet, 10 inches in length and 3 to 3½ inches in diameter. Your tuna should be very fresh, sashimi quality and deep red in color. Using very fresh tuna is important, since it will not be cooked through. Preparation of this dish should be completed at least 4 hours before you plan to serve it. Serves 8.

1	whole Ahi tuna fillet, about 1½ lbs (690 g)
¼	cup (40 g) peeled, grated fresh ginger
4	garlic cloves, minced
¼	cup (30 g) lemon zest
¼	cup (10 g) finely chopped fresh cilantro
½	teaspoon salt
½	teaspoon freshly ground black pepper
3	tablespoons (45 ml) olive oil
	Julienned carrots and white radishes, for garnish

THE SAUCE

½	cup (120 ml) light soy sauce
2	tablespoons (30 ml) balsamic vinegar
2	tablespoons (30 g) clear honey
2	tablespoons (30 ml) fresh lemon juice
	Peels from ginger
½	cup (120 ml) toasted sesame oil

Sear the whole tuna fillet in 1 tablespoon of oil, over high heat, until evenly browned to approximately ⅛-inch depth on all surfaces, including ends. Remove from pan and leave to cool to room temperature. Mix the ginger, garlic, lemon zest, cilantro, salt, pepper and 2 tablespoons olive oil, and roll the tuna in this mixture to cover all surfaces well. Place in a tightly covered container and refrigerate for at least three hours.

Place the soy sauce in a saucepan and bring to a boil. When reduced by half, add the balsamic vinegar and reduce by half volume again. Add the honey, lemon juice and ginger and simmer for five minutes. Stir in the sesame oil and remove from heat. When cool, strain the dressing mixture through a fine sieve and chill.

To serve, cut the tuna into ⅜ inch (1cm) thick slices. Place a bit of lettuce on individual salad plates and top with julienned carrots and white radishes. Arrange 3 tuna slices on each plate, as shown. Stir the sauce well and spoon it over the cut faces of the tuna. Serve immediately.

A medium-dry white wine will go best with this dish. My own preference would be a Burgundy-style chardonnay.

Shellfish for All Seasons

Freshly caught live Dungeness crab

The waters of the Pacific Northwest offer an incredible variety of fish and shellfish. When Michel lived in Seattle and Alaska, he would often get fresh seafood directly from local fishermen and, sometimes, on a day off, he would go fishing himself. Michel still fishes today at a nearby lake. When time permits, he also likes to fish on the Mediterranean, which is only an hour away from Saint-Rémy.

As a child in British Columbia, I fished with my cousins and friends nearly every morning from April to September. The local waters were filled with shellfish for the taking. Mussels, abalone, oysters and scallops would cling to rocks in the shallow tide pools and could be gathered at low tide. The sands were alive with clams revealing their presence by spurting geysers of water. At night, the crab pots were taken out into the bay and when retrieved in the morning, they were filled with crabs crawling over each other and trying to free themselves. The thought of crab and corn chowder, made with fresh crabmeat, locally grown sweet corn, and new potatoes, still makes my mouth water.

In the spring, shrimp beds formed at the mouth of a local creek that flowed into the bay. Locally, these small bay shrimp were called pearl shrimp and had wonderful sweet flavor when simply boiled in salted water and peeled. Abalone is my own ultimate shellfish treat. We gathered them by diving just a few feet below the surface of what many people, used to warmer climates and waters, would think of as ice water. Abalone meat is a solid, off-white sphere of meat with a tough, rubbery texture. Preparing it involves slicing it sideways, into ¼-inch slices and pounding the slices with a meat hammer until tender. It has a most appealing flavor when breaded and sautéed in butter. Unfortunately, abalone stocks are endangered and their harvesting is now severely limited.

Dungeness Crab Cakes

Dungeness is a west coast crab variety with slightly sweet flesh. Crab cakes are a favored preparation for this delicious crustacean and they are great as a starter or as a main dish. If Dungeness crab is not available, other crabmeat can be used instead. Serves 10.

3	tablespoons (45 ml) Dijon mustard
1	large egg yolk
2	tablespoons (30 ml) white wine
2	teaspoons (10 ml) Worcestershire sauce
¼	cup (60 ml) tomato sauce
½	teaspoon paprika
¼	teaspoon cayenne pepper
1	tablespoon finely chopped fresh rosemary
1	tablespoon finely chopped fresh thyme
5	tablespoons (75 ml) olive oil
¾	cup (30 g) finely chopped fresh cilantro
4	cups (200 g) soft, dry white bread crumbs
1	lb (450 g) Dungeness crab meat
½	green bell pepper, seeded finely chopped
½	red bell pepper, seeded and finely chopped
3	large shallots, finely chopped
4	large garlic cloves, finely chopped
3	medium new potatoes, boiled, peeled and diced
5	tablespoons (75 g) unsalted butter
	Salt and freshly ground pepper

Note *that this dish is best when prepared the day before cooking and serving.*

In a food processor, mix the Dijon mustard, egg yolk, wine, Worcestershire sauce, tomato sauce, paprika, cayenne, rosemary and thyme, pulsing until well blended. Slowly add the oil and continue pulsing until the mixture is well blended and has a mayonnaise-like consistency. Place in a small bowl, cover and refrigerate.

Mix ¼ cup of the cilantro with 2 cups of breadcrumbs in a medium bowl and set aside. Remove excess liquid from the crabmeat by pressing it into a sieve. In a large bowl, combine the bell peppers, shallots, garlic and remaining cilantro and breadcrumbs. Add the crab-meat, diced potatoes, and chilled Dijon mixture, and mix gently until all ingredients are just combined. Shape into 10 patties. Carefully coat the patties with the cilantro breadcrumb mix and, if serving the following day, refrigerate overnight in a tightly covered container.

Preheat the oven to 400° F (200° C), line a baking pan with foil and coat lightly with oil.

Heat the butter in a large skillet over medium heat until it bubbles. Sauté the crab cakes on both sides until golden brown. Place them in the baking pan and bake until hot all the way through (about 5 to 7 minutes). Serve immediately, with tartar sauce or cocktail sauce.

A medium-dry Chablis or less oakey chardonnay is the perfect complement to this dish.

Salmon and Asparagus Terrine

Many home cooks hesitate to try making pâtés or terrines because they think them difficult. They are in fact, relatively easy to make and are wonderful starters that your guests will definitely enjoy. Salmon terrine makes an ideal light starter for either lunch or dinner. This terrine is best if prepared on the day before it is to be served. Serves 12.

2½ lbs (1.1 kg) thin asparagus spears
2¼ lbs (1 kg) fresh, skinless salmon fillet,
       boned and chopped
2   egg whites
½   cup (120 ml) whipping cream
     Salt and freshly ground black pepper
     Paprika, for accent
12   lemon wedges, for garnish

Terminology

Pâtés are baked in ceramic containers called 'terrines' but terrine is also a name for dishes closely related to pâtés that are baked in the same containers.

Preheat the oven to 400° F (200° C).

Trim off the hard bottoms of the asparagus spears. Blanch the asparagus in salted, boiling water, immediately chill them in a bowl of ice water, and then dry them and cut them into 1-inch sections.

In a food processor, blend the salmon, egg whites, cream, salt, and pepper, until completely smooth. Line the inside of a terrine mold or bread loaf pan with foil. Put a layer of salmon mousse at the bottom and then alternate layers of asparagus, lying parallel to the length of the pan, and salmon mousse. The top layer should be a salmon layer.

Place the terrine mold in a larger, deep baking pan, half-filled with hot water and cook for approximately 25 minutes, until just cooked through. Test by inserting a clean, thin knife into the middle of the terrine. If salmon sticks to the knife when it is pulled out, the terrine is not done. When cooked through, let cool then cover and refrigerate until ready to serve.

To serve, remove the terrine from the mold, cut into ½-inch slices and allow the slices to come to room temperature on individual plates. Garnish both the terrine slices and the plate with a dusting of paprika and place a lemon wedge at the side of the terrine. A sprig or two of parsley and a small bunch of salad greens or a few cooked asparagus spears, with dressing, will set off the terrine on the plate. For an additional decorative touch, place a small smoked salmon rosette on each plate, as shown.

❁ *A light, fruity white wine, a lighter rosé or sparkling rosé, or Champagne is the perfect accompaniment.*

Chicken Liver and Mushroom Pâté

This pâté is ideal as a starter or hors d'oeuvres served on baguette slices or water crackers with a piece of olive for accent. This recipe is one that never fails to please, even though it is one of the easiest to make. Chicken livers should be readily available at most supermarkets and any poultry butcher's shop. Serves 12.

1	cup (240 g) unsalted butter
2	lbs (900 g) trimmed chicken livers
½	lb (230 g) mushrooms
1	large shallot, chopped
½	cup (120 ml) whipping cream
1	teaspoon Provence herbs
1	teaspoon Poultry Seasoning
1	teaspoon Beau Monde seasoning
¼	cup (60 ml) Armagnac, cognac or brandy
4	tablespoons (60 g) unsalted butter, melted
	Toast points or toasted baguette slices

In a large skillet, heat the butter over medium heat, until it begins to bubble. Add the chicken livers, mushrooms, shallots, cream, Provence herbs, Poultry Seasoning, and Beau Monde seasoning. Cook until the chicken livers become firm but are still slightly pink in the center. To test doneness, simply slice a liver in half and check the color. Add the brandy and carefully ignite from the gas flames or with a long match, gently moving the pan until the flame dies. Remove from the heat and let cool to room temperature.

When cooled, purée the mixture in a food processor, until completely smooth. Spoon into one or more molds (terrines or loaf pans can be used) lined with plastic wrap and pour the melted butter over the top. Refrigerate at least 6 hours until ready to serve.

To serve, remove pâté from the mold, cut into ½ inch slices, and allow the slices to come to room temperature on individual plates, about 30 minutes. Serve with slices of toasted bread and garnish with sprigs of parsley, a few salad greens and slices of cherry tomato.

A fairly oakey California chardonnay will go very nicely with this pâté.

Prepare *the pâté at least six hours before you plan to serve it. It should, however, be served at room temperature, in order to maximize the flavor.*

Pâtés *can be made from other meats, seafood or vegetables. One of our favorites, in Provence, is Pâté de Sanglier, a delicious, chunky pâté, made with wild boar meat.*

Restaurant Life in Saint-Rémy

La Table de Michel's terrace at lunchtime

Restaurant life is a continuous circle of procurement, preparation, cooking, serving and the inevitable chores of cleaning up, closing, and opening again. Think of having lunch and dinner parties every day in your home. And then imagine that you have at least 50 guests for every meal and a menu with five or six choices for each of three or four courses. The routine requires planning for menu specials and changes that are based upon the season and available foods.

In Provence, every day, except Sunday, is market day. Each village in the area has its open-air market on a different day where local producers display their products for sale.

Local producers also make deliveries of fresh produce, wines, other beverages, and specialties such as smoked salmon and poultry directly to the restaurant. A trip to the large commercial market in Avignon, which is only open to 'the trade', is required twice each week for staples and hard goods. Fresh fish arrives early each morning, except on Sundays, at a local fish market.

The restaurant day begins early in the morning by setting tables and preparing lunch. After lunch

there is time for the staff to eat and have a break until it is time to prepare for the evening meal. On some days that time is used to plan menu specials for the following days. On other days there is time for a walk around the village or up into the surrounding hills. When the weather is fine, as it is most of the year, these short treks are wonderful therapy. There is nothing like a stroll in the hills on a beautiful day to recharge the batteries so you are ready to greet the evening's guests.

During 'the season', which lasts from Easter until the end of September, the restaurant is open seven days a week with service from late morning until the last dinner guests leave. Some guests linger later at night which provides a chance to get to know them a bit. You meet some very interesting people and always have an opportunity to learn something new.

In late fall and early spring, when most tourists have abandoned Provence, the restaurant closes from Sunday afternoon until Tuesday lunch. When I have the chance to be there, usually just one weekend each month, we entertain a few friends and neighbors on the Sunday or Monday night. These are delightful affairs since we can join our guests at the table and have a truly relaxed evening.

On such occasions we abandon the normal menu and get creative. The restaurant menu is traditional French with a decidedly Provence influence. So, for these evenings, the dishes are whatever we feel inspired to make on the spur of the moment. They are often dishes from, or at least inspired by, other cuisines. Sometimes we taste new wine releases from local producers or open a bottle or two of something special that we have been saving in the cellar.

One of our friends refers to these as 'Surprise-Us Dinners' and we often do just that. Michel may make a more unusual but traditional French dish, such as *Tête de Veau* (calf's head) or *Boudin Noir* (blood sausage). You never know what may come out of the kitchen when Michel gets creative; you only know that it is going to be delicious. His talent for combining ingredients that most people would not normally think of always makes for a most memorable experience.

Once in a while, Michel turns the kitchen over to me. Michel and many of our friends like a bit of spice so, when I have charge of dinner, I often make a meal consisting entirely of Asian, Oriental or Cajun dishes that I have learned in my travels to the

Tasting a newly released wine and comparing opinions

Far East and the southwestern United States. When I am at the restaurant, I usually take responsibility for staff meals and make dishes that are not part of the restaurant's normal fare. These are simple meals, such as Italian meatloaf, Chinese stir-fries, and Asian noodle dishes, or French Dip sandwiches, a particular favorite of Michel's from his days in America.

There are many rewards in the restaurant business. Visitors come to Provence from the far corners of the earth and many return at least every year or two. When guests return several times during the course of their holiday visits, we know they have really enjoyed their experiences at La Table de Michel. Quite often, first-time guests arrive and tell us that their friends who had visited previously recommended the restaurant. When that happens, there is an instant connection.

MEAT DISHES

FILET AU POIVRE   87
(THE CLASSIC FRENCH PEPPER STEAK)

FILET D'AGNEAU EN CROÛTE   88
(LAMB LOIN WITH MUSHROOM DUXELLES IN PUFF PASTRY)

BŒUF EN DAUBE À LA PROVENÇALE   89
(PROVENCE STYLE BEEF STEW IN RED WINE)

LAMB CANNONS IN RED CURRANT SAUCE   91
CHEF NEIL DEMPSEY, ZIBA RESTAURANT, LIVERPOOL

ROAST SIRLOIN ENCRUSTED IN ENGLISH MUSTARD   92

PORC RÔTI BELLAGIO   93
(ROAST PORK LOIN WITH HERBS IN PANCETTA)

VEAL PARMIGIANA   94

VEAL MARSALA   95

ITALIAN SAUSAGES WITH MIXED BEANS AND POLENTA   97

Meat Dishes

Beef, lamb, veal, or pork are staple ingredients, almost everywhere in the world. All can be prepared in a vast number of different ways with great results. Lean cuts of red meat are loaded with protein and other essential dietary nutrients, and contain only a little more fat than a same-sized skinless chicken breast.

As always, quality ingredients make a tremendous difference in the end result of your cooking. The best beef, veal and lamb are naturally raised. That is grass-fed, outside on a farm, as opposed to cereal-fed in a feedlot. The best beef and lamb is also hung to age for at least 20 days. The beef and lamb that our friend, Andrew Sharp, sells in England is hung for 35 days and you can taste the difference that it makes.

With all red meats, the degree of cooking is often a controversial subject. On quite a few occasions I have been in restaurants with friends who wanted their steak well-done, only to be told by a server "the chef will not do that." Whether at home or in a restaurant, if one of your primary objectives is to please your guests, as I believe it should be, accommodating their wishes just makes good sense. I personally prefer roasts and steaks cooked medium-rare or pink but not very rare. Pork should always be completely cooked but not to the point that it dries out. Some form of coating can really help to seal in the juices.

In many cases, several different cuts of meat will produce equally successful results for a single recipe. Where that is the case, we have included alternate cuts under 'Variations'. Long ago, Michel taught me that simpler cooking methods for red meats often produce the best dishes and that a delicious sauce can turn an ordinary dish into a spectacular one.

Accolades that Mean the Most

When the great chefs of Seattle dine out, many of them dine at Deville's.
Michel Deville (center) and assistants Byron Hall (right) and Merlyn Baker showed off his restaurant's "cooking bourgeois".

For Michel, the accolades that mean the most are the opinions of his professional chef peers. Other professionals' views of one's work always provide the most demanding evaluations. For a 1979 article in the Seattle Post-Intelligencer newspaper, food critic and writer, Julie Smith, interviewed most of the highly regarded chefs in the Seattle area. She asked them which restaurants, other than their own, were their favorites. She wrote, "All week long, the city's great chefs cook the crème de la crème for the customer. Presumably their palates are primed for the nonpareil. So when the great chefs of Seattle . dine out, where do they dine? Deville's on Broadway gets the most votes."

Everywhere Michel has been, other chefs have remarked very favorably about his cooking talents and creativity. I remember, some years ago, meeting the owner-chef of one of the most highly acclaimed French restaurants in London. Over a glass of wine, he told me that, when he had a night out, his favorite place to dine was Chez Maria in Richmond. He said, "I go to Michel's place for the best of classic, traditional cooking in a comfortable environment, without the pretensions of many other restaurants." You know you are doing something right when chef peers say such things about your work.

Filet au Poivre
The Classic French Pepper Steak

*This is the first dish that Michel taught me in the earliest days of our friendship.
It is a true classic and has delighted sophisticated palates for decades. It is always a
success and, best of all, is extremely easy to prepare. Serves 6.*

6	beef tenderloin steaks (6 to 8 oz/180 to 240g each) about 1 inch thick
¼	cup (25 g) cracked black pepper
1	tablespoon (15 g) unsalted butter
1	tablespoon (15 ml) olive oil
½	cup (120 ml) cognac or Armagnac
1½	cups (360 ml) Brown Sauce (page 30)
⅓	cup (75 ml) heavy cream

Coat each of the steaks generously on both sides with cracked pepper.

In a large saucepan or skillet, heat the butter and oil over medium-high heat until the
butter begins to bubble. Add the steaks and cook on each side until medium rare (about 4
minutes per side) or, if you wish, medium (about 5 to 6 minutes per side). Pour the brandy
over the steaks, let it warm slightly and ignite it from the gas flame by gently tilting the pan
into the flame. If using an electric stove, ignite the brandy with a long match. In either case, be
very careful not to burn yourself when igniting the brandy. Once the flames have died, remove
the steaks from the pan and set aside in a 140° F (60° C) oven.

Add the cream to the pan, stirring continuously, and stir in the brown sauce. Reduce again
until nicely thickened. Take the steaks from the oven and stir any residual juices into the sauce.
Place the steaks on individual serving plates, pour sauce liberally over each steak, and serve
with side dishes.

Although *using
tenderloin is tradi-
tional, New York or
Sirloin cuts work
equally well and
some people think
that they have more
flavor.*

Variation

A variation is *Filet de Bœuf au Fromage Bleu.* Eliminate the cracked pepper and brandy
from the recipe, and, instead place a thick slice of blue cheese, such as English Stilton, on each
of the steaks, after you have turned them over in the skillet. Crumble an additional 2 to 3
ounces of the cheese into your sauce and mix it in, as you reduce it.

*A full-bodied, chunky red wine will make the most successful accompaniment to this dish. We recom-
mend older Clarets from Bordeaux or cabernet sauvignons from America. A California petite sirah or
an Italian Tiganello would be another good choice. With the intensity of the pepper and brandy sauce,
the wine needs to be able to hold its own. Lighter, less full-bodied wines simply will not work as well.*

Filet d'Agneau en Croûte
Lamb Loin with Mushroom Duxelles in Puff Pastry

This dish never ceases to delight. It is a very easy dish to make, even though working with puff pastry may take a little bit of practice before you get comfortable with it. Serves 6.

Duxelles *is a mushroom mixture used to thicken or augment a stuffing or a sauce and to intensify its flavor.*

6	lamb fillets (6 oz/180 g each)
2	tablespoons Provence herbs
	Salt and freshly ground pepper
1	tablespoon (15 g) unsalted butter
1	tablespoon (15 ml) olive oil
2	puff pastry sheets (about 10 x16 inches, each)
1	cup (170 g) mushroom purée
1	egg, beaten with 1 teaspoon (15 ml) milk
1½	cups (360 ml) Brown Sauce (page 30)

MUSHROOM DUXELLES PASTE

1	tablespoon (15 g) unsalted butter
1	shallot, finely chopped
2	cups (300 g) minced mushrooms (shiitakes, if available)
2	tablespoons (30 ml) cream
	Salt and freshly ground pepper

For the *duxelles*, melt the butter in a saucepan over medium-high heat and sauté the shallots, until just browned. Add the mushrooms and continue sautéing, until cooked through. Add the cream, stirring continuously, and continue cooking until the mixture reduces and thickens to a paste. Remove from heat and set aside.

Pre-heat the oven to 375° F (190° C). Sprinkle each of the lamb fillets lightly on all sides with Provence herbs, salt and pepper. In a large saucepan or skillet, heat the butter and olive oil over medium heat until the butter begins to bubble. Sear the lamb fillets very quickly on all sides, until just lightly browned. Remove the lamb fillets from the pan and set aside to cool. Remove the pan from heat and reserve the seared lamb juices in the pan.

Cut the puff pastry sheets to size, allowing enough overlap to easily wrap each fillet. Place one tablespoon of *duxelles* on each fillet. Wrap the fillets in puff pastry and squeeze the edges together to seal in the meat completely. Brush the surface of the pastry with the egg and milk mixture. Place the wrapped fillets on a foil-covered baking sheet. Bake until pastry turns to a rich golden brown color and remove from oven.

For the sauce, stir the brown sauce into the pan with the reserved meat juices. Season to taste with salt, freshly ground pepper, and Provence herbs. Place the pastry-wrapped fillets on individual serving plates, pour sauce liberally over each fillet and serve.

❀ *A full-bodied, sophisticated red wine will make the most successful accompaniment to this dish. I would recommend a mature Claret from Bordeaux, an Hermitage from Burgundy, or a cabernet sauvignon from the New World. California zinfandels or petite sirahs would be other good choices.*

Boeuf en Daube à la Provençale
Provence Style Beef Stew in Red Wine

The "mother" of all stews, daube is a classic French dish of slowly braised beef, red wine, vegetables, and seasonings. This is Michel's own recipe from Provence. Traditionally, this dish is prepared over the course of three days: one day to marinate, one day to cook, and one day to mature flavors. Serves 12.

4-5	lbs (2 kg) lean stewing beef, cut into cubes
1	tablespoon Provence herbs
	Salt and freshly ground black pepper
2	onions, halved and cut into ½-inch slices
4	carrots, cut into ½-inch pieces
1½	cups (360 ml) full-bodied red wine
2	tablespoons (30 ml) cognac or other brandy
4	thick bacon slices, chopped
1	tablespoon (15 ml) olive oil
3	garlic cloves
	Peel of ½ orange, cut into small slices
2	bay leaves
2½	cups (600 ml) beef stock (page 28)
½	cup (70 g) pitted black olives (not canned)
1	cup (40 g) chopped fresh parsley

Season the beef cubes with the Provence herbs, salt and pepper. In a bowl, combine the beef, half the onions, half the carrots, red wine and brandy. Be sure the wine and cognac cover most of the solid ingredients. Cover and refrigerate for at least 6 hours.

Preheat the oven to 275°F (140°C). Separate the beef from the marinated vegetables and wine, reserving these for later use. Pat the beef dry with paper towels. Sauté the bacon in a large Dutch oven over medium high heat until golden. Remove bacon and set aside, leaving the bacon fat in the pot. Add the oil, and sauté the beef, in batches on all sides, about 10 minutes (do not crowd the pan). Remove the last batch of beef and sauté the remaining onions and carrots in the same pan, stirring frequently until browned, about 10 minutes. Remove from heat.

Return the bacon and all the beef to the Dutch oven. Add the reserved wine marinade and vegetables, garlic, orange peel, bay leaves, and beef stock. Cover with a tightly fitting lid and braise in the oven for 3 to 4 hours, until beef is fork tender. Remove from oven and skim off excess surface fat. Add the olives, taste, and adjust seasoning with salt and pepper. If making a day ahead, cool to room temperature and refrigerate overnight. Remove from the refrigerator and let stand until returned to room temperature before reheating over low heat. Serve in shallow bowls with a sprinkling of parsley over each serving.

A full-bodied red wine, such as a Claret from Bordeaux or a cabernet sauvignon from America, will go very well with the Daube. A spicy California zinfandel or petite sirah will also work well.

Originally, *a daube was cooked in a daubière, a heavy casserole or pot with a concave lid. In the days of wood fires, the lid would be filled with water to help radiate heat around the stew.*

Guest Chef NEIL DEMPSEY

Ziba at the Liverpool Racquet Club

In our travels, Michel and I sometimes find really great, lesser known restaurants and inspired chefs who have yet to be discovered by the international culinary community. One such recent discovery is Ziba Restaurant at the Racquet Club in Liverpool, where Neil Dempsey is executive chef.

Raised in England, Neil's early interest in cooking began when hunting and fishing with his grandfather and wanting to see his game and fish become tasty meals. His first restaurant job, at age 15, was as a dishwasher at a restaurant where he was exposed to the buzz of a kitchen with flaming skillets and chefs tossing sautés. The chef there became his first cooking mentor, starting Neil on his culinary journey. He received his formal training as a chef at Coliquette Street Catering College in Liverpool.

After completing his training, Neil was hired as a *commis chef* in a small restaurant in Cheshire. He moved on to the renowned Grosvenor Hotel in Chester, under the direction of Chef Simon Bradley, and then, to Hambarry Manor in Hartfordshire. His career progressed, with the appointment as Sous-chef at the Hope Street Restaurant in Liverpool and in 2004, he became executive chef at Ziba.

Ziba features a spacious dining room and a long bar, where the drinks are generous and the Irish bartenders provide conversational entertainment. Service in the dining room is prompt, courteous and charming. The food includes traditional local dishes, such as a delicious 'sausage and mash', made with the benefit of Neil's classic training, and creative new dishes, all perfectly prepared and beautifully presented. The wine list is extensive and caters for every taste and budget.

The Liverpool Racquet Club was first established in 1874 as a gentlemen's club. In 1981, the club and all its records were totally destroyed by fire, during street riots protesting race discrimination. The club moved to the historic Hargreaves Buildings in 1982. After extensive alteration and renovation, the club re-opened in 1985. In 2003, brother and sister team, Martin and Helen Ainscough, local hoteliers and restaurateurs, acquired the club and completed the final stages of its renovation. Facilities include eight luxurious sleeping rooms, excellent gym facilities, squash courts, a spa and treatment rooms. For me, however, the restaurant is the highlight and I never miss the chance to dine there when I visit Liverpool.

Ziba Dining Room and Bar

Lamb Cannons in Red Currant Sauce
Chef Neil Dempsey, Ziba Restaurant, Liverpool

The term 'lamb cannons' is an English name for what Americans call the eye of the loin. In the British Isles, where they have excellent mutton, it is often used for these sorts of dishes. The addition of red currant preserves to the basic brown sauce gives the lamb a distinctive flavor. Serves 6.

18	small new potatoes
2½	lbs (1.1 kg) lamb eye of the loin
3	large garlic cloves, minced
1	medium onion, chopped
2	tablespoons (30 g) unsalted butter
1	tablespoon finely chopped fresh thyme
2	cups (480 ml) Brown Sauce (page 30)
2	tablespoons (40 g) red currant preserves
½	cup (120 ml) full-bodied red wine
	Salt and cracked black pepper

Preheat the oven to 400° F (200° C). Blanch the potatoes in salted boiling water for approximately 5 minutes, remove from the water and set aside. Rub the lamb loin with the minced garlic, working the garlic into the meat. Place the lamb loin in a heavy (preferably enamelled cast iron) baking dish, surround it with the chopped onions and blanched potatoes. Bake for about 45 to 50 minutes. Remove the baking dish from the oven, reduce oven heat to 140° F (60° C), transfer the lamb loin and potatoes to another baking dish, cover and keep hot in the oven.

Put the first baking dish with the remaining meat juices and chopped onion on a stovetop burner, over medium-high heat. Add the butter, thyme, brown sauce, red currant preserves and red wine, stirring until all ingredients are blended with the cooked onions and meat juices. Continue cooking, stirring frequently, until the sauce reduces by about one-third and thickens.

Remove the lamb and potatoes from the oven, cut the lamb into ½-inch slices, and slice the potatoes. Arrange portions on dinner plates, pour sauce over the lamb, and serve.

✿ *With this dish, a really chunky, full-bodied red wine is in order. More robust Bordeaux, with lots of tannins, similar American or Australian cabernets or American petite sirahs or zinfandels should do the trick.*

Roast Sirloin Encrusted in English Mustard

If you are partial to a Sunday roast of beef, this recipe is guaranteed to please. As with all roasts, the key is keeping the meat nice and juicy. The mustard paste seals in the meat's natural juices and assures tenderness and flavor. Serves 8.

½	cup (60 g) dry English mustard
	Cold water
4	lb (1.8 kg) whole sirloin of beef
2	tablespoons (15 g) cracked black pepper
1	tablespoon Provence herbs or finely chopped fresh rosemary
2	cups (480 ml) Brown Sauce (page 30)

Variations

This recipe calls for sirloin but other cuts of beef, such as prime rib or top round, also work well.

Note *that, although the mustard paste is very spicy, cooking entirely eliminates the spiciness and only a very slight flavor is retained from the mustard.*

Pre-heat the oven to 425° F (220° C).

Mix the dry mustard with enough cold water to make a paste. Coat the sirloin on all surfaces with the paste. Sprinkle cracked pepper and herbs over the paste coating. Place the roast in a roasting pan and cook in the oven for 15 minutes.

Reduce heat to 325° F (160° C) and continue cooking for about 1 hour. Remove the roast from the oven and let it stand for 10 to 15 minutes before carving it.

For the sauce, place the juices from the roasting pan in a skillet over medium heat. Add the brown sauce, stirring continuously, and simmer, until your sauce thickens to a creamy consistency. Season to taste with salt and freshly ground pepper.

Carve the roast into thin slices, place on individual plates, pour the sauce over the meat, and serve.

Almost any medium-to-full-bodied red wine will make a suitable accompaniment to this dish. American cabernet sauvignons, merlots or cabernet-merlot blends are all good choices, as are Clarets and Italian Barolos.

Porc Rôti Bellagio
Roast Pork Loin with Herbs in Pancetta

Pork is sometimes the forgotten meat. However, when properly prepared, it is an excellent alternative to other meats. This recipe, embellished with garlic, herbs, and pancetta, is adapted from a dish I first tasted in Bellagio, on the shores of Lake Como in Northern Italy in 1993. Serves 8.

¼   cup (10 g) finely chopped fresh rosemary
¼   cup (10 g) fresh thyme leaves
¼   cup (10 g) finely chopped fresh oregano
3   large garlic cloves, finely chopped
2   tablespoons (30 ml) olive oil
1   tablespoon (15 g) Dijon mustard
3   lbs (1.4 kg) pork top loin or tenderloin
    Salt and freshly ground pepper
12   medium-thick slices of pancetta
      or smoked bacon
1½   cups (360 ml) Brown Sauce (page 30)

Note *that this dish requires pre-preparation, at least two hours before final preparation and cooking.*

In a mini food processor or blender, blend the rosemary, thyme, oregano, garlic, olive oil and mustard together until smooth. Coat all surfaces of the pork loin with the herb and garlic mixture and sprinkle salt and pepper lightly over all surfaces. Place the roast in a baking dish, fat side down, and cover the top, sides and ends with the pancetta or bacon. Cover with plastic wrap and refrigerate for 2 to 3 hours.

Pre-heat the oven to 425° F (220° C). Let the pork come to room temperature while the oven preheats. Roast the pork for 15 minutes and then reduce heat to 350° F (180° C), and cook for about 1 hour. A meat thermometer inserted into the center of the roast should read 180° F (80° C) when fully cooked to medium. Remove from oven, transfer the roast to a platter and let stand for 10 minutes.

Place the roasting pan on the stovetop over medium heat. Add the brown sauce, stirring continuously, and continue cooking, until the sauce thickens to a creamy consistency.

Carve the roast into ½-inch thick slices, place on plates with a bit of the pancetta or bacon, and pour the sauce over the meat and serve.

Almost any medium-to-full-bodied red wine, such as cabernet, merlot or pinot noir will go well with this dish. Italian Barolo Brunello or Tiganello are also very good choices.

Veal Parmigiana

This is an easy to make classic Italian dish, found in Italian restaurants around the world. I learned this recipe at age 19 from Maître d' and Chef, Egon Shultz, at the Casa Villa Restaurant in Seattle. It has been refined and perfected over many years and I am sure you will always find it a success. Serves 6.

2	tablespoons (30 g) unsalted butter
2	tablespoons (30 ml) olive oil
12	veal cutlets (about 3 oz/90 g each)
1½	cups (150 g) grated mozzarella
1	cup (100g) grated Parmesan
2	cups (300 g) fine dry breadcrumbs
1	tablespoon minced fresh oregano
1	tablespoon minced fresh thyme
1	tablespoon minced fresh rosemary
	Salt and freshly ground black pepper
3	eggs
¼	cup (60 ml) milk
3	cups (300 g) thin sliced mushrooms
3	cups (720 ml) Provençal Tomato Sauce (page 33)

Pre-heat the oven to 400° F (200° C). Melt the butter and olive oil in a large foil-covered baking pan in the oven, until the butter just begins to brown, and then remove the pan from the oven, making sure that the melted butter and oil cover the whole surface of the foil.

On a heavy cutting board, pound the veal cutlets with a meat hammer on both sides until they are completely flat (about ¼-inch thick). Mix the grated cheeses together in a bowl and set aside. Combine the breadcrumbs, herbs, salt and pepper in a flat-bottomed serving dish. Whisk the eggs and milk together until smooth and place in a shallow bowl. Dip each cutlet in the egg mixture, then into the breadcrumbs, coating both sides completely, and place the breaded cutlets in the baking pan. Bake for about 8 to 10 minutes. Remove from oven, turn over the cutlets and cover each with sliced mushrooms, tomato sauce and grated cheese, in that order. Return to the oven and continue baking for approximately 5 to 6 more minutes. Turn on the broiler and broil until the cheese is lightly browned. Remove from oven, let stand for 3 minutes and serve.

❀ *A medium-to-full-bodied Italian red wine, such as a Barolo, Brunello, Tiganello or Chianti, or an American merlot, will go best with this dish.*

Veal Marsala

This is a somewhat more subtly flavored veal dish from Italy that never fails to please even the most discerning palates. It is a relatively lighter main dish, so starters can be a bit more generous in their proportions, but take care not to have starters that are very heavily flavored, as they will detract from the subtle and sophisticated flavor of the veal. Serves 6.

18	veal medallions (about 3 oz/90 g each)
	Salt and freshly ground black pepper
3	tablespoons (45 g) unsalted butter
2	tablespoons (30 ml) olive oil
2	cups (200 g) thinly sliced mushrooms
1	teaspoon finely chopped fresh oregano
1	teaspoon ground fresh fennel seeds
1	teaspoon finely chopped fresh rosemary
2	cups (480 ml) Brown Sauce (page 30)
½	cup (60 ml) Marsala wine
¼	cup (60 ml) heavy cream

On a heavy cutting board, pound the veal medallions with a meat hammer on both sides, until they are completely flat (about ¼-inch thick). Season the cutlets with salt and pepper. Melt 2 tablespoons of butter and the olive oil in a large skillet over medium-high heat, until the butter bubbles and place the medallions in the skillet (you may need to do this in batches, depending on the size of your pan). Cook approximately 2 to 3 minutes on each side, remove from pan and keep hot in a 140° F (60° C) oven.

In the same skillet, add the remaining butter and sauté the mushrooms with the herbs until just browned. Add the brown sauce and Marsala wine stirring continuously until the liquids begin to boil. Add the cream, stirring frequently and reduce until the sauce reaches a thick, creamy consistency. Season to taste with salt and pepper. Remove the veal from the oven and pour any residual juices into your sauce, stirring them in. Place the veal medallions on individual plates, pour sauce over each and serve.

Variations

For Veal Saltimboca, another classic Italian veal dish, press a couple of sage leaves and a wafer-thin slice of Parma Ham or Prosciutto onto each veal medallion before cooking and delete the mushrooms and cream from the recipe.

Medium-bodied red wines will go best with this dish. My favorites would include a Beaune or Mercurey from Burgundy, or a California or Oregon pinot noir.

Vineyard in winter — Beaumes de Venise, France.

Italian Sausages with Mixed Beans and Polenta

During World War II, many affluent Italians who feared persecution by the Fascists went to live in France. One such family moved to Sorgue, near Avignon and Michel's family. The lady became friends with Michel's mother and showed her many Italian dishes. This dish, which is a typical family meal in the Piedmont region of Italy, is a particular favorite. Serves 8.

2	cups dry red beans (300 g)
2	cups dry white beans (300 g)
16	Italian sausages
2	tablespoons (30 ml) olive oil
6	slices thick pancetta or bacon, chopped
1	large shallot, finely chopped
2	garlic cloves, finely chopped
½	teaspoon chopped fresh thyme
½	teaspoon chopped fresh oregano
¼	cup (60 ml) red wine
2	cups (480 ml) Provençal Tomato Sauce (page 33)
	Salt and freshly ground black pepper
1	tablespoon (15 g) unsalted butter
8	slices pre-cooked polenta

Note *that preparation for this dish begins the evening before you plan to serve it.*

Soak the red and white beans overnight in cold water. Drain and rinse beans, and boil for 1 to 1½ hours, until tender, drain and set aside. In a saucepan, over medium-high heat, cook the sausages, until they are cooked through and nicely browned, remove from the pan, set aside and keep hot in a 140° F (60° C) oven. Pour off the cooking fat from the sausages. Add the olive oil, chopped bacon, shallots, garlic, thyme, and oregano to the pan and cook, until the bacon pieces are cooked but not browned (about 4 to 5 minutes). Add the wine, tomato sauce and cooked beans to the pan. Simmer, for about 20 to 25 minutes, stirring occasionally. Season to taste with salt and freshly ground black pepper.

At the same time, in a separate saucepan, melt the butter over medium-high heat, and sauté the polenta slices, until they are a nice golden brown and heated through. Season to taste with salt and pepper.

To serve, place two sausages on each dinner plate, with a serving of the mixed beans in sauce, and a slice of polenta.

Medium to full-bodied red wines, such as American cabernet sauvignons or petite sirahs and Italian Barolos or Brunellos will complement this dish most effectively.

POULTRY DISHES

Shish Taouk   101
(Lebanese Barbequed Chicken)

Sautéed Chicken Breasts in White Wine and Cream Sauce   102

Coq au Vin   103
(Chicken in Red Wine)

Rover's Chicken   105
Chef Thierry Rautureau, Rover's Restaurant, Seattle

Roast Hen with Wild Rice and Mushroom Stuffing   106

Su-Su Chicken Curry   107

Poulet Rouge   109
(Tandoori Chicken in Mild Red Curry Sauce)
Chef Mehernosh Mody, La Porte des Indes Restaurant, London

Roast Turkey with Celery and Mushroom Stuffing   110

Poultry

What would we do without chicken? It is relatively inexpensive and is one of the most versatile foods on the planet. You can make an unlimited variety of wonderful dishes with chicken and it is the easiest of all with which to experiment by varying ingredients such as herbs, spices, and sauces.

The quality of poultry is just as much an issue as it is for meat and fish. In most areas there are local, smaller producers or small producer cooperatives, which are usually the best sources for assuring quality. Poultry grown many hundreds of miles away is much less likely to be as fresh or flavorful as locally grown products. Naturally raised poultry can be more flavorful than mass-produced poultry that is grown in large warehouse-like facilities. A few pennies per pound difference in price can definitely be worth it for to quality, freshness, and flavor.

As with so many other ingredients, avoiding overcooking is the key to successful poultry dishes. Overcooked poultry becomes dry, tough, and flavorless. This is true, whether you are sautéing, roasting, or stir-frying.

We have included a recipe for roast turkey and you might wonder why, since it is such a common dish. My parents always had an 'open door policy' for holiday dinners like Thanksgiving and Christmas. That tradition has continued with my own family and our holiday tables are always filled with family, friends, and other guests who are away from their own families and homes at the holidays. Over the years, many guests have remarked about how much they liked our roast turkey and, particularly, how moist and juicy it was. For this reason, even though it is standard holiday fare, we thought it worth including.

Middle Eastern Delights

M*y introduction to Lebanese food came from my wife, Ani, who grew up in Beirut. Lebanese cuisine is among the world's most delightful. Many dishes are time consuming to prepare but well worth the effort. However, since the focus of this cookbook is ease of preparation and attended cooking time, we have included only one of the many Lebanese dishes that we truly love. That dish is* Shish Taouk, *char-broiled chicken breast cubes.*

A Lebanese meza *is truly a feast fit for a king or a sultan. A typical Lebanese restaurant menu will offer at least 25 small dishes that can serve as appetizers before a main course or, if you prefer, as an entire meal in themselves. And, if you have any room left for dessert, sweet Lebanese pastries and fresh fruit, followed by a cup of freshly brewed Arabic coffee, makes a delightful end to the meal.*

Typical meza *dishes include flavorful dips that are eaten with warm pita bread used as 'scoops'. They include* Hommos bi Tahini, *chickpeas puréed with sesame paste, lemon juice and garlic;* Baba Ghannouj, *fire-roasted eggplant puréed with sesame paste and garlic; and* Labneh, *drained yogurt.* Warak Inhab *are stuffed grape leaves.* Falafel *are puréed fava bean and chickpea patties, deep-fried and served with a tahini sauce.* Sambousiks *are pastries filled with meat;* Fatayir, *with spinach; and* Boeregs, *with cheese. One of the most popular Lebanese salads is* Tabbouleh, *the famous parsley, mint and cracked wheat salad.*

Mezas also include meat dishes. Kibbeh, *which may be the most famous of all Lebanese dishes, comes in many variations;* Kibbeh Neyeh *is minced raw lamb with bulgur wheat. Meat dishes grilled on skewers over a wood charcoal fire include* Shish Taouk *(see above),* Shish Kebab, *usually made with lamb but sometimes beef cubes, and* Kefta Kebab, *made with minced lamb.*

Shish Taouk
Lebanese Grilled Chicken

This really is the easiest of all chicken dishes. It can be prepared in 10 minutes, and cooked later in another 5 to 10 minutes. Usually as part of a mixed grill, it is always one of the dishes Ani and I order when we are out at one of our favorite Lebanese restaurants. Serves 6.

3	garlic cloves, minced
¼	cup (60 ml) olive oil
¼	cup (60 ml) fresh lemon juice
	Salt and freshly ground black pepper
6	boneless, skinless chicken breast halves, cut into 1-inch cubes

In a food processor or blender whip the garlic, olive oil, lemon juice, salt and pepper together. Put the chicken cubes in a bowl, pour the marinade over them and toss to be sure that all the chicken cubes are coated. Cover and refrigerate for 30 minutes to 1 hour and no longer, or the chicken will lose its texture.

Pre-heat an outdoor grill or set the oven to broil. Thread chicken cubes onto the skewers. Place skewered chicken on the grill, turning to be sure that all sides are cooked evenly. Note that this dish will cook very quickly so be sure to watch carefully. If broiling in an oven, place the skewered chicken cubes on a baking pan lined with foil, and broil 6 inches from the heat, turning once. Season with more salt, if necessary, and serve.

Chef's Tip

If you are using bamboo skewers, soak them in water for 10 to 15 minutes before using them, which will help prevent them from burning.

Variations

If you wish, you can add onion and bell pepper chunks between the chicken cubes on the skewers.

With Lebanese food, cold beer may, in fact, be the best choice. But Shish Taouk also goes nicely with more robust white wines, such as west coast chardonnays and almost any red wine that you like.

Sautéed Chicken Breasts in White Wine and Cream Sauce

Sautéed chicken breasts are the epitome of versatility. With simple variations in herbs, spices and sauces, you can produce many different dishes that share the same basic preparation. This recipe is one that we have developed over time, after trying many variations. Serves 6.

6	boneless, skinless chicken breast halves
	Salt and freshly ground pepper
1	tablespoon finely chopped fresh rosemary
1	tablespoon Poultry Seasoning
1	teaspoon Beau Monde seasoning
1	tablespoon (15 g) unsalted butter
1	tablespoon (15 ml) olive oil
½	cup (120 ml) dry white wine
¼	cup (60 ml) heavy cream

Variations

Herb substitutes for the rosemary include Provence herbs, tarragon, fennel and/or thyme. For a spicier alternative, sauté very thinly sliced shallots and garlic in the butter and oil until just golden brown before adding the chicken breasts, and then add ½ teaspoon of curry powder, cayenne pepper or Szechuan Seasoning with the rest of the herbs.

Sprinkle the flesh side of the breasts with salt, pepper, rosemary, Poultry Seasoning and Beau Monde seasoning.

Melt the butter and oil in a large skillet, over medium heat, until the butter begins to bubble. Place the chicken breasts seasoned-side-down in the skillet and sprinkle the top sides of the breasts with the rest of the seasonings. Sauté on one side until just golden brown, then turn over and sauté until the breasts are just cooked through. Breasts are cooked when they are firm to touch and no longer pink in the middle of the thickest part.

Pour the white wine over the breasts and then transfer just the breasts to a bowl and keep warm in a 140° F (60° C) oven. Stir the white wine and cooking juices over low heat, until the liquid is reduced by half, and then add the cream, stirring continuously until the sauce thickens. Take the chicken breasts from the oven, pour the residual cooking juices into the sauce and stir until fully mixed in. Season to taste with salt and pepper. Place the chicken breasts on individual serving plates, pour the sauce over them and serve.

This dish goes particularly well with lighter, dry white wines such as Meursaults, Montrachets or lighter chardonnays. With the spicier variation, a Burgundy-style red also works well.

Coq au Vin
Chicken in Red Wine

This is a traditional French chicken stew that has been enjoyed in countless restaurants and homes for generations. There are a large number of different recipes for this dish. This is one that is easy to make and never fails to please. Serves 8 to 10.

¼ teaspoon ground cloves
¼ teaspoon ground coriander
¼ teaspoon cumin powder
¼ teaspoon salt
¼ teaspoon freshly ground black pepper
2 large chickens, skinned and cut into pieces
1 large onion, chopped
2 large carrots, cut into ½-inch slices
1 leek, white and pale green parts chopped
1 bay leaf
2 garlic cloves, finely chopped
3 cups (720 ml) full-bodied red wine
½ cup (120 ml) port
3 tablespoons (45 ml) olive oil
2 tablespoons (15 g) all-purpose flour
4 cups (960 ml) poultry stock (page 28)
2 tablespoons chopped parsley

Note *that preparation for this dish begins the evening before you plan to serve it.*

The night before serving, make a rub by mixing together the cloves, coriander, cumin, salt and pepper. Rub the chicken pieces with the spice mixture and put in a large covered container with the onion, carrots, leek, bay leaf, garlic and remaining spices from the rub. Pour in the red wine and port and refrigerate overnight.

The next afternoon, remove the chicken pieces from the container. Heat the oil in a large, heavy stockpot over medium-high heat until hot (just before the smoking point). Reduce the heat to medium and sauté the chicken pieces until lightly browned, remove from the pot and set aside.

Sprinkle the flour into the pot, stirring continuously and slowly with a wooden spoon or spatula and cook for about 2 to 3 minutes, until the flour is mixed smoothly with the oil. Put the chicken pieces back in the pot and add the rest of the marinated ingredients and liquid with enough poultry stock to cover all the ingredients completely. Bring to a rolling boil for 3 minutes, reduce heat to medium-low, and simmer uncovered for approximately 1 hour or until liquid is reduced by half, stirring occasionally. When done, the liquid should coat the wooden spoon, without running off. Serve in fairly deep dishes or bowls and garnish with chopped parsley.

This dish goes well with a full-bodied red wine, such as a Claret from Bordeaux or an American cabernet.

Guest Chef THIERRY RAUTUREAU

Rovin' with Thierry

Internationally renowned chef Thierry Rautureau began his culinary apprenticeship in the French countryside at age 14. With a warm wit and cheerful personality, he is an inspired hand in the kitchen. His specialties feature seafood, game, sauces and vegetarian cuisine. He has created Rover's, a very special restaurant in Seattle.

As Michel did many years ago, Thierry has combined his classic French artistry with the bounty of ingredients from local waters, fields, and farms. Thierry has been featured in numerous food magazines and articles, as well as nationally broadcast television programs.

Gourmet Magazine said, "A perfect expression of its ebullient and creative chef owner, Thierry Rautureau, Rover's is relaxed and highly original. Rautureau serves up Northwest contemporary cuisine that, like its creator, has a distinct French accent and celebrates the freshest possible ingredients in refined dishes." Michel and I both wholeheartedly agree. Any dinner at Rover's is definitely a treat, as Thierry's numerous awards and international recognition demonstrate.

Seattle Magazine called Rover's "The Best Restaurant in the city." When we talk with other chefs and restaurant owners in Seattle, Thierry's name invariably comes into the conversation, when they speak of the chefs whose work they most respect.

Thierry's degustation (tasting) menus are always an adventure, with dishes like Oxtail and Foie Gras Terrine with Carrot-Cumin Salad and Bing Cherry Relish or Maine Lobster with Roasted Beets and Lobster Pastis Sauce with Sea Urchin Roe. Service is just right with Thierry's crew in the dining room, always attentive to every guest's needs and wishes.

Unlike many renowned restaurants, Rover's is happy to accommodate special dietary requests and has offered a multi-course vegetarian menu for many years. Thierry goes out of his way to see that his guests get what they want and not just what he wants them to have.

I have dined at Rover's on many occasions and every visit has been thoroughly enjoyable. The atmosphere is very pleasant, conducive to conversation and a relaxed meal, where one never feels rushed. Not long ago, I attended a mutual friend's birthday party at Rover's, where the entire restaurant had been reserved for the party of more than 60 guests. The whole event, from cocktails on the terrace through dinner and dessert was truly a production worthy of Stephen Spielberg and the special menu is still being talked about months later.

Rover's exterior

Rover's Chicken
Thierry Rautureau, Rover's Restaurant, Seattle, Washington

This dish from Rover's earliest days is one that never fails to please. You will find Thierry's recipe easy to prepare and cook, while at the same time, quite unique. Please note that this dish requires advance preparation. Serves 6.

3	cups (1 lb/450 g) dry black beans
6	cups (1.4 liters) poultry stock (page 28)
1	carrot, chopped
1	medium onion, peeled and chopped
1	celery stalk, chopped
2	bay leaves
3	sprigs fresh thyme, finely chopped
4	cloves
6	shallots, peeled and chopped
3	tablespoons (45 ml) olive oil
1	bottle (750 ml) white wine
2	cups (480 ml) heavy cream
9	ounces (260 g) goat cheese
3	tablespoons (45 g) unsalted butter, at room temperature
6	boneless, skinless chicken breast halves
	Salt and ground white pepper

Soak the black beans 6 to 8 hours prior to cooking, in enough cold water to completely cover them.

Put the poultry stock in a medium saucepan over medium-high heat. Drain the black beans and add them to the pan with the carrot, onion, celery, bay leaves, thyme and cloves. Bring to a boil and skim off any impurities. Reduce heat to medium and continue cooking, until the black beans are nearly soft and the liquid has reduced by half, about 1½ hours. Remove from the stovetop and keep warm in a 140° F (60° C) oven.

In a separate saucepan, over medium-high heat, sauté the shallots in 1 tablespoon of oil until they are translucent. Add the wine and reduce by half. Stir in the heavy cream and continue cooking until the liquid reduces by half again. Remove from heat and let cool for about 5 to 7 minutes. Strain the mixture into a blender, add the goat cheese and butter, and blend until smooth and fully combined. Return the sauce to the pan, cover and keep hot over very low heat.

Season both sides of the chicken breasts with salt and pepper. In a large skillet, heat the rest of the oil over medium heat. Cook the chicken breasts on one side, until nicely browned, turn and continue cooking, until just cooked through. Remove from heat, cut each breast into diagonal slices and arrange on individual plates. Pour sauce generously over the chicken slices, add a serving of black beans on the side, and serve.

A light, medium-dry chardonnay will complement this dish most effectively.

Roast Hen with Wild Rice and Mushroom Stuffing

Wild rice is not actually rice but a rice-like aquatic grain and the only grain truly native to North America. It grows wild, in the marshes of the upper Midwest, and has a naturally rich, nutty flavor. If they are available, shiitake or morel mushrooms really enhance this dish. Serves 8.

2	cups (400 g) wild rice
2	roasting hens, about 2 lbs each
2	tablespoons (30 g) unsalted butter, at room temperature
I	tablespoon (15 ml) olive oil
I	large shallot, finely chopped
2	garlic cloves, finely chopped
¼	cup (60 ml) dry white wine
I	cup (150 g) dry bread crumbs
2	cups (200 g) diced mushrooms
½	teaspoon finely chopped fresh rosemary
I	pinch ground dry sage
¼	teaspoon cayenne
	Salt and freshly ground black pepper
2	large eggs, beaten
¾	cup (180 ml) poultry stock (page 28)

Rinse the wild rice in a fine sieve, in cold water. In a saucepan over medium-high heat, cover and cook the wild rice in 5 cups of water for 35 to 40 minutes, until the rice is nearly tender but still just a bit chewy. Remove from the heat, drain off excess water and let stand to cool.

Preheat the oven to 425° F (220° C). Rinse the hens inside and out in cold water and dry them with paper towels. Using your fingers, rub the butter over all outside surfaces of the hens, making sure to get butter into the spaces between legs, wings and bodies. Heat the oil in a large skillet over medium heat and lightly sauté the shallots and garlic until just translucent. Remove from heat and let cool. In a large bowl, combine the wild rice, shallots, garlic, wine, bread-crumbs, mushrooms, rosemary, sage, cayenne, salt, black pepper, and eggs. Using your hands, mix these ingredients together, adding poultry stock, ¼ cup at a time, until you have a well-mixed, doughy stuffing. Moisture should be just visible. If it is too dry, mix in a bit of water.

Stuff the inside cavities of the hens with stuffing, pressing it in so that the cavities are completely filled, without any air pockets. Roast for 15 minutes, reduce the heat to 325° F (160° C) and continue cooking for about 40 minutes, testing with a meat thermometer after 35 minutes, to gauge the degree of doneness, 165° F (75° C). Remove from oven, let stand 10 minutes and then carve the meat from the bones, remove the stuffing and serve.

Medium-dry white wines or light-to-medium-bodied red wines will complement this dish.

Su-Su Chicken Curry

When people hear the word "curry" they often think of India and hot, spicy dishes. In fact, curry simply refers to any number of different spice blends, which are not always very spicy. This recipe is adapted from a southern Chinese curry with the addition of cream, which tempers the curry's spiciness. Serves 8.

1	tablespoon (15 g) unsalted butter
1	tablespoon (15 ml) olive oil
2	large shallots, thinly sliced
3	garlic cloves, very thinly sliced
2	tablespoons (30 ml) soy sauce
1	tablespoon Provence herbs
2	tablespoons mild yellow curry powder
8	boneless, skinless chicken breast halves, cut into 1-inch cubes
1	bell pepper, cored, seeded and cut into ¼-inch strips
2	cups (200 g) sliced mushrooms
¼	cup (60 ml) white wine
¼	cup (60 ml) rice wine
	Salt (or more soy sauce) and freshly ground black pepper
½	cup (120 ml) heavy cream or crème fraîche
8	cups (1.4 kg) cooked white rice, kept warm

In a wok or large skillet, heat the butter and oil over medium heat until bubbling. Add the shallots, garlic, soy sauce, Provence herbs, and curry powder and sauté until the shallots and garlic are translucent. Add the chicken and bell pepper. Continue sautéing until chicken pieces are nearly cooked through. Add the sliced mushrooms and continue sautéing, stirring continuously until the mushrooms are just cooked.

Add the white wine and rice wine and season to taste with salt, or more soy sauce, pepper and more curry powder. Then add the cream, stirring until you have a rich yellow sauce. To serve, spoon over rice.

Note that the timing of the introduction of ingredients is very important. Be sure not to let the wine and cream boil while cooking. The bell pepper and mushroom slices should be just cooked and not too soft.

Medium-dry white wines like Chablis and Petit Chablis or west coast chardonnays will go best with this dish

The Doorway to India

Nearly 400 years ago, when Frenchmen from Alsace immigrated to Quebec, some of their neighbors traveled in the opposite direction, establishing a small colony on the southeastern tip of India. Like the Acadians in Quebec, and Cajuns in Louisiana, the French settlers in Pondicherry blended their tradition of Alsace cuisine with the local ingredients and spices they found in India.

La Porte des Indes (The Doorway to India) restaurant is located in Central London near Marble Arch. The French-Indian cuisine is unique, incorporating the flavors of southern India in an array of colors and tastes that please both the eye and the palate. Chef Mehermosh Mody and proprietor Sherin Alexander-Mody have brought the exceptional cuisine of Pondicherry and its surroundings to London's West End, in a truly memorable setting. A friend introduced me to La Porte des Indes, just after it opened in 1993, and I have been going back ever since whenever I am in London.

The restaurant is spacious, with high ceilings and authentic southern Indian décor, palm trees and tropical flower arrangements. The Blue Dome, pictured at right, is high above a grand marble staircase that connects the two levels of the restaurant. A meal at La Porte des Indes is always a treat. It is a perfect venue for parties and special occasions. We have celebrated birthdays and anniversaries there, with friends who have always been delighted with the food and service.

Mehernosh and Sherin have become friends of mine and have shared a number of recipes with me, which I now make at home. Their menu is expansive, featuring more than 60 truly exotic dishes. The Menu de Maison is a sampling of ten different signature dishes, including my own personal favorite, Poulet Rouge, with the recipe on the facing page.

This dish requires somewhat more preparation time and effort than most of our recipes but it is well worth the little bit of extra effort that is involved. Most of the preparation

takes place the day before you are going to serve this dish and the final cooking and assembly of your ingredients is actually quite quick, about 30 minutes. The dish is typically served with plain Basmati or Pilau rice, cooked with a little bit of saffron powder, and Naan bread. You may need to visit an Indian specialty food store to find the authentic spices used in this recipe.

Poulet Rouge
Tandoori Chicken in Mild Red Curry Sauce

Chef Mehernosh Mody, La Porte des Indes Restaurant, London
Note that this dish requires preparation the night before you plan to serve it. Serves 8

4	boneless, skinless chicken breasts
2	tablespoons (30 ml) fresh lemon juice
2	teaspoons red chili powder
1	cup (230 g) whole milk yogurt
8	garlic cloves, chopped
2	tablespoons (20 g) grated fresh ginger
4	fresh, small red chilies, chopped
2	tablespoons garam masala powder
2	teaspoons finely ground cumin
2	teaspoons ground coriander
2	tablespoons (30 ml) vegetable oil

ONION SAUCE

¼	cup (60 ml) vegetable oil
1	bay leaf
1	cardamom pod
3	ground cloves or ¼ teaspoon powdered
1	cinnamon stick
1	large yellow onion, sliced
2	tablespoons (30 ml) water

POULET ROUGE SAUCE

4	garlic cloves, finely chopped	2	tablespoons garam masala powder
2	tablespoons (30 g) unsalted butter	3	tablespoons tandoori masala powder
2	tablespoons paprika	1½	cups (345 g) whole milk yogurt
		2	cups (480 ml) heavy cream

Make shallow diagonal cuts on both sides of the chicken breasts, coat with lemon juice and chili powder, rubbing the powder into the cuts and all over the flesh and set aside in a bowl. In a blender or food processor, purée the yogurt, garlic, ginger, chilies, garam masala, cumin, coriander and 2 tablespoons oil. Coat the chicken breasts with the purée, cover the bowl, and refrigerate overnight.

Preheat the oven broiler. Place the chicken breasts on the rack of your broiler pan and broil about 8 inches beneath the top broiler element, broiling until the chicken just begins to char. Remove from the oven, turn once, put back in the oven and continue broiling until it just begins to char. Remove from the oven, let stand to cool, shred the chicken breasts by hand and set aside.

For the onion sauce, heat the oil in a sauté pan. Add the bay leaf, cardamom pod, cloves, cinnamon stick, and the onions and simmer gently until the onions are translucent. Add the water and bring to a boil. Simmer until the onions are cooked to a pulp (about 30 minutes) and set aside to cool. Remove the cinnamon stick, bay leaf and cardamom pod, and then purée the mixture in a blender. Note that the Onion Sauce can be made up to several days ahead and refrigerated.

For the Poulet Rouge sauce, mash the garlic with a little water to make a paste. Melt the butter in a pan, put in the garlic paste and brown lightly. Stir in the paprika, garam and Tandoori masala and sauté for a few seconds before lowering the heat and adding yogurt. Stir continuously for 1 to 2 minutes and then add the onion purée and mix well. Add the cream, return to a boil, reduce the heat to medium, and simmer for 10 minutes. Add the shredded chicken and continue to simmer for 2 to 3 minutes until the meat is heated through. Add salt to taste and serve with Saffron Basmati or other long grain rice.

This dish goes particularly well with cold beer, like India pale ale, or a lighter pinot noir or merlot.

Roast Turkey with Celery and Mushroom Stuffing

Contrary to some opinions, roast turkey can be prepared and served other than on Thanksgiving and Christmas. Like chicken, it has the advantages of being quite inexpensive and, when properly prepared, makes a wonderful meal with lots of leftovers for snacks, sandwiches and soups. This recipe is one that has been developed and refined, over many years, with lots of early experimentation. Serves 12.

1	whole turkey (12 to 15 lbs/5.5 to 7 kg)
½	cup (120 g) unsalted butter
	Salt and pepper

THE STUFFING

4	cups (1¼ lbs/600 g) diced celery
4	large shallots, finely chopped
3	garlic cloves, finely chopped
1	tablespoon finely chopped parsley
1	tablespoon finely chopped sage
1	tablespoon finely chopped rosemary
1	tablespoon finely chopped thyme
1	teaspoon mild yellow curry powder
12	cups (600 g) dry bread cubes
3	cups (300 g) sliced mushrooms
1	cup (240 ml) medium-dry white wine
2	large eggs, beaten
2 to 3	cups (480 ml to 720 ml) poultry stock (page 28), at room temperature

Use a meat thermometer *to assure your turkey is cooked through, 165° F (75° C) in the middle of the breast or thigh.*

Preheat the oven to 425° F (220° C). Remove the neck and giblets from the turkey cavity, and set aside for later use. Place the turkey in a large, heavy roasting pan. Smear half of the butter over all outside surfaces of the turkey, being sure to get some butter into the spaces between legs and body. Season well all over with salt and pepper. Tuck the wings under the bird.

For the stuffing, heat the remaining butter in a large skillet over medium heat until it begins to bubble and sauté the celery, shallots, garlic, parsley, sage, rosemary, thyme, curry powder, and salt and pepper, to taste, stirring frequently until the shallots and garlic are translucent. In a large mixing bowl, mix the bread cubes, mushrooms, wine and eggs and then add in the sauté mixture. Gently mix all of these ingredients together with the stock, adding wine ½ cup at a time until you have a moist mixture that clings together easily.

Stuff the bird's cavity and neck flap with the stuffing mixture, pressing it in to completely fill the entire cavity. Use poultry skewers to seal the neck flap and butcher's twine to tie the legs together. Roast the turkey for 20 minutes, then reduce the heat to 325° F (160° C) and continue to cook about 12 minutes per pound of turkey weight. Remove from oven and let stand for 10 to 15 minutes. Remove the stuffing from the bird into a serving dish and keep hot in a 140° F (60° C) oven. Carve the turkey and serve.

Turkey Gravy

When you remove your bird from the roasting pan, there should be lots of cooking juice and fat. Place the roasting pan on the stovetop over medium-low heat and add 1 to 2 cups of water or poultry stock, stirring continuously. In a small bowl, mix 2 tablespoons corn starch with ¼ cup cold water, whisking until there are no lumps. Slowly add to the gravy, stirring continuously until the gravy thickens. Season to taste with salt and pepper, and serve.

Variations

This recipe works equally well with roasting chickens and can also be used for roast goose. We usually make lots of extra stuffing and cook it, covered with foil, in a separate deep baking dish in a 325° F (160° C) oven, for 1 to 2 hours. Simply double the ingredients for the stuffing to have plenty of extra for seconds and to accompany leftover turkey. Test the inside temperature of the stuffing, whether inside or outside the bird. The temperature should be 165° F (75° C) to assure safety.

Turkey Soup

After your turkey dinner, carve off all of the leftover meat that you want to save for later meals. Cut up the turkey carcass and put it in a large stockpot. Just follow the Poultry Stock recipe (page 28). Now you have turkey stock as the base for soup. Turkey stock works well as a base for Chicken, Rice and Butternut Soup (page 54), Soupe Marché (page 55) and New Orleans Style Gumbo (page 67) and you can experiment with other ingredients, such as cauliflower florets, with rice or noodles, or carrots and cilantro, which make very nice turkey-based soups.

Helpful Hints for Health & Safety

As with all poultry and many other ingredients, overcooking will always produce a less-than-ideal result. Also remember that poultry is particularly susceptible to contamination, requires careful handling and should always be completely cooked through. These suggestions should help you to stay out of danger.

1. Do not leave your turkey out at room temperature any longer than it takes to finish dinner and carve off the remaining meat.
2. Make sure you have completely removed all stuffing from the inside and neck flap cavities.
3. Immediately put the carcass into a stockpot, to make stock, or refrigerate it.
4. If making stock, freeze your broth or make soup from it, as soon as it is ready.

Roast turkey, in this recipe, has enough flavors to enable it to go with a variety of either red or white wines. Oakier chardonnays as well as medium-bodied reds, such as Burgundies or merlots, work equally well.

FISH AND SEAFOOD

Fish & Seafood

In North America, the word 'seafood' is used to describe both fish and shellfish. Shellfish refers to bivalves (clams, mussels, oysters, scallops, etc.) and crustaceans (crab, prawns, lobster, etc.). In other countries, a distinction is made in terminology. The term 'fish' includes sea or freshwater creatures that have gills for breathing, while 'seafood' is all shellfish and crustaceans. Whatever you call them, sea creatures are an important and delicious contribution to our diets and cooking.

Michel and I are both lucky to have lived in places around the world where the sea, lakes and rivers offer an incredible variety of fresh fish and shellfish. There are few things that live in the sea from which either of us I would shy away.

In this book we have focused on ingredients that are easy to find at your local market. These include salmon, sea bass, cod, sole, crab, scallops, prawns, and shrimp. Most seafood recipes lend themselves very well to substitution when the fish called for in a recipe is not available. For example, many whitefish, including cod, snapper and sea bass or other flatfish can substitute for sole. Also,

one crustacean will easily take the place of another in most recipes.

Fish is an important component in a healthy diet because of its beneficial fatty acids, which help to reduce 'bad cholesterol' levels. Some scientific research studies show a correlation between eating a mainly seafood diet and the fact that, on average, Japanese people live longer with lower incidence of major illness than people in other countries. However, Japanese consumption of Scotch whisky is second in the world only to the United Kingdom, so I'm hoping that also plays a part in better health and longevity.

The Culinary Olympics

The Culinary Olympics are held every four years and chefs from all over the world compete for medals, just as athletes do in the Summer and Winter Olympics. In 1976, when Michel was living in Seattle, he was selected to compete in this prestigious event, which was to be held in Frankfurt, Germany. The competition judges the taste and originality of cooking, as well as the displays that the chefs create. There are medals awarded in many categories, covering different regional cuisines. Everything must be perfect in order to win a medal. The taste must be exquisite and the display of foods, dishes, and backdrops must be both original and artistic.

Michel's main dish was to be Pacific halibut and, for his display, he arranged with his fish supplier, in Seattle, to procure a huge, 150-pound halibut to serve as the backdrop for his seafood display. He arranged for the fish to be flown directly to Frankfurt in a refrigerated container. This was truly a logistics challenge and he had to assure that his fish would arrive in Germany in pristine condition. He had other food for the competition in smaller containers.

When he arrived in Frankfurt, he had to clear immigration and customs. Immigration was not a problem and the German customs inspectors had no issue with the other packaged foodstuffs that Michel brought. The giant halibut, however, was another matter. There was nothing in their rule books that mentioned a whole, unprocessed 150-pound fish of any kind, let alone something called 'halibut', for which there is no equivalent word in German. Michel explained that halibut was like sole or turbot but the inspectors knew that those fish were much smaller. After an hour of discussion, explaining, and begging, the inspectors flatly refused to allow the fish to stay in Germany, so it had to be returned on the next plane to America.

Michel was in a quandary. Without a great display, his chances of winning a medal would be impossible. And then he had an idea. Simply for curiosity, he had brought two geoducks, the giant Pacific Northwest, long-necked clams. Hardly anyone in Europe was familiar with these unusual looking creatures. In the Olympic Hall, Michel made a display of shellfish, crustaceans, mussels, and smaller clams, and placed the geoducks as the centerpiece of the display. As the judges made their way to Michel's display, they all commented on the giant clams and their huge necks. And then they tasted Michel's dishes. When the medals were announced, with great ceremony, Michel and his team were awarded two gold medals.

Jumbo Prawns Flambéed with Pernod

This is an adaptation of a dish that I originally tasted at the Mirabeau, when Michel was the restaurant's Executive Chef. The flambéed Pernod liqueur, which has a distinct anise flavor, gives this dish a unique character and, although the cream may make the dish sound very rich, it is actually quite light. Serves 6.

3	tablespoons (45 g) unsalted butter
30	large, fresh jumbo prawns, peeled and de-veined
6	tablespoons (90 ml) Pernod liqueur
1½	cups (360 ml) whipping cream or crème fraîche
2	teaspoons chopped fresh parsley
	Salt and freshly ground pepper

Melt the butter in a large sauté pan over medium heat until it bubbles and sauté the prawns until they are just cooked through (about 3 to 4 minutes). Pour the Pernod over the sautéed prawns, let warm slightly and ignite with a long match. When the flame dies, stir in the whipping cream, with salt and pepper to taste. Continue cooking, until the cream and cooking juices reduce by about one-third. Garnish with chopped parsley and serve.

Our recipe for Basmati rice with peppers, shallots and garlic (page 133), cooked with a little saffron, makes a great side dish with the prawns.

This dish *makes an excellent starter if you simply reduce the recipe by half.*

❀ *A light, dry, somewhat acidic white wine should accompany this dish.*

The Bounty of the Sea

Fresh catch at the market

If you are fortunate to live by the sea, you will have an ever-changing array of fish and other seafood readily available at your local market. In Brittany, Dublin, London, Marseilles, San Francisco, Seattle, Sydney, and Vancouver as well as the Atlantic seaport cities in North America, fish markets often source the morning's catch directly from the fishermen. In recent years, with economically viable airfreight, fresh ocean fish and other seafood are often available far away from the sea. Within 24 hours of being caught, fresh fish and shellfish from a coastal city can be delivered to a market in Chicago or Geneva.

Today, 'flash-freezing' and vacuum packaging make quality fish and seafood available in most areas. Flash-freezing is not as good as having fish caught in the morning but when that is not possible, flash-frozen fish are a fine substitute and they can certainly be preferable to 'fresh' fish that are several days out of the water.

Cooking most fish is really quite easy, although I often talk with people who say they find it difficult and are reluctant to try it. The key, once again, is to avoid overcooking. Most fish should be just barely cooked through and even not quite entirely cooked in the middle. In fact, fish does not need to be cooked at all, as the Japanese have proven with sushi and sashimi. Unfortunately, not everyone appreciates raw fish. For this reason, all of the fish dishes we have included in this book require at least some cooking. Seared Ahi Tuna (page 77) is cooked very lightly on the surface and left completely raw in the middle. Even guests who would usually not think of eating raw fish always seem to enjoy the dish.

Black Cod in White Wine and Butter Sauce

In the Northwest, black cod, a very rich tasting fish, is sometimes called sablefish or Cape Sable. True cod or lingcod can work as a substitute. This is a very light, delicate dish that should be accompanied by suitably lighter side dishes. Serves 6.

2	tablespoons (30 g) unsalted butter
1	teaspoon (15 ml) olive oil
6	cod fillets (6 ounces/180 g, each)
1	tablespoon fresh thyme leaves
	Salt and freshly ground black pepper
½	cup (120 ml) white wine
1	teaspoon ground paprika
2	tablespoons (30 ml) heavy cream
6	lemon wedges

Melt the butter and olive oil in a large skillet, over medium heat until the butter begins to bubble.

Place the cod fillets in the skillet, sprinkle with thyme, salt and pepper, and cook about 3 to 4 minutes per side, until the fish is just cooked through. Pour the white wine over the fish, quickly remove the fish fillets to an ovenproof dish and keep hot in a 140° F (60° C) oven.

Stir the white wine and cooking juices continuously, until well blended and beginning to reduce. Add the cream and paprika, stirring continuously, until the sauce reduces to a creamy consistency. Remove the cod fillets from the oven and pour any residual cooking juices into your sauce, stirring until blended.

Place one fillet on each dinner plate, pour the sauce over the fish and serve with a wedge of lemon. Note that this sauce is not particularly effective on most side dishes and the specified quantity will only be enough for the fish.

❁ *A lighter dry, Burgundy-style white wine will go best with this very delicate fish dish.*

Variations

Other lighter white fish, such as hake or perch, can be used with this recipe instead of cod. It also works well with some South Pacific or Hawaiian fish varieties, such as Opakapaka or mahi-mahi. For those fish, add one teaspoon of soy sauce to your sauce, in place of the paprika. Hollandaise or mornay sauces (page 31) also work well with this dish.

Sole Amandine

This is a truly classic, simple dish that never fails to please. Michel first made Sole Amandine in the kitchens of the Savoy Hotel in London, where the local Dover sole was forever popular. With few ingredients and minimal preparation time, it is a dish that you can count on whenever you are short on time. It is also quite a sophisticated dish and lends itself well to both casual dinners and more festive occasions. Serves 6.

3	cups (360 g) all-purpose flour
1½	cups (360 ml) milk
12	sole fillets, about 3 to 4 oz (90 to 120 g) each
	Salt and freshly ground black pepper
4	tablespoons (60 g) unsalted butter
½	cup (60 g) flaked almonds
6	lemon wedges

This delicate fish *goes best with a seafood starter or a lighter green salad, such as bib or butter lettuce, with a light dressing. Boiled new potatoes, shredded potatoes or rice and vegetables, such as fresh garden peas, baby asparagus or small green beans, and baby carrots go nicely as side dishes.*

Put the flour in a shallow dish or bowl, wide enough to accommodate the length of each sole fillet. Put the milk in another bowl. Dip each of the sole fillets in the milk and then coat thoroughly with flour. Season on both sides with salt and pepper.

Melt the butter in a large skillet over medium-high heat, until it begins to bubble. Place the sole fillets in the skillet and cook until golden brown (approximately 2 to 3 minutes per side). Remove the sole fillets from the pan and keep hot in a 140° F (60° C) oven, until ready to serve. Put the flaked almonds into the pan and sauté lightly, until the flakes begin to brown.

Place sole fillets on each dinner plate, sprinkle the sautéed almonds on top, and serve.

 For this dish, almost any lighter, medium-dry white wine that you like will work. Meursault, Mâcon Villages or white Graves, as well as Chassagne Montrachet are ideal.

Salmon in Puff Pastry

Served as either a main dish or starter, this dish never fails to elicit unending praise. Wild salmon, from either the Atlantic or Pacific waters, is a real treat, on any menu. Puff pastry seals in the juices and flavors of the fish, which is enhanced by a light rosemary and white wine sauce. Serves 8.

2	puff pastry sheets (about 10x16 inches, each)
8	salmon fillets, about 1½ inches thick, 4 to 5 inches long and 3 inches wide, skin and bones removed
¼	cup (60 ml) unsalted butter, melted
2	teaspoons finely chopped fresh basil
2	teaspoons finely chopped fresh dill
	Salt and freshly ground black pepper
1	egg and 1 teaspoon milk, beaten together
1½	cups (360 ml) Béchamel Sauce (page 31)
½	cup (120 ml) dry white wine
1	tablespoon finely chopped fresh rosemary
	Ground paprika
	Cayenne pepper

Pre-heat the oven to 375° F (190° C). Line a baking sheet with foil and grease lightly. Cut the puff pastry sheets into sections, sized to wrap around the individual salmon fillets. Place each salmon fillet on a puff pastry section, brush the salmon fillets lightly with melted butter and sprinkle with basil, dill, salt, and pepper. Fold the pastry edges together, pinching with your fingers to seal into parcels, and place the parcels seam side down on the baking sheet, spaced well apart. Brush the top and sides of each parcel with the egg and milk mixture. Bake until the puff pastry is golden brown, about 15 to 20 minutes.

Meanwhile, put the béchamel sauce in a small saucepan, over medium heat, whisk in the white wine and rosemary and season to taste with paprika and cayenne. Pour sauce onto each dinner plate, place a salmon and puff pastry parcel on top of the sauce and serve.

Note *that it is important that your sauce is ready at the same time that the salmon parcels come out of the oven. Starting the sauce just a minute or two after you place the salmon parcels in the oven will help. The sauce can be kept hot over a very low heat for several minutes.*

Less oakey white wines, such as Meursault, Montrachet, Pouilly Fuisse or lighter New World chardonnays, will go extremely well with this dish. A chilled lighter red wine, such as a Beaujolais, also goes nicely.

An Evening in Paris

The Arc de Triomphe

There is nothing better than an evening in Paris or, for that matter, an entire week in Paris. It is a truly magnificent city with wide boulevards, beautiful architecture, and an amazing array of art, culture and scenery. But, of course, it is the Parisian restaurants and food that I look forward to most.

Just a few streets from the Eiffel Tower, at 20 Rue de Monttessuy, is one of the most wonderful restaurants on earth. It is small, with only about two dozen seats and a delightful atmosphere. It is called Vin sur Vin and I have been eating there for nearly 20 years. The owner, Patrice, is a gracious host with a warm, outgoing personality and a vast knowledge of wine and food. His presence alone would make the restaurant worth visiting but when Patrice welcomes you to Vin sur Vin you soon discover that it is just the beginning of an evening you are sure to remember.

The menu, like the restaurant, is relatively small with only a few choices for each course. All dishes are presented with flair and an explanation. The wine list is substantial, with a large selection of vintages from all the winemaking regions of France, as well as carefully selected choices from other countries. Patrice is always willing to suggest wines that will complement your meal perfectly and fit your budget. We have recommended Vin sur Vin to many people and have received nothing but compliments from everyone.

Filet de Sole avec Crevettes Roses
Pan Fried Sole Stuffed with Bay Shrimp

This is an adaptation of a dish I first tasted at Vin Sur Vin some years ago and have often prepared at home ever since. It works equally well as either a starter or main course. Halve the recipe if serving as a starter. Serves 8.

8	sole fillets
1	cup (240 ml) milk
	Salt and freshly ground black pepper
½	lb (230 g) bay shrimp
2	tablespoons (30 ml) olive oil
1	tablespoon (15 g) unsalted butter
2	cups (480 ml) Béchamel Sauce (page 31)
½	cup (120 ml) dry white wine
1	teaspoon Beau Monde seasoning
½	teaspoon Szechuan Seasoning or cayenne
1	teaspoon paprika

Cut the sole fillets in half, lengthwise, removing any bones, and soak in the milk for 10 minutes. In a baking dish, lightly salt and pepper the sole fillet halves and roll 6 to 8 shrimp in each. Heat the oil and butter in a large skillet over medium-high heat, until bubbling but not browned, place the rolled sole fillets in the pan and cook until the underside is a rich golden brown (approximately 3 to 4 minutes). Carefully turn each of the rolled sole fillets over, being sure not to let any of the shrimp fall out, and repeat cooking for the other side. Remove the rolled sole fillets from the skillet to a baking dish and keep warm in a 140° F (60° C) oven.

Add the béchamel sauce to the skillet, heat until it bubbles, stir in the white wine, Beau Monde seasoning, and Szechwan Seasoning, and season to taste with salt and pepper. Continue stirring for 3 to 4 minutes until the sauce reduces to a creamy consistency.

Place the rolled sole fillets (2 for main dishes and 1 for starters) on individual plates, pour the sauce over them and serve.

Either a lighter New World chardonnay or a medium-dry white Burgundy, such as a Chablis, Montrachet, Saint Aubin, or Meursault is the ideal complement to this dish.

Chef *GUILLAUME LEBURN* and
Owner-chef *PATRICK GUILBAUD*

Making Irish Eyes Smile

And taste buds, too! The Irish are well known for their lively music, literature, pints of Guinness and hospitality. In recent decades, Ireland has also become known as a leading culinary center, with a worldwide reputation for quality ingredients and great restaurants.

I lived in Ireland with my family for eight years and traveled to all areas of the country. On one of my earliest visits, before living there, an Irish cousin introduced me to Restaurant Patrick Guilbaud in Dublin. I have now been dining there for more than 20 years.

The restaurant is located on Upper Merrion Street, next to the world class Merrion Hotel. The décor is open and fresh, looking out onto the hotel's gardens.

Executive Chef, Guillaume Lebrun's menu offers a broad range of delicacies, all creatively prepared and beautifully presented. The highlight is the 'chef's tasting menu', a daily creation that one must order, without knowing what will be served. My own first reaction to this was incredulity. It sounded like, "Sorry, you will just have to trust us, as we know best." With my North American biases, I was not particularly pleased. With some considerable hesitation, I decided to give in and see what would happen.

The entire menu was superb and now, I almost always opt for the tasting menu, whenever I dine there. Service is simply superb, with manager and Maître d', Stephane Robin, presiding over the staff. Any guest's request, within reason, receives an immediate Irish response of, "sure now, leave it to us," often with a French-Irish accent.

Patrick, himself, who originally came from Brittany, in northern France, followed a successful career with his own restaurant in Cheshire, opening Restaurant Patrick Guilbaud in 1981. Since then, his Dublin restaurant has set the standard by which all other gourmet restaurants in Ireland are judged.

In many ways, Patrick was a key leader in the meteoric rise of fine dining in Ireland, where there are now a number of great restaurants and talented Irish chefs. Still, in our opinion, none have managed to completely equal, let alone surpass, the standards set by Patrick Guilbaud, Ireland's first to earn a Michelin star and now the only restaurant in the country with two. It has received Ireland's "Restaurant of the Year" award several times, including 2006.

Sea Bass à la Plancha
Chef Guillaume Lebrun, Restaurant Patrick Guilbaud, Dublin

Wild sea bass is a favorite fish of ours and is generally available, in most areas, during the majority of the year. The white flesh is tender, without being overly delicate and can be served with a variety of sauces. This recipe from Restaurant Patrick Guilbaud always gets lots of compliments. Serves 6.

¾ cup (120 g) chopped shallots
4 tablespoons (60 ml) olive oil
1 garlic clove, crushed
1 bay leaf
1 sprig fresh thyme
¾ cup (180 ml) white wine
1 cup (240 ml) poultry stock (page 28)
12 heads baby fennel, trimmed
12 green onions, trimmed
3 slices of orange peel
½ cup (120 g) unsalted butter
6 sea bass fillets, scaled with skin left
    on, about ¾-inch thick
6 lemon segments, skinned and chopped
    Salt and freshly ground black pepper
6 sun dried tomatoes, sliced into ¼-inch strips
6 lemon segments, skinned
6 sprigs fresh dill

Soak the shallots in 3 tablespoons of the olive oil for 5 minutes. In a 3-quart saucepan, over medium-high heat, cook the shallots, garlic, bay leaf and thyme in the same 3 tablespoons of olive oil, until the shallots are translucent. Add the white wine and continue cooking until the liquid reduces by half. Add the poultry stock, bring to a boil, then add the fennel and cook until tender, about 1 hour. Add the green onions 3 to 4 minutes before the fennel is ready. Remove the fennel and green onions, and keep warm in a 140° F (60° C) oven. Add the orange peel to the saucepan and continue cooking, until the liquids reduce by half again. Remove the bay leaf, thyme and orange peel. Whisk in the butter, until it is completely blended into the sauce. Reduce heat to low and keep the sauce hot.

To cook the sea bass fillets, heat 1 tablespoon of olive oil over medium heat in a medium skillet. Place the bass fillets in the pan, skin-side-down and cook for about 3 to 5 minutes depending on thickness, until the skin begins to brown. Turn the fillets over and cook for a further 1 to 2 minutes.

To arrange, place two fennel heads and two green onions on individual dinner plates. Add the chopped lemon segments to the sauce and pour sauce over the fennel. Place a sea bass fillet partially on top of the fennel on each plate, and garnish with sun-dried tomato slices, a lemon segment and a sprig of dill.

❀ *For this dish, almost any medium-dry white wine, such as a Chablis, Macon Villages or lighter American chardonnay, that you like will work well.*

Salmon Wrestling in Alaska

Michel has always enjoyed fishing, from his childhood in Provence to his days in Alaska, Seattle, and England. He is always ready to fish on the sea, lakes, or rivers anytime the opportunity presents itself. And of course, he has never had any difficulty figuring out what to do with the fish he has caught.

While living in Alaska, Michel was invited on a fishing trip to the Kenai Peninsula, which is south of Anchorage. Michel became increasingly excited as the trip dates grew closer. King salmon has always been one of his very favorites, both for catching and for eating, and he had heard that salmon fishing at the mouth of the Kenai River was particularly good at that time of year.

Pacific King salmon can grow to a length of 5 feet and weigh more than 100 pounds but are more typically 30 to 36 inches, weighing 20 to 30 pounds. Michel would be perfectly happy with any size but hoped for a few "normal" ones and could already see them on the grill.

The day finally came and they were off to the Kenai with an experienced local guide. Fishing from the bank of the river, with brightly colored flies for bait, it seemed an eternity before anyone had a strike. In reality, it was only a few minutes, and soon other members of the party had caught six fine salmon, one of them a 24-pound beauty. Michel finally had a strike on his line. He played the line for more than two hours, by reeling in slowly and then watching as the fish swam away, taking his line out again. Gradually, his quarry began to tire and was coming closer to the shore. One of Michel's friends got ready with the net they had brought to take the fish from the water.

Michel brought the salmon right to the water's edge but, now, there was a problem. This was not the "normal" catch he had hoped for. It was an enormous King salmon and it was far too big for the net. Both of Michel's friends and the guide had to get into the cold water in order to wrestle the giant fish onto the shore. The salmon turned out to be a near-record catch weighing 96 pounds and measuring 56 inches from nose to tail. It became a fine meal for Michel and his friends, as well as patrons at the Captain Cook Hotel, where Michel was Executive Chef and Director of Food and Beverage.

Grilled Salmon with Soy Sauce, Lemon and Herbs

This recipe is the result of many years of experimenting with different techniques for grilling salmon. I have tried foil wraps, frequent basting and many other preparations, all of which were quite good. This is my own personal favorite. For this recipe, I always buy whole salmon fillets with the skin left on. Serves 8.

1 or 2 whole salmon fillets
    (about 4 lbs/1.8 kg total)
½   cup (120 ml) soy sauce
    Juice of 2 lemons
1   tablespoon total, finely chopped fresh
    rosemary and dill or thyme
1   teaspoon freshly ground black pepper

Preheat an outdoor grill with a cover that closes. Mix the soy sauce and lemon juice in a bowl and set aside. Remove the pin bones from the salmon.

Place the fillet(s) skin down, on a large baking tray, baste liberally with the soy and lemon juice mixture and let stand for a few minutes. Sprinkle the herbs and pepper over the salmon. Place fillet(s) skin side down on the grill and close the cover. Depending on the size and thickness of your fillets, cooking should take approximately 7 to 10 minutes. To be sure, lift a bit of flesh with a fork to test doneness. The salmon is done when the flesh is still very slightly moist (almost raw), in the thickest part of the middle of the flesh. To serve, have a large platter ready by the grill and simply use a spatula to lift the flesh from the skin.

Variations

You can use Provence herbs instead of those listed. If you do not have a covered grill, broiling the fish in the oven broiler is an acceptable, though not ideal, alternative. In that case, you should cook the fish on the flesh side rather than the skin side. It will have a harder, crusty brown surface when it is ready to serve. You can mitigate this by additional basting with the soy-lemon mixture during the broiling process.

Chef's tip

To remove the pin bones from the salmon, run your fingers over the thick side of the flesh to expose the bones and remove them with a pair of pliers, pulling directly from the flesh, without tearing.

❀ *For my tastes, a French Chablis or Chassagne Montrachet is the perfect wine to accompany this dish, but less oakey American chardonnays or a Semillon Blanc are likely to be less expensive and just as effective.*

Thailand Beckons

Thai cuisine has become famous throughout the world with Thai restaurants found in virtually every major city across the globe. Thai cuisine is a blend of indigenous, as well as Chinese and Indian foods, evolved over centuries, as different peoples from Southern Asia migrated to Thailand. Although Thai dishes can be very spicy, almost all Thai restaurants, in Thailand and abroad, are prepared to turn down the heat for guests who wish them to do so.

My own first exposure to Thai cuisine was in New York on a business trip in the mid-1970s and then in Southeast Asia also while on business. I found an amazing range of flavors and tastes while working in Bangkok and on side trips to Phuket and Chiang Mai. Noodles and rice are Thai staples and are almost always combined with other ingredients including meats, fish, and vegetables. Pad Thai is fried flat noodles that are typically served with a choice of beef, chicken, seafood, or tofu accompanied by cilantro and chilies. Another traditional dish is Mee Crob, which is puffed rice noodles coated with caramelized palm sugar and served as an accompaniment to hot curry dishes.

Seattle Weekly's Roger Downey in writing an article about Thai food said, "Most of us made the acquaintance of Thai cooking when looking for something healthy, fast, and cheap. Thai food is all those things, but it is much more – one of the wonders of the culinary world, in fact." His observation is entirely correct, which you will discover, if you open your mind and mouth to the wonders of traditional Thai cooking with all of its spice and zest. Downey also said, "Remember, Thai food's not too hot if you eat it the way Thais do, with lots and lots of glorious jasmine rice."

Thai Green Cream Shellfish Curry

The most common Thai green curries can be very spicy. This is a milder preparation that retains more than a hint of spiciness but without the fire. The white wine and cream take the edge off the curry sauce. This is a dish you can successfully serve to friends who say that they "do not like spicy foods." Serves 8.

3	tablespoons (45 g) unsalted butter
1	tablespoon (15 ml) toasted sesame oil
3	shallots, finely sliced
4	garlic cloves, very finely sliced
1	green bell pepper, cored, seeded and cut into ¼-inch strips
1	red or orange bell pepper, cored, seeded and cut into ¼-inch strips
2	tablespoons Provence herbs
½	cup (120 ml) dry white wine
32	prawns, shelled and deveined
32	sea scallops
½	lb (230 g) small whole mushrooms
2	cups (480 ml) Thai green curry sauce
1	cup (240 ml) heavy cream
	Salt and freshly ground black pepper

Heat the butter and oil in a large saucepan or skillet over medium-high heat until the butter bubbles. Add the shallots and garlic, and sauté until just beginning to brown. Add the peppers, Provence herbs and half the wine, and sauté until the peppers just begin to soften. Add the prawns and scallops and continue cooking, stirring frequently until the prawns begin to turn bright orange in color. Add the mushrooms and the remaining wine. Stir in the curry sauce and then the cream. Continue stirring until the sauce thickens to a creamy consistency. Season to taste with salt and pepper. Serve over white rice (Jasmine, Basmati or American long-grain), or Chinese rice noodles.

Note *that using a commercially available curry sauce is every bit as good as making the sauce from original ingredients and far less work. The quality of commercial curry sauces is excellent. You can also use Thai green curry paste mixed with water.*

A medium-dry Burgundy style white wine, like Petit Chablis, Montrachet, Meursault or a lighter, less oaken California chardonnay, goes well with this dish.

Cooking for a Crowd

Cooking successfully for a crowd requires a somewhat different approach and plan than cooking for a nice comfortable group of six or eight. Holiday and special occasion dinner parties at home, with as many as 18 to 24 guests, are a fairly regular occurrence at least several times each year.

Your first reaction to this may be, "Are you out of your mind? I am not even attempting to cook dinner for 24 people at my house." Cooking for a larger group is, in fact, quite manageable and does not need to be a formal sit down dinner. It requires a bit of planning and some consideration of your home and menu.

When planning, avoid anything that has to be 'cooked to order' and focus on dishes that can be made ahead and held until it is time to serve them. Salads and soups can be difficult for your guests to manage on their laps, instead of on a table. Instead, choose starters like Crab Cakes, Avocado Mousse, Chicken Liver Pâté, or Salmon Terrine. All can all be prepared well ahead of time and are easy to handle.

Avoid anything for main dishes that requires on-the-plate surgery such as anything with bones. Roasts of beef, lamb, or pork, carved in the kitchen and served on a platter work well as do baked veal dishes, which are easy to serve on a platter. For poultry, Sautéed Chicken Breasts, Shish Taouk, Poulet Rouge, and Su-Su Chicken Curry are good large crowd choices. Salmon in Puff Pastry, Grilled Salmon and Paella Seattle are all great for larger groups. You can serve everything on platters, in bowls and on trays and let your guests help themselves buffet-style.

For dessert, choose something you can make in the morning or the day before and serve without a lot of last-minute fuss. Crème Brûlée, Tarte Tatin, Death by Chocolate, Gâteau au Chocolat, and Chocolate Mousse all meet those criteria.

Paella Seattle
A Northwest Adaptation of a Spanish Classic

I first tasted Paella while attending a conference in Barcelona more than 25 years ago. Although most of the standard Spanish ingredients are now available in America, that was not the case at the time. This recipe is based on the original but uses ingredients that were more readily available in Seattle in 1980. Serves 12.

8	mild Italian sausages
2	tablespoons (30 g) unsalted butter
¼	cup (60 ml) olive oil
4	skinless, boneless chicken breast halves, cut into 1-inch cubes
1	lb (450 g) prawns, shelled and de-veined
1	lb (450 g) sea scallops
2	large shallots, finely chopped
4	garlic cloves, thinly sliced
1	red bell pepper, cored, seeded and cut into ¼-inch strips
1	green bell pepper, cored, seeded and cut into ¼-inch strips
½	lb (230 g) mushrooms, sliced
1	tablespoon finely chopped fresh oregano
1	tablespoon finely chopped fresh rosemary
	Salt and freshly ground black pepper
½	teaspoon cayenne
3	cups (720 ml) Provençal Tomato Sauce (page 33)
1	cup (240 ml) dry white wine

3	cups (720 ml) poultry stock (page 28)
¼	teaspoon saffron
3	cups (600 g) Arborio rice
2	cups (300 g) fresh or frozen green peas

Cook the sausages in a large skillet over medium-high heat, until cooked through, remove from the skillet, set aside to cool, and cut into ½-inch slices. Pour off excess sausage fat from the skillet. Melt half of the butter and oil in the skillet, until the butter begins to bubble. Add the chicken pieces, prawns and scallops and sauté, until the chicken pieces begin to brown and the prawns turn bright orange. Remove from the skillet and set aside.

Add the rest of the butter and oil with the shallots and garlic, and sauté until the shallots turn translucent. Add the bell peppers, mushrooms, herbs, salt, pepper, cayenne, tomato sauce, and white wine, stirring frequently until all is well mixed. Just cover these sautéed ingredients with poultry stock, add the saffron and bring to a boil, then stir in the Arborio rice grains and simmer for about 20 to 25 minutes, until the rice is fully cooked. Add the sausages, chicken, prawns, scallops and green peas, and cook for about 3 to 4 minutes, until all ingredients are hot. Season to taste with salt, cayenne, and freshly ground black pepper, and serve.

This dish has a very robust flavor, so full-bodied, somewhat spicy red wines make the best accompaniment. I like Italian Barolos or Tiganellos and California zinfandels or cabernets.

PASTA AND RICE

Pasta & Rice

Pastas and rice are to Italy, Spain and the Far East what potatoes are to Ireland. When I was a child, my mother often served rice but, since my parents were both Irish, potatoes were the only starch at most meals. The only pasta I tasted in my early childhood was spaghetti, which was always served with canned tomato sauce, ground beef, and cheese.

As a teen, I discovered that pasta was so much more than I had ever known. Eating at the homes of friends whose parents were from Italy, I tasted lasagna, ravioli, tortellini, gnocchi, linguine, and Fettuccini Alfredo. One friend's Italian mother served amazing homemade sauces and she showed me how to make her special tomato sauce, which she had learned from her grandmother as a young girl in Italy. Some months later, I ate in an Italian restaurant owned by a schoolmate's parents and my love affair with Italian cuisine began.

Flat Italian noodles range from very thin angel hair to wider linguine or fettuccini and very wide lasagna. Tube-shaped pasta includes macaroni and penne and larger tubes that are used to make cannelloni. Farfalle looks like small bow ties and fusilli is twisted into spiral shapes.

Pasta has Asian roots as well. Noodles are a popular part of the Asian diet from Seoul to Singapore. *Chow mien, dan min* (Chinese egg noodles), *gan mien* (Chinese wheat noodles) and *naeng myun* (Korean noodles made with buckwheat flour and potato starch) are just a few of the many types of noodles you can find in the Far East. In Japan, entire restaurants are devoted to noodle soup dishes, and if you visit, a chorus of loud slurping may surprise you. The local patrons eat their soup noodles and demonstrate their appreciation audibly. No matter the type, Italian, Asian or other, I do love pasta.

There are dozens, if not hundreds, of rice varieties. White rice, brown rice and wild rice, long-grain and short-grain, as well as Arborio rice, which is used to make risotto, are the most common varieties. Risotto is especially nice with other ingredients for either side dishes or starters. It takes care in cooking but the extra effort is definitely worthwhile and, when you make a perfect risotto, your guests are sure to love it.

American rice growers produce many varieties including domestic versions of Chinese, Japanese, basmati, jasmine and Egyptian rice, and the quality is outstanding. Interestingly, more rice is grown in California than in any other country, with the possible exception of China. Most supermarkets also carry a large number of pre-packaged rice medley selections such as a blend of white, brown, and wild rice.

Asparagus and Mushroom Risotto

This is one of the easiest risottos to make. It makes a very interesting side dish and, with the asparagus and mushrooms, can eliminate the need for a vegetable side dish. It is also light enough that it can go with even the most subtle and delicately flavored fish main dishes. If available, chanterelle, shiitake or morel mushrooms are wonderful in this dish. Serves 6.

1½   cups (300 g) Arborio rice
1   tablespoon (15 ml) olive oil
4½   cups (1 liter) poultry stock (page 28), warmed
1   teaspoon Provence herbs
¼   teaspoon Beau Monde seasoning
1   bunch asparagus (1¼ lbs/570 g), cut into ½-inch pieces
½   lb (230 g) small whole mushrooms
½   cup (120 ml) dry white wine
1   tablespoon (15 g) unsalted butter
    Salt and freshly ground black pepper
½   cup (25 g) freshly grated Parmesan

Note *that cooking this dish will require at least 20 minutes of nearly undivided attention, and that continuous stirring is absolutely essential. Only by tasting will you be able to tell when the risotto is done. It should be just cooked through but still firm.*

Combine the rice and oil in a large saucepan, over medium heat and cook, stirring continuously with a wooden spoon or spatula, until the rice becomes translucent. Add 1 cup of poultry stock and stir continuously until the liquid is almost completely soaked up by the rice, and then add the next ½ cup of stock. Reduce the heat to medium-low, add the Provence herbs, Beau Monde seasoning, and a bit of salt and pepper, stirring continuously and repeating the ½ cup of stock additions, until the risotto is nearly done. When you have used 3 cups of the stock, add the asparagus and mushrooms. When you have used all the stock, add the white wine and continue stirring, until it is also absorbed and then test doneness. If the risotto is not completely cooked, add water ¼ cup at a time, until the risotto is completely cooked. Stir in the butter and remove the pan from the heat. Season to taste with salt and pepper, top the risotto with a sprinkle of grated Parmesan and serve.

Variations

There are innumerable risotto variations. One of our favorites uses small, green garden peas (petit pois) instead of asparagus. You will want to add the peas to the risotto later in the cooking process, after you have added approximately 3½ cups of the poultry stock, as peas cook more quickly than asparagus.

Basmati with Peppers, Shallots and Garlic

Basmati is originally an Indian variety of rice, although it is now grown in many other countries. It is a long-grained, aromatic and flavorful white rice that cooks fluffy, without becoming sticky. This recipe makes for a more interesting side dish than plain rice and goes nicely with almost any main dish. Serves 8.

1	tablespoon (15 g) unsalted butter
1	bell pepper, cored, seeded and diced
2	large shallots, thinly sliced
3	garlic cloves, minced
¼	teaspoon Bouquet Garni or Provence herbs
¼	teaspoon mild yellow curry powder
2	cups (400 g) basmati rice
½	teaspoon salt
3	cups (720 ml) cold water
	Salt and freshly ground pepper

Melt the butter in a medium saucepan, over medium-high heat, until it begins to bubble. Add the bell pepper, shallots, garlic, herbs and curry powder and sauté, stirring frequently, until the shallots are translucent. Add the rice and salt to the saucepan and stir until the rice grains are coated with butter. Add the cold water, turn the heat to medium-high, bring to a rolling boil and then immediately reduce heat to simmer. Cover and continue cooking until the water is fully absorbed and the rice is cooked through, about 12 to 15 minutes. Be sure to check the rice after 10 minutes and every minute or two, thereafter. As soon as the rice is cooked, remove it from the heat, season to taste with salt and pepper, stir with a fork, place a clean dish towel over the top of the saucepan and cover with a lid. The cloth will absorb excess moisture and prevent the rice from becoming sticky. Let the rice stand for 5 minutes before serving.

Note *that an electric rice cooker is guaranteed to give you perfectly cooked rice every time, provided that you closely follow the manufacturer's instructions. With a rice cooker, the peppers and shallots should be sautéed separately and mixed in with the rice after it is cooked.*

A Family Affair

Brendan in the kitchen with Papken

Cooking with my children has been one of my great joys. Involving children, at an early age, in the entire process of menu planning, shopping, preparation, and cooking, exposes them to quality foods and, if you are lucky, encourages them away from less healthy choices. My three children, Papken, Alana and Fiona, all have an interest in food and cooking and being with them in the kitchen is always a treat.

Both Michel and I have involved our sons and daughters in our home entertaining from very early ages. On school holidays Michel's youngest, eleven-year-old Andrea, sometimes comes to the restaurant and learns from Michel and the other chefs. On trips to markets we have shown our children how to select food products for quality and freshness. At home, we have taught our children techniques for preparation and cooking, as well as presentation, and more recently, for the older ones, food and wine pairings.

Cooking and food wisdom, passed down from generation to generation, is one of the most valuable gifts you can give your children. Now young adults, my children are all quite accomplished cooks. My daughter Alana will often call Ani or me with a cooking question, which delights us because it gives us a chance to connect with her now that she lives away from home. She also likes to share stories from her recent dinner parties and makes me chuckle when she says she inherited her "entertaining genes from both parents, but the wine genes... they came entirely from you, Dad."

Fettuccini Fiona

I created this pasta dish for my youngest daughter, Fiona, who has cooked with me at home since she was a very small child. She is away at university now but still comes home often and takes charge of complete meals or acts as my sous-chef, when we are entertaining company. Serves 8.

6	thick bacon slices, diced
3	tablespoons (45 ml) olive oil
1	shallot, finely chopped
¼	cup (60 ml) dry white wine
2	cups (200 g) sliced mushrooms
2	cups (300 g) fresh or frozen green peas
1	tablespoon finely chopped fresh rosemary
1	tablespoon finely chopped fresh basil
1½	cups (360 ml) Béchamel Sauce (page 31)
¾	cup (75 g) grated Swiss cheese
1½	lbs (690 g) fresh egg fettuccini
1	tablespoon (15 g) unsalted butter
	Salt and freshly ground pepper

This dish *makes either an appealing starter or, in larger portions, an excellent main dish.*

Sauté the bacon pieces in a large skillet, over medium heat, stirring frequently, until fully cooked but not crisp. Remove the bacon pieces, set aside, and pour off the fat from the skillet. Add 1 tablespoon of olive oil to the pan, add the shallot and cook, until translucent. Add the wine, mushrooms, peas, rosemary and basil, stirring frequently, until the mushrooms and peas are just cooked. Reduce the heat to low, add the béchamel sauce, stirring continuously, until the sauce is well blended and just begins to bubble. Add ½ cup of the grated Swiss cheese, a bit a bit at a time, stirring continuously, until the cheese melts and blends with the sauce. Season to taste with salt and pepper, reduce to low heat and keep hot.

To prepare the fettucini, bring a large saucepan of salted water, with 1 tablespoon of olive oil, to a rolling boil and cook the fettuccini, stirring occasionally until just cooked al dente. Drain the pasta well in a colander, first adding a burst of cold water to stop the cooking process. Place pasta in a large, warm serving bowl, and stir in the butter and a bit more olive oil. Pour the heated sauce over the pasta, tossing to cover all of the noodles.

Garnish with bacon bits, grated cheese and a sprig of basil and serve with *crostinis* (thin baguette slices with melted cheese), as shown.

Full-bodied, slightly oakey chardonnays or medium-bodied red wines, such as pinot noirs or merlots, will go best with this dish, complementing the cheese and bacon flavors.

Linguine with Prawns in a Sun-dried Tomato Cream Sauce

Linguine is thin, flat pasta, about midway between fettuccini and angel hair. This is a very simple pasta side dish that should only be served with more flavorful meat or poultry main dishes and can also be served as a main dish. Serves 6.

4	tablespoons (15 ml) olive oil
1	garlic clove, thinly sliced
¼	teaspoon dry oregano, crushed
1	lb (450 g) prawns, shelled and deveined
3	ounces (90 g) sun-dried tomatoes, cut into ¼-inch strips
½	cup (70 g) pitted black olives (not canned)
1	cup (240 ml) Provençal Tomato Sauce (page 33)
¼	cup (60 ml) dry white wine
2	tablespoons (30 ml) heavy cream
	Salt and freshly ground pepper
1	lb (450 g) fresh egg linguine
¼	cup (25 g) grated Parmesan

Variations

This is a dish with which you can experiment to your heart's content. To lighten this dish, eliminate the tomato sauce, olives and sun-dried tomatoes, and substitute green peas, lima beans and zucchini slices. You can also substitute chicken for the prawns.

Heat 2 tablespoons of olive oil in a skillet over medium heat and sauté the garlic with the oregano, until the garlic is translucent. Add the prawns, sun-dried tomatoes and olives, and sauté, stirring frequently, until the prawns are just cooked through. Add the tomato sauce, stir in the white wine, and continue cooking until the sauce is just below the boiling point. Stir in the cream and continue stirring until the sauce thickens to a creamy consistency. Season to taste with salt and pepper, and keep warm over low heat.

Bring a large saucepan of salted water, with 1 tablespoon of olive oil, to a rolling boil. Add the linguini to the boiling water and cook, stirring occasionally, until the pasta is just cooked, al dente. Drain well in a colander, first running a burst of cold water over the pasta to stop the cooking process. Place pasta in a large, warm serving bowl and stir in the last tablespoon of olive oil. Pour the heated sauce over the pasta, top with grated Parmesan and serve.

Smoked Salmon Pasta with Swiss Cheese Sauce

This is a simple pasta dish that works equally well as a main dish or starter. Any thin, flat or curly pasta can be used. The choice of smoked salmon is yours, as either cold-smoked lox style or warm-smoked varieties work equally well. Serves 6.

3	tablespoons (60 ml) olive oil
2	tablespoons (30 g) unsalted butter
1	large shallot, finely chopped
1	tablespoon minced fresh oregano
1	tablespoon minced fresh thyme
¼	cup (60 ml) dry white wine
1½	cups (225 g) green peas
2	cups (200 g) sliced mushrooms
¾	cup (180 ml) Béchamel Sauce (page 31)
¾	lb (360 g) smoked salmon, cut into small pieces
½	cup (50 g) grated Emmenthal or Jarlsberg cheese
	Salt and freshly ground pepper
1½	lb (690 g) fresh egg pasta (Fettuccini, Linguine, Penne or Farfalle)

In a large skillet, over medium heat, heat 1 tablespoon of olive oil with 1 tablespoon butter, and sauté the shallots with the oregano and thyme, until the shallot pieces turn translucent. Add the white wine, green peas and mushrooms, and simmer, until the vegetables are just cooked. Reduce the heat to medium-low, add the béchamel sauce and smoked salmon pieces, and slowly add the grated cheese, stirring continuously, until the sauce is well blended. Season to taste with salt and pepper, and keep warm over low heat.

Bring large saucepan of salted water, with 1 tablespoon of olive oil, to a rolling boil. Add the pasta to the boiling water and cook, stirring occasionally, until the pasta is just cooked, al dente. Drain well in a colander, first running a burst of cold water over the pasta to stop the cooking process. Place the pasta in a large, warm serving bowl and stir in the remaining butter and olive oil. Pour the heated sauce over the pasta, toss gently to coat the pasta completely with sauce, and serve.

Variations

This dish is also very nice made with risotto instead of pasta. Just follow the Asparagus and Mushroom Risotto recipe (page 132) and cook the risotto, adding the salmon, mushrooms and peas at the same stage as the asparagus and mushrooms. Heat the béchamel sauce and mix in the grated cheese separately. Mix the sauce with the risotto just before serving.

Wild Rice with Mushrooms and Herbs

Wild rice is one of nature's great gifts. It is an aquatic grain that grows wild in the marshlands of the upper Midwest and is the only grain native to the North American continent. Technically, it is not rice but another rice-like grain. This makes a perfect side dish for more flavorful meat, poultry and game dishes. Serves 8.

2	cups (400 g) wild rice
5	cups (1.2 litres) poultry stock (page 28)
2	cups (480 ml) water
¼	teaspoon Provence herbs
¼	cup (40 g) pine nuts
I	tablespoon (15 g) unsalted butter
I	tablespoon (15 ml) olive oil
I	shallot, finely chopped
½	lb (230g) diced shiitake or button mushrooms
	Salt and freshly ground black pepper

Note *that cooking wild rice requires more liquid and takes longer to cook than regular rice.*

Variations

You can use beef stock instead of poultry stock if your main dish is meat. To accompany fish dishes, vegetable stock works well.

Rinse the wild rice thoroughly in a fine sieve under cold water. Put the washed rice in a large, deep saucepan. Add the poultry stock and water. Add the herbs and bring to a boil over medium-high heat. Stir, reduce heat and simmer, covered, for 35 to 45 minutes, or just until the kernals puff open. Perfectly cooked wild rice is slightly split, yet still holds its shape. The rice should be soft and a little bit chewy, but not mushy. Remove the rice from the heat, drain off excess liquid and let stand, covered, for 3 to 5 minutes.

Toast the pine nuts under the broiler, until just golden brown, and set aside. Heat the butter and olive oil in a skillet over medium heat, until the butter begins to bubble, and sauté the chopped shallot and mushrooms until tender. Add the shallots, mushrooms and pine nuts to the cooked rice and mix together. Season to taste with salt and pepper, and serve.

Polenta Gratin with Broccoli and Mornay Sauce

In parts of northern Italy, polenta is as much a part of the daily diet as bread. It is made from ground corn and is usually yellow. This is a side dish that incorporates both polenta, for a starch, and broccoli, for a vegetable. It works well as a light main dish for vegetarian friends. Serves 12, as a side dish, or 6, as a vegetarian main dish.

½ cup (120 g) unsalted butter
2¼ cups (400 g) dry polenta
8⅓ cups (2 liters) vegetable stock (page 29)
1 cup (240 ml) milk
Salt and freshly ground pepper
10 ounces (300 g) Emmenthal or
Gruyère cheese, grated
2 lbs (900 g) small broccoli florets
2 cups (480 ml) Mornay Sauce (page 31)
2 tomatoes, each cut into wedges
Sprigs of parsley, for garnish

Preheat the oven to 400° F (200° C). Heat the butter in a large skillet, over medium heat, until it bubbles. Add the dry polenta and sauté, stirring, until it turns golden brown. Whisk in the vegetable stock slowly, and stirring continuously, cook until the polenta thickens and bubbles (about 10 to 15 minutes). Add the milk gradually, until the mixture reaches the consistency of loosely cooked hot breakfast cereal, such as Cream of Wheat. Season to taste with salt and pepper.

Butter the bottom and sides of a large baking pan. Fill with alternating layers of polenta and grated cheese, with polenta on the bottom and cheese on the top layer. Bake for about 40 minutes and then remove from the oven to cool. Leave the oven temperature at 400° F (200° C).

Bring 2 cups of salted water to boil over medium-high heat, add the broccoli florets, cover the saucepan and steam the florets, until they are just cooked through and retain a rich green color. Remove from the saucepan, drain and set aside.

Cut the baked polenta gratin into approximately 3-inch squares or circles and place on a large baking sheet. Arrange 3 or 4 small broccoli florets on top of each polenta gratin square and pour Mornay sauce over them. Put the baking sheet in the oven and bake for approximately five minutes or until the Mornay sauce turns golden brown. Remove from the oven, place on individual plates, garnish with tomato wedges and sprigs of parsley, and serve.

POTATOES

Potatoes

When Ani and I lived in Ireland with our children we noticed that most restaurant meals featured at least two or three different choices of potato dishes. The potato is, after all, the Irish national flower. No, that is not really true, but potatoes have played a major role in Irish history and are still featured very prominently in the Irish diet.

In 1997, Michel and I teamed up for a special dinner in Dublin, for clients and other guests of my company. The theme for the dinner was "An Evening in Provence," with a five-course menu comprised of traditional Provence dishes. We borrowed the usually breakfast-only restaurant kitchen and dining room in a friend's small Georgian boutique hotel. The dinner was a great success and we received many compliments. However, a number of guests remarked with surprise that we served an entire five-course meal without including a single potato, which was taken as some sort of Irish sacrilege.

The birthplace of the Irish white potatoes that we eat today was actually on a high plateau in the Andean Mountains of South America. Spanish Conquistadors introduced potatoes to Europe when they returned from their expeditions to the New World. Like rice, there is an incredible variety of different types of potatoes in the world and countless different potato dishes. Mashed potatoes and breakfast potato cakes are old standards, as are grated, fried potatoes (hash browns). Simple boiled potatoes or piping hot baked potatoes with butter, salt, and pepper can be just great.

Different potato varieties have different characteristics. If not overcooked, potatoes with thin, smooth skins, in white, red and yellow colors, remain firm and moist. These 'waxy' potatoes are usually best for boiling or steaming. Russet potatoes with thicker brown, almost leathery, skins cook dry and fluffy and are best for baking.

Some people avoid potatoes thinking that they have too many calories or carbohydrates. In fact, a potato has approximately the same calories as a same-sized apple. It is the other ingredients and the frying in butter, or serving with lots of butter and sour cream or mayonnaise that account for calories. Potatoes are low in fat and sodium and high in nutritional value. They are relatively inexpensive. Perhaps it is my Irish genes but potatoes are one food that I would never be without.

Baked, roasted, fried, steamed, boiled, potatoes can be a meal, a snack, an accompaniment, an extender, a soup, a salad or an ingredient in cakes and bread.

Pommes de Terre au Gratin
Au Gratin Potatoes

Au gratin potatoes have been served in French homes and restaurants for several centuries. In addition to having a wonderful taste and being easy to make, this dish has the added advantage of being one that can be prepared a day in advance, and baked or reheated without losing any flavor. Serves 8.

8	medium white or yellow, thin-skinned potatoes (about 4 lbs/1.8 kg)
1	tablespoon (15 ml) olive oil or vegetable oil
3	cups (720 ml) cream or half and half
1½	cups (150 g) grated Emmenthal or Jarlsberg cheese
	Salt and freshly ground black pepper

Variations

For a somewhat lighter dish, omit the cheese from this recipe. To embellish the flavor, add a sprinkling of herbs, such as minced chives, parsley, thyme or Provence herbs.

Preheat the oven to 400° F (200° C). Peel the potatoes and cut them into ⅛-inch thick slices. A mandoline or food processor with an adjustable slicing attachment makes this very easy. Coat the inside of a 12-inch gratin dish or other baking dish with the oil.

Arrange half of the potato slices, overlapping in the baking dish. Pour half the cream over the potato slices, scatter evenly with half the grated cheese, and season with salt and pepper. Arrange the rest of the potato slices on top of the cheese in the same way. Repeat the cream, grated cheese, and salt and pepper steps.

Bake in the oven for approximately 40 minutes, until the potatoes are completely tender and the top is golden brown. Test doneness by piercing the potatoes with a fork. Remove from the oven and let stand 2 to 3 minutes before serving.

If you are going to refrigerate the potatoes for later use, let them cool to room temperature, cover and refrigerate. You can also keep this dish hot, in a 140° F (60° C) oven, for up to 30 or 40 minutes, until ready to serve it.

Croquettes de Pomme de Terre
Potato Croquettes

Potato croquettes are an elegant alternative to French fries. They take a little extra time and care in preparation but are delicious and eye-catching. One of the earliest dishes that Michel taught me in the early 1970s, croquettes also make great hors d'oeuvres. Serves 8.

8	medium, white, thin-skinned potatoes, peeled and quartered (about 4 lbs/1.8kg)
2	large eggs, separated
	Salt and freshly ground black pepper
1	cup (120 g) all-purpose flour
1½	cups (180 g) fine dry unseasoned breadcrumbs
2½	cups (600 ml) vegetable or peanut oil

Variations

To serve croquettes as hors d'oeuvres, add ½ cup of diced, cooked chicken meat or bacon and ½ cup (50 g) of grated cheese to the recipe, at the same time as the egg yolks.

Preheat the oven to 250° F (120° C). Put the potatoes in a large saucepan, over medium-high heat, with enough cold water to just cover them, and boil until fully cooked (about 15 to 20 minutes). Test doneness with a fork. Remove the saucepan from the heat and drain the potatoes in a large colander. Put the potatoes in a large bowl and, with a potato masher or electric hand mixer, mix the potato pieces until they are smooth.

This next step is essential. Your croquettes will succeed only if the potatoes are quite dry. Cover a baking dish or pan with aluminum foil and spread the potatoes out on the foil. Bake the potatoes for approximately 30 to 35 minutes, to remove excess moisture. Take the potatoes out of the oven and place them in a mixing bowl. While the potatoes are still hot, add the egg yolks and beat slowly with a mixer, until completely and smoothly blended. Add salt and pepper, to taste. Note that you will want the potatoes to have a consistency that will mold easily, without losing shape.

When the potato mixture has cooled, use your hands to make 1-inch diameter logs. Place these side by side, but not touching, on a baking sheet, and refrigerate for at least 2 hours. (You may store them like this, covered with plastic wrap, for a day or two before cooking them.) To finish, roll the molded potato logs in the flour, coating them completely. Gently beat the egg whites. Dip the flour-coated croquettes in the egg whites and then roll them in the breadcrumbs, until evenly coated.

In a deep fryer or skillet, heat the oil to 350° F (180° C) and fry 3 to 5 croquettes at a time, until rich golden brown. Remove them from the hot oil and place them on paper towels set on a plate. Keep warm in a 140° F (60° C) oven while frying the remaining croquettes.

There are Mashed Potatoes

Michel explaining technique

And there are mushed potatoes, if not cooked properly. The key to great mashed potatoes is a combination of timing, technique and attention to detail. First, be sure that the potatoes are just cooked through but still firm. Then be sure to drain off all excess water. Melting the butter and heating the milk, before adding them to the mash helps to get the potatoes mixed smoothly. Finally, add milk a bit at a time and be careful not to mix too vigorously or your mash will be smooth but not light and fluffy. When mashed potatoes are just nicely moist and fluffy they are delicious but knowing these key steps is what will make the difference between great and just okay.

As Michel often says, "cooking is easy, as long as you follow the rules." Of course, before you can follow those rules, you have to know what they are.

Chefs like Michel cook instinctively and their instincts are immensely helped by a foundation of classic training and years of experience, trial and error. For most of us who may not have been blessed with creative genius or the benefit of formal culinary training and long experience, there are more challenges. Even when we think we have carefully followed a recipe, the result is sometimes not always what we expect. Remember that "cooking mistakes" are not always the fault of the cook. Mistakes can be caused by problems with recipes. Many recipes take quite a bit for granted and sometimes leave out important details.

Some of the things I have learned over the years, and now take for granted myself, are things I might never have learned from recipes. Many years ago Michel taught me never to use paprika in cooking other than for accent unless the recipe also contained wine, vinegar or lemon juice. Just following recipes with paprika and one of the other ingredients, I might never have understood the broader 'rule'.

Two other examples of important cooking techniques are when to sprinkle or just dump ingredients into a dish, as it is cooking, and when a little bit of water is truly needed. Always sprinkle sugar into hot liquids, while stirring continuously. A spoonful of water in salad dressings helps the oil and vinegar mix together more easily. The oil should be added last when making dressings since herbs and other dry ingredients tend to cling together in oil.

Many recipes include instructions to "season to taste." Taste is, of course, quite individual. Even if you like your food very salty or spicy, your guests may not. So, remember this when cooking for others and be sure to taste your dishes, along the way, to assure the best results.

Classic Mashed Potatoes

Plain and simple but oh so delicious, fluffy mashed potatoes with a bit of butter or gravy are a treat. Most of us first tasted mashed potatoes at our family dinner tables as small children. As a youngster, it was one of the very first dishes I learned to make, under the watchful eyes of my own mother. Serves 8.

3 lbs (1.4 kg) waxy potatoes, peeled,
   washed and halved or quartered
¾ cup (180 ml) whole milk or light cream
½ cup (120 g) unsalted butter, melted
   Salt and freshly ground pepper

In a large saucepan, cover the potato chunks with cold, salted water. Cover the saucepan, and over medium-high heat, bring the water to a rolling boil. Uncover and reduce heat, so the potatoes are boiling gently. Continue boiling until the potato chunks are just cooked through.

Drain the potatoes, and, to evaporate excess water, return them to the pot, uncovered, over very low heat for a few minutes, or into a preheated oven at 200° F (90° C) for 10 to 15 minutes. Heat the milk (or cream), without boiling. Place the potatoes in a large mixing bowl and mash gently with a potato masher. Using an electric hand mixer on lower speed, mix the potatoes, adding the melted butter. Then add half the warm milk (or cream) and continue mixing until fully blended. Slowly add more milk, until the mash is smooth and fluffy. Season to taste with salt and pepper, and serve.

Note *that melting the butter and heating the milk helps to make mixing smoother and avoids lumps in the mash. Removing excess water, after boiling, also helps to assure a smoother mash.*

Fried Potatoes with Provence Herbs

This dish is a suitable side dish for almost any main dish. These potatoes are easier to make and have a bit more eye and taste appeal than plainer alternatives. Serves 8.

8	medium white, yellow or red thin-skinned potatoes, peeled and cut into 1 inch cubes
1	tablespoon (15 g) unsalted butter
2	tablespoons (15 ml) olive oil
1	teaspoon Provence herbs or a blend of chopped fresh thyme and rosemary
	Salt and freshly ground black pepper

Heat the butter and oil in a large skillet over medium-high heat, until the butter begins to bubble. Add the potatoes and herbs, and sauté, tossing frequently, until evenly browned and cooked through (about 25 to 30 minutes). Season to taste with salt and pepper and serve.

Note that, if you master the skill of tossing ingredients in a skillet, it is the easiest way to turn diced potatoes.

These potatoes will also hold nicely, over very low heat on the stovetop or in a 140° F (60° C) oven, for up to an hour, as long as they are covered.

Pictured from top to bottom:
Fried Potatoes with Provence Herbs
Shredded Potatoes with Shallots
Curried Roast Potatoes with Parsley

Shredded Potatoes with Shallots

Also known as hash browns, shredded potatoes make a simple accompaniment to many main dishes, as well as a tasty side dish for a hearty breakfast with eggs, bacon, ham or sausage, and toast. I use garlic and shallots sparingly for this recipe, so that the flavor of the potatoes can still come through. Serves 8.

6	large white or yellow potatoes, peeled and shredded
2	garlic cloves, very thinly sliced
I	medium shallot, finely sliced
I	tablespoon (I5 g) unsalted butter
2	tablespoons (30 ml) olive oil or vegetable oil
	Salt and freshly ground black pepper

Preheat the oven to 225° F (110° C). Put the freshly shredded potatoes in a baking dish and bake for about 25 to 30 minutes, to dry them. Remove from the oven. Mix the shredded potatoes, garlic and shallots together in a large bowl. Melt the butter and oil in a large heavy skillet over medium-low heat until it bubbles. Add the potato mixture, spreading it evenly across the bottom of the pan.

Cook until the bottom is a rich golden brown, flip the potatoes and continuing cooking until the other side is also a rich golden brown. Using a fork, gently remove a couple of potato shreds from the middle of the potatoes and taste test to be sure that they are fully cooked. If not, reduce the heat to low and cover the skillet until the potatoes are done.

Variations

Cover the potatoes with grated cheddar cheese (approximately 1½ cups/150 g), immediately after turning them in the skillet. The cheese will melt over and into the potatoes while the second side is browning.

Curried Roast Potatoes

The curry in this recipe introduces an element of surprise and gives a kick of spiciness to the roasted potatoes. Note that using small waxy potatoes and leaving the skins on enhances the overall flavor of the dish. Just be sure when using hot curry powder that the flavor does not overwhelm the main dish. Serves 8.

2	tablespoons (30 g) unsalted butter
3	tablespoons (45 ml) olive oil
I	teaspoon curry powder
24-32	small new potatoes (about 3 lbs), washed, with skins left on
	Salt and freshly ground black pepper
½	cup (20 g) chopped parsley

Preheat the oven to 350° F (180° C). Heat the butter and oil with the curry powder in a large, oven-proof skillet over medium-high heat until the butter begins to bubble. Add the potatoes and season lightly with salt and pepper. Continue cooking for 1 to 2 minutes, turning the potatoes to coat them with the curry powder, butter, and oil. Transfer the pan to the oven and roast, until the potatoes are cooked through (about 25 to 30 minutes).

Test doneness with a fork. When the fork tines slide in and out of a potato without any resistance, the potatoes are done. Serve in a serving dish or on individual plates, and sprinkle a bit of parsley over the potatoes.

Variations

Using Provence herbs, or fresh chopped rosemary or thyme, instead of curry, for those who are not fans of curry.

Creamed Stuffed Baked Potatoes

This recipe, sometimes called Twice Baked Potatoes, is one that Michel often featured on banquet menus at the hotels where he was in charge of catering. It is easy to make and holds well in an oven, without losing flavor or becoming dry, for up to an hour or slightly more. Serves 8.

8	medium russet potatoes, washed and pierced a few times with a fork
2	tablespoons (30 ml) olive oil
	Salt and freshly ground black pepper
1	cup (240 g) sour cream, at room temperature
1	cup (40 g) finely chopped chives
¼	cup (60 g) unsalted butter
1	bell pepper, cored, seeded and finely diced
8	slices smoked bacon, fried crisp and crumbled
1½	cups (150g) grated cheddar or Emmenthal cheese (optional)
	Ground paprika, for accent

Preheat the oven to 400° F (200° C). Coat the potatoes with the oil and season with salt and pepper. Place the potatoes in the oven, spaced evenly across and directly on the oven rack. Bake for approximately 40 minutes or until the skin is crisp and the potatoes are tender. Test with a fork or thin knife. Remove the potatoes from the oven and let cool for about 10 to 15 minutes.

Using a sharp knife cut off the top of each potato, sideways as shown in the photo. Using a spoon, carefully scoop the cooked potato flesh into a large bowl, without tearing the potato skins, and set the skins aside. Add the sour cream, chives, butter, bell pepper, and crumbled bacon. Using an electric mixer on low speed, or a large whisk, blend the ingredients together.

Carefully refill each of the potato skins with the mixture, again being careful not to tear the skins. Arrange the potatoes on a large baking sheet and bake for 6 to 7 minutes at 375° F (190° C). (If you wish to top with cheese, sprinkle the potato tops with the cheese now.) Turn the oven to broil and broil until the surface begins to brown. Remove from the oven, sprinkle lightly with paprika, and serve, or keep warm in a 140° F (60° C) oven for up to 1 hour.

Breakfast Potato Cakes

Mashed potatoes refrigerated overnight make wonderful potato cakes either for breakfast or as a side dish for lunch or dinner. Whenever I make mashed potatoes for dinner, I always make extra for later use as breakfast potato cakes. I first tasted this treat on a fishing trip to a lodge at the northern tip of Vancouver Island. Serves 6.

6	cups (1.5 kg) Classic Mashed Potatoes (page 143)
¼	cup (30 g) all-purpose flour
1	egg plus 1 egg yolk, beaten with a teaspoon of water
1½	cups (225 g) unseasoned breadcrumbs
1	tablespoon (15 g) unsalted butter
1	tablespoon (15 ml) olive oil
	Salt and freshly ground pepper
1	cup (100 g) grated cheddar cheese (optional)

Wet your hands with cold water and form the mashed potatoes into patties, about 4 inches in diameter and ¾-inch thick.

Place the flour, beaten egg and breadcrumbs each in separate shallow bowls. Coat the potato patties with flour, then dip in the egg and coat with breadcrumbs.

Heat the butter and oil in a large skillet over medium heat until bubbling and cook the patties, until they are a nice rich golden brown, about 4 to 5 minutes per side, turning carefully when flipping to the second side. If the patties are browning too quickly, reduce the heat to medium low and cook slowly, to ensure a thicker crust. If you want to add the grated cheese, do so right after you turn the patties onto the second side.

VEGETABLES

Vegetables

The world's gardens and farms offer an almost endless variety of delicious vegetables and other related delights. Michel and I have only included vegetables in this cookbook that are, for the most part, readily available in most areas throughout the year. Some frozen vegetables, such as corn, peas, and green beans, can be nearly as good as fresh ones. I honestly cannot think of a single vegetable, squash or mushroom I have ever tasted that I did not like as long as it was not overcooked.

Some years ago my son, Papken, and I spent a few days as guest chefs at a close friend's backcountry restaurant in Montana. The restaurant's menu featured hamburgers, hot dogs, deep-fried chicken, fish, potatoes, and onion rings with lots of ketchup. For the time that Papken and I spent there, my friend, who owned the restaurant, and I collaborated to introduce a truly international menu, which included a number of the dishes in this cookbook.

Every night, one of the regulars came with his wife. On the first night, as the man enthusiastically devoured his *Filet au Poivre*, his wife noticed that he was also eagerly eating the buttered garden peas and baby carrots that we had served. She exclaimed, "How come you never eat vegetables when I cook them?" His instant response was, "You never cooked them like this." And her retort was, "Hell no, I don't! They're raw." Eventually she did venture a bite, with a bit of goading encouragement from her husband, and much to her own surprise became an instant convert to cooking vegetables al dente.

You may notice the frequent use of mushrooms in our recipes. Ordinary white and brown mushrooms are readily available everywhere and chanterelle, shiitake, and other mushrooms are also available in most places. Michel and I think of morels and *cèpes* as the king and queen of mushrooms.

Squash is another of nature's great gifts and is wonderful in soups as well as on its own.

Fava Beans in Mint Sauce

Fava beans, also known as broad beans, are one of the oldest known cultivated plants. Fresh fava beans come in large, long, thick pods and are available in North American markets from April through October. This recipe is adapted from traditional preparations served in Mediterranean countries. When fresh fava beans are unavailable, frozen lima beans make a good substitute. Serves 6-8.

2 lbs (900 g) Fava beans, shelled and skinned (see Chef's tip)
2 tablespoons (30 g) unsalted butter
1 large shallot, finely chopped
2 garlic cloves, finely chopped
½ cup (60 g) finely chopped bell pepper
1½ cups (350 g) Béchamel Sauce (page 31)
½ cup (120 ml) dry white wine
3 tablespoons (10 g) finely chopped fresh mint
¼ cup (60 ml) heavy cream
Salt and freshly ground black pepper

Chef's tip

Note that fava beans must be shelled from their long pods, then blanched and skinned. Blanch the beans in boiling salted water for 1 minute, and then transfer into iced water to avoid further cooking and cool. Free the bean from its skin by piercing the skin with a sharp knife along the bean's outer curve. Gently squeeze out the tender bean inside.

Bring a large saucepan of salted water to a boil, over medium-high heat, add the shelled and skinned fava beans and cook until tender, about 3 to 5 minutes. Drain the beans and set aside.

Heat 1 tablespoon of the butter in a medium saucepan over medium-high heat, add the shallots, garlic, and bell peppers, and sauté until the shallots are translucent and just barely beginning to brown. Add the béchamel sauce, the white wine, remaining butter, and mint, and cook, stirring continuously, until the sauce is completely blended. Stir in the cream until fully blended in. Season to taste with salt and pepper, stir the beans into the sauce, heat for 2 to 3 minutes, and serve.

Green Beans with Almonds

*Fresh green beans, from garden or farm, can complement virtually any main dish.
In late spring or summer, Michel gets fresh green beans from small local producers in
Provence. Thanks to the region's rich soil and sun, these green beans have a wonderful
natural flavor. All they need is a little butter and olive oil, salt and pepper. The
almonds in this recipe add an extra visual touch, as well as great flavor. Serves 6.*

I	lb (450 g) fresh green beans, stemmed
I	tablespoon (15 g) unsalted butter
	Salt and freshly ground black pepper
¼	cup (40 g) flaked almonds, toasted

Bring 2 cups (480 ml) of salted water, in a saucepan, to a rolling boil over medium-high heat.

Add the beans, and boil for about 3 minutes, or until the beans are just cooked al dente. Note that the beans should be a bright green color, as shown. Turn off the heat, drain the beans well, return them to the saucepan and cover it.

Add the butter to the beans, season to taste with salt and pepper, and toss to coat the beans with butter. Mix in the almonds. Cover the saucepan and let stand for 2 minutes before serving.

Variations

*This recipe works
equally well with
trimmed asparagus
spears or Brussels
sprouts.*

Herbs and Spice
and Everything Nice

Seasoning dishes involves both science and art. The science is in knowing what seasonings work well with other ingredients and the art is in using your senses to add just the right amount of particular herbs and spices to achieve the flavors you want. The right combinations and quantities of seasonings can make a real difference in the taste of your dishes.

The fresh herbs we use most frequently are rosemary, basil, thyme, and parsley. We also often use fresh tarragon, sage, and cilantro, as well as, for convenience, some dried herbs, such as Provence herbs, bay leaves, and oregano.

Dried herbs deteriorate over time and storing them in a dark cupboard will help to prolong their shelf life. You can tell when dry green herbs are past their prime when their color darkens and fades. Replacing dried herbs every year or so will help assure they are at their best.

As you can tell from our recipes, Michel and I use salt and freshly ground pepper in nearly every dish. We have some chef friends who claim to use nothing else, most of the time. We often use different types of salt and pepper for different recipes, but in most cases, ordinary salt and freshly ground black pepper will suffice. Sea salt and kosher salt have more intense flavor than ordinary salt, and, freshly ground pepper has more flavor than the pre-ground, packaged variety.

I always keep four different curry powders on my kitchen shelves; mild yellow Madras, hot Bombay, garam masala, and tandoori masala. I also use paprika, both as a seasoning in dishes, and as a decorative accent when plating dishes. Although spices tend to hold up longer than dry herbs, they too lose their potency, in time, and like dried herbs, should be replaced every year or so.

Nutmeg and cinnamon, in both powder and stick form, are two other standards. For spicy dishes, I use cayenne, chili powder, and red pepper flakes. Filé powder is used for gumbo and other Cajun dishes, and cardamom pods or powder are called for in many Indian recipes. Red chilies are an ingredient in many dishes from Southeast Asia and some regional Chinese cuisines, such as Szechuan and Mandarin.

Fresh spices at the market in Arles

Butternut Squash with Nutmeg and Thyme

Butternut squash is simply a treat. There are many ways to prepare it but this is the one I choose most often. One advantage of butternut squash is that it is available most of the year, almost everywhere in North America and Europe. Serves 8.

2	medium butternut squash
2	tablespoons (60 g) unsalted butter, melted
2	tablespoon (15 ml) olive oil
1½	tablespoons (10 g) fresh thyme leaves
1½	tablespoons (10 g) finely chopped fresh basil
½	teaspoon ground nutmeg
	Salt and freshly ground black pepper
	Sprigs of thyme, for garnish

Variations

This recipe also works with acorn squash. If using acorn squash, add 1 teaspoon of brown sugar to the recipe when you add the herbs and nutmeg.

Preheat the oven to 400° F (200° C). Cover the bottom of a large baking pan with foil. Cut the squash in half, lengthwise and remove the seeds and soft, stringy bits. Place the squash halves, cut side up, with ½ tablespoon of melted butter and ½ tablespoon of oil in each squash cavity. Bake for about 30 to 35 minutes or until the squash is fully tender. When done, remove from the oven and let stand to cool for 10 to 15 minutes.

Scoop the squash flesh out of its skins, put it in a large bowl, and discard the skins. Mash the squash with a potato masher until nearly smooth. Stir in the thyme, basil, and nutmeg, and season to taste with salt and pepper. Place in an ovenproof serving dish and return to the oven for about 8 to 10 minutes, until the surface begins to brown. Remove from the oven and serve, or use a spoon to place on individual dinner plates. Garnish with sprigs of thyme.

Cauliflower with Cheddar Sauce

This dish is oh so easy to make and oh so good. Cauliflower is one of our staple vegetables at the restaurant and at home. Simple cauliflower florets, steamed and served with butter, salt and pepper, are always well received by our guests. This recipe's cheese sauce adds a bit of color and a very rich flavor, without losing the tastiness of the cauliflower itself. Serves 6.

1	large cauliflower, stem removed and broken or cut into florets
1½	cups (360 ml) Béchamel Sauce (page 31)
¾	cup (75 g) grated cheddar cheese
	Salt and freshly ground black pepper
¼	cup (10 g) finely chopped fresh parsley

Variations

This recipe also works with broccoli florets or a mix of both cauliflower and broccoli.

In a steamer or covered saucepan, steam the cauliflower florets until they are just done (tender, but still firm). Remove from the heat, drain, and then place in a bowl lined with paper towel to absorb excess water. Keep hot in a 140° F (60° C) oven.

Warm the béchamel sauce in a small saucepan over low heat, stirring frequently and add the cheese, a bit at a time, until it is fully melted and well blended into the sauce. Season to taste with salt and pepper.

Arrange the cauliflower florets on individual plates and pour the sauce over the florets. Garnish with a sprinkling of chopped parsley and serve.

Steamed Cabbage with Bacon and Shallots

This is a delicious recipe that we first encountered in Ireland, when one of our Irish friends, Nicola Hampton, prepared it with Michel and me in my home kitchen in Dublin. You should cook this dish just before your guests sit down to eat. Serves 6.

6	thick, smoked bacon slices, diced
1	shallot, finely chopped
¼	cup (60 ml) Béchamel Sauce (page 31)
2	tablespoons (30 g) unsalted butter, melted
1	head cabbage, trimmed, washed and cut into ¾-inch thick slices
	Salt and freshly ground black pepper

Note *that this dish does not hold well. Be sure to have the sauce and cooked cabbage ready at the same time.*

Sauté the bacon in a skillet over medium-high heat until the bacon is cooked but not crisp. Remove the bacon bits from the skillet and set aside on paper towels. Pour off excess bacon grease and sauté the chopped shallots until they are translucent.

Heat the béchamel sauce in a small saucepan over low heat. Whisk in the melted butter, shallots and bacon, until well blended, and keep warm over low heat, stirring frequently.

Bring 2 cups of water to a rolling boil in a large pot, add the cabbage leaves, cover the pot, and steam for about 5 minutes, until fully cooked but still firm. Remove cabbage from the heat and drain well. Pour the sauce over the cabbage, tossing lightly to coat the cabbage evenly with the sauce, and serve.

A Garden in the Sun

The Herbfarm Garden, Woodinville, Washington

Using fresh herbs and other ingredients from your garden can be a wonderful added attraction for your meals. If you enjoy gardening, it also adds extra satisfaction to your cooking. I love being able to use fresh herbs from our garden. There is no doubt about their freshness because I pick them when I am going to use them. You don't need a large garden since fresh herbs grow well in planters and some vegetables, such as tomatoes and peas, also grow well in planters.

In Provence, many of the top restaurants have their own vegetable gardens and orchards and the produce available locally from small producers is fantastic. There is something extra special about making dishes with ingredients that you have grown yourself. One of the most celebrated restaurants in the Pacific Northwest, The Herbfarm, actually began as a fresh herb business. Chef Jerry Traunfeld is a master at creating original dishes with seasonal herbs grown in the restaurant's own gardens.

In warmer climates like Provence or the southern USA, growing seasons are longer and it is not unusual for people to have citrus trees in their home gardens. One of my dearest friends, who lived in Southern California, had orange, grapefruit, lemon, lime and kumquat trees in his backyard, as well as a vegetable garden and a 40-foot tall avocado tree at the entrance to his driveway, all contained on a half-acre property. Whenever I visited, we cooked together and made many dishes using ingredients from the garden.

When my family and I lived in Dublin, we had apple trees, pear trees, fennel and other herbs, and a rhubarb plant that had to be pared back every year to keep it from taking over the garden. Ani made rhubarb cobblers and preserves that were absolutely delicious.

Growing your own ingredients can be a bit like cooking in that there can be surprises. The weather doesn't always cooperate, insects and animals can consume your crops, and sometimes it is just a mystery, when things don't grow properly. Even with such difficulties, the joy that comes with cooking things from your own garden makes the effort very worthwhile.

Spinach with Swiss Cheese Sauce

With due regard for Popeye the Sailor Man, his cans of spinach and all the children who might wish to avoid it, fresh spinach, properly prepared and cooked is just delicious. This dish works well as a side dish with more flavorful meat and poultry main dishes. Note this dish is best made just before serving as it does not hold or reheat well. Serves 8.

1½   cups (360 ml) Béchamel Sauce (page 31)
½   cup (120 ml) dry white wine
1½   cups (150 g) grated Jarlsberg or
       Emmenthal cheese
½   teaspoon paprika
       Salt and freshly ground black pepper
2½   lbs (1.1 kg) spinach, stemmed

Combine the béchamel sauce and wine in a small saucepan over medium heat, stirring until well blended. Stir in the cheese, a bit at a time, until it is also fully blended into the sauce. Stir in the paprika and season to taste with salt and pepper. Keep the sauce hot over low heat, stirring frequently.

Bring two pints salted water to a rolling boil in a large stockpot, over medium-high heat. Add the spinach leaves. Cover and cook for approximately two minutes, until the water comes back to a boil, and then stir the leaves in the boiling water to be sure that all are just lightly cooked.

Turn off the heat and drain the spinach well in a colander, pressing down slightly. Return the spinach to the warm stockpot. Pour the cheese sauce over the spinach, tossing gently until evenly mixed, and serve immediately.

Mixed Seasonal Vegetables with White Wine and Herbs

This dish is one for which your own imagination is an important ingredient. This recipe calls for green peas in the pod, baby carrots, and small yellow pinwheel squash but you can easily substitute other vegetables such as sweet corn, lima beans or zucchini slices. Serves 8.

2	cups (480 ml) water
½	cup (120 ml) white wine
½	lb (230 g) of fresh green pea pods
½	lb (230 g) baby carrots
½	lb (230 g) small yellow pinwheel squash, halved
I	tablespoon (15 g) unsalted butter
I	teaspoon finely chopped thyme
	Salt and freshly ground black pepper

Combine the water and the wine with a pinch of salt in a large saucepan, and bring to a boil over medium-high heat.

Add the vegetables, cover and cook until they are just done, al dente. Remove the saucepan from the heat and drain well. Stir in the butter and thyme, and season to taste with salt and pepper.

Note that some vegetables take longer to cook than others, so be sure to factor that in when cooking mixed vegetable dishes. For example, garden peas cook faster than corn and a quite a bit faster than carrots. So plan the cut size and order of introducing different vegetables to the boiling water accordingly to assure that all vegetables are done at the same time.

Stuffed Zucchini with Rice and Herbs

Stuffed zucchini makes a very nice appearance on the plate and, best of all, is relatively easy to make. It has the advantage of holding quite well and can be prepared an hour or two in advance and reheated, just before serving. You can use any zucchini variety, in season. Serves 6.

1½ cups (225 g) American long-grain
     or Basmati rice
3 medium green or yellow zucchini
1 tablespoon (15 ml) olive oil
¼ cup (25 g) finely chopped shiitake
     or button mushrooms
¼ cup (40 g) finely chopped onions
¼ cup (50 g) diced tomatoes
½ teaspoon crushed dry oregano
2 garlic cloves, finely chopped
     Salt and freshly ground black pepper
2 tablespoons (30 g) unsalted butter, melted

Prepare the rice of your choice.

Preheat the oven to 350° F (180° C). Trim the zucchini stems and cut the zucchini in half lengthwise. Carefully scoop out the centers from the zucchini sections with a spoon and chop the centers. Leave about ¼-inch thick shells and set aside.

Heat the oil in a skillet, over medium heat, and sauté the mushrooms, onion, tomato, oregano, garlic and chopped zucchini centers, stirring occasionally. Continue sautéing, until the chopped onions are translucent. Add the cooked rice, stirring until all ingredients are nicely blended. Season to taste with salt and pepper and remove from the heat. Place the hollow zucchini sections, upright, on a baking pan lined with foil and lightly oiled. Fill each of the zucchini sections with the rice and vegetable mixture.

Bake the stuffed shells for about 15 to 20 minutes until the zucchini shells are cooked through. Remove from the oven, arrange on individual plates and drizzle the melted butter over the stuffed zucchinis.

Manzo Brothers Produce Stand, Pike Place Market, Seattle

Tomates Gratinées
Tomatoes with Breadcrumbs, Herbs & Parmesan

This small side dish is one that is extremely easy to make and, like Stuffed Zucchinis (page 161), can be made ahead and reheated just before serving. The red tomatoes add a touch of color to your dish and, with the breadcrumbs, cheese and herbs, the flavor is very nice. Serves 8.

4	medium tomatoes, just ripe
3	tablespoons (45 ml) olive oil
	Salt and freshly ground black pepper
½	cup (25 g) fresh breadcrumbs
2	tablespoons (10 g) finely grated Parmesan
2	teaspoons dry thyme or Provence herbs

Preheat the oven to 400° F (200° C).

Cut each tomato in half, sideways, and remove the stems. Line a baking pan with foil and brush lightly with oil. Arrange the tomato halves, cut side up, on the foil. Drizzle about ½ teaspoon of olive oil onto each tomato half and season with salt and pepper.

Using your fingers, top each of the tomatoes with breadcrumbs, cheese and herbs, in that order. Bake the tomatoes for approximately 10 to 12 minutes, until the cheese browns slightly, without letting the tomatoes become too soft or mushy. Remove from the oven and serve.

Note that overcooking the tomatoes will severely impair the flavor. Your tomatoes should be completely cooked but still a bit firm to the touch.

Variations

When they are available locally, you can also use sweet yellow tomatoes for this recipe. The bright yellow color makes a nice presentation on a plate and, like the red ones, contrasts nicely with green vegetables.

DESSERTS

Desserts

What more can we say? Nothing takes the place of a sweet, delicious dessert to top off a fine meal. In keeping with the 'simple-to-make' theme of this book we have opted for less demanding dessert recipes, so only one of these involve any baking. Two, however, rely on packaged, pre-made puff pastry.

Michel and I both like fresh fruit desserts, which can be light and very healthy. One other advantage of fresh fruit desserts is that they lend themselves easily to using whatever fresh fruits are in season and locally available. Both of us, however, share a weakness for chocolate, ice cream, and liqueurs, so the dessert recipes we offer here emphasize fresh fruits and at least one of our 'weakness' ingredients.

I serve dessert wines only on rare occasions and seem to always choose either a French sauterne or a muscat, which is another sweet wine served either as an aperitif or with dessert. In recent years, truly delightful dessert wines are also being produced in America.

You will notice that some of our desserts call for Crème Anglaise. This sauce can be used as a topping or garnish for many different desserts and the recipe is very simple.

Crème Anglaise

1	cup (240 ml) milk
2	tablespoons (25 g) sugar
½	teaspoon vanilla extract
3	egg yolks, beaten

In a heavy saucepan, over medium heat, combine the milk, sugar and vanilla. Bring mixture almost to the boiling point. Beat the egg yolks in a separate bowl until well blended. Whisk half of the hot milk and sugar mixture into the eggs then return this to the saucepan. Cook until thickened, stirring continuously, for about 5 minutes, taking care not to let it boil, as it will curdle. Let cool, cover and refrigerate until ready to use.

Chef's Tip. Add ½ teaspoon of cornstarch to the eggs when you beat them. That helps to keep the Crème Anglaise from curdling, even if it gets a bit too hot when you add the milk to the beaten eggs.

An Evening to Remember

In 1992, Ani and I rented a large 'mas' (Provence farmhouse) in the hills above Aix-en-Provence, for the month of July, with four of Ani's five sisters. It was the summer of their mother's 70th birthday. The sisters came for parts of the month, with their husbands and children. Other friends and two of my cousins from Ireland also visited. The house had seven bedrooms and a very large family kitchen, with a table that sat 16. It was built in the 18th century and had 100 hectares (240 acres) of land, with vineyards, vegetable gardens, woods and a stream running through the property. Most evenings we cooked at the house and had an average of 13 people at the dinner table. It was one of the best family vacations we ever had.

One night, Ani and I went with several others to a restaurant that had been recommended to us, in a small, nearby village called Brignoles. The restaurant was on the second floor of a 17th century house in the middle of the village. The proprietor-chef was a great, gregarious bear of a man, with a huge handlebar moustache. His name was Jean-Louis Bienvenue and he absolutely lived up to his last name, which means 'welcome' in French. Our group of family members and friends were the restaurant's only guests that night. Jean-Louis's wife, Véronique, was a petite, soft-spoken woman who waited tables. After dinner, Jean-Louis prepared a special 'off-the-menu' dessert with fresh pineapple, which he and Véronique enjoyed as well by joining us at the table. The entire dinner was excellent and the conversation was so entertaining that, before we knew it, nearly half a bottle of Armagnac had been consumed and it was two o'clock in the morning.

Sometime later I found that the restaurant had closed but I had not forgotten Jean-Louis, Véronique, the evening, or the dessert. So, I created my own replica recipe and christened it Ananas Véronique in honor of that evening and our very gracious host and hostess.

Ananas Véronique
Caramelized Pineapple with Brandy Sauce and Ice Cream

This is a dessert that you can serve any time that fresh pineapples are available. The sauce adds a sophisticated touch and complements the natural tartness of the pineapple. Serves 8.

1	tablespoon (15 g) unsalted butter
4	tablespoons (60 ml) cognac
	Juice of one large, ripe orange
4	tablespoons (50 g) granulated sugar
1	whole ripe pineapple, trimmed, cored and cut into bite-sized pieces
2	oranges, peeled, sectioned and skinned
6	scoops of vanilla ice cream
¼	cup (60 ml) blackberry syrup

Melt the butter in a sauté pan over medium-high heat, until it bubbles and add the cognac, orange juice, and sugar, stirring continuously until the mixture caramelizes and thickens.

Place the pineapple pieces in the pan, turning them until the liquid coats the pineapple and continue cooking until the pineapple pieces are warmed through. Remove the skillet from the heat.

Place one scoop of ice cream on each dessert plate and arrange the caramelized pineapple pieces around. Pour the rest of the liquid over the pineapple and ice cream, and then drizzle the blackberry syrup over the top. Serve immediately before the ice cream melts.

Variations

A few fresh berries and orange slices add color and complements the caramelized warm pineapple wedges. This dish also works with fresh peaches or nectarines instead of pineapple.

Gâteau au Chocolat Jean Banchet
Dark Chocolate Torte with Hazelnuts and Grand Marnier

This is a recipe adapted from one that Chef Jean Banchet showed Michel in their early days together in London. This is a dessert that you can prepare ahead of time and serve after dinner without any fuss. It is rich but not too filling, as the portions are small. Serves 12.

16 ounces (450 g) semi-sweet chocolate, broken into pieces

8 ounces (230 g) unsalted butter, at room temperature

1½ cups (300 g) granulated sugar

12 large eggs, separated

1 cup (100 g) powdered hazelnuts

1 tablespoon (15 ml) Grand Marnier liqueur

1 teaspoon (5 ml) vanilla extract

1 cup (240 ml) Crème Anglaise (page 165)

Powdered sugar, for garnish

Berries, orange slices and mint leaves, for garnish

Jean Banchet c. 1982

Preheat the oven to 250° F (120° C). Lightly butter a 10-inch round baking pan and set it aside. Melt the chocolate pieces and butter in the top of a double boiler over medium-low heat, stirring occasionally until they are fully melted and smooth. Add 1¼ cups of the sugar, stirring until the sugar is nearly dissolved.

Whisk the egg yolks in a medium bowl and then whisk approximately one quarter of the chocolate-butter mixture into the egg yolks. Whisk this mixture into the rest of the chocolate-butter mixture in the double boiler. Continue cooking, stirring continuously until the mixture begins to thicken. Remove from the heat and set aside to cool. Stir in the hazelnuts, Grand Marnier, and vanilla extract.

Beat the egg whites in a large bowl with the remaining ¼ cup of sugar, until they form stiff peaks when the beater is lifted.

Spoon ⅓ of the chocolate mixture into the egg whites and gently fold together. Gradually fold in the remaining chocolate mixture until all ingredients are just blended together and then spoon into the baking pan. Bake for 3 hours, remove from the oven, let cool to room temperature, cover and refrigerate for at least 3 hours. Cut into individual portions, place on dessert plates with Crème Anglaise, sprinkle with powdered sugar and garnish with berries, orange slices and mint leaves. For a decorative touch, pour lines of berry sauce on top of the Crème Anglaise and stroke up and down with a knife to make the pattern shown.

Mousse au Chocolat
Chocolate Mousse

This is a dessert that Michel included in his original Ten Classic French Recipes that You Can Make at Home *cookbook. This version is relatively lighter than many chocolate mousse recipes, which guests always appreciate. Best of all, the taste is superb. Serves 8.*

2 cups (480 ml) heavy whipping cream

1 teaspoon (5 g) granulated sugar

8 ounces (230 g) semi-sweet chocolate, broken into pieces

GARNISH OPTIONS

    Berries in season

    Whipped cream

    Red berry sauce

    Chocolate shavings

    Mint leaves

    Pirouette cookies

Whip the cream with the sugar until it forms stiff peaks and refrigerate.

Melt the chocolate in the top of a double boiler, until the chocolate is just fully melted and smooth. Remove the melted chocolate to a medium bowl and let stand to cool slightly. Gently fold the whipped cream into the melted chocolate until they are completely blended.

Spoon the mousse into small individual dessert glasses or cups and place in the refrigerator to chill, for at least 2 hours. Garnish to your liking and serve.

Note that it is very important that you remove the melted chocolate from the heat as soon as it is fully melted. If you overcook the chocolate, it will turn thick and dull and look like icing instead of melted chocolate. Stirring the melting chocolate gently is important for the same reason. And, finally, be gentle when folding the whipped cream into the melted chocolate.

Chocolat Très Magnifique

Whether we grew up in Canada with Cadbury, Rowntree, and Smarties or in America with Hershey's, Snickers, and M&Ms, chocolate played a part in most of our diets. As children, we all had hot cocoa and, for a real treat, chocolate ice cream or a hot fudge sundae. I do not remember ever turning those down or any of my friends doing so either.

One important reason that so many people like chocolate and, in fact, describe themselves as 'chocoholics' is that chocolate is a psychoactive food and has psychochemical effects in the central nervous system. Chocolate is made from the seeds of the cacao tree, *theobroma cacao*, originally grown in the tropical forests of Central and South America and now in other tropical climes. In Greek, "theobroma" literally means "food of the gods." Eating chocolate trig-

Joél Durand, Saint-Rémy de Provence

gers the release of endorphins, the body's endogenous opiates.

I spent one summer month as a high school student, working as a candy maker's helper in a local candy factory. Physically, it was the single hardest civilian job I ever had. I spent endless hours stirring huge cauldrons of molten chocolate, cooking over gas flames with a heavy four-foot long wooden spatula. When the candy batches were ready, two of us would pick them up by the cauldron handles and pour the molten mixtures onto large greased steel slab tables

that had rails to prevent the nearly boiling mass from running onto the floor. My arms were covered with burns and my muscles ached in ways I had never known.

It was a true factory operation and produced large volumes of chocolates that contained preservatives, and allowed the product to be stored for months before delivery to retail outlets. The chocolates were nice and people bought and ate them in all the quantities the factory could produce.

As with all food, quality in chocolates ranges from ordinary to extraordinary. It was only in my 30s that I discovered the existence of really amazing gourmet chocolates and I was completely hooked from that point forward.

Only a few chocolatiers produce truly extraordinary gourmet chocolates. These are individuals with the same passion for chocolate making that great chefs have for creating superb dishes and meals.

In discussing this topic, Michel and I had no trouble agreeing on the two chocolatiers we know who amaze us most. In many ways, they are both quite similar in their approach to creating truly great and memorable chocolates, although they come from very different backgrounds. They are Joel Durand in Saint-Rémy de Provence and Fran Bigelow in Seattle. Both have melded science and art in the finest traditions of European chocolate making, and both are true artists in every sense of the word.

By coincidence, Joel's shop is located right next to our restaurant in Saint-Rémy. He moved to Provence from Brittany seven years ago and since then has combined inspirational chocolate making talent with native ingredients from Provence and the Mediterranean. His alphabetically coded signature chocolates contain flavors of thyme, rosemary, lavender, violet, honey, jasmine, and olives.

A total perfectionist in his art, Joel has an easy way about him and readily charms even those customers who express reluctance to sample his 'odd-sounding' confections. Then he watches as they taste and their initial skeptical looks turn to broad smiles.

Joel's creations are in great demand. He ships freshly made chocolate treats to customers all over the world. In the spring of 2005, a 20-person Japanese food magazine photography crew traveled specially to Saint-Rémy to shoot photographs for a feature article about Joel and his products in a Japanese gourmet food magazine.

When Fran founded Fran's Chocolates in 1982, it was a two employee operation in a quaint Seattle neighborhood. She opened her business with the goal of creating and selling extraordinarily high quality chocolates, caramels, and desserts to customers who valued the distinction between mass marketed chocolates and truly exquisite chocolate confections. Her objective was to provide the ultimate taste experience by cooking with only the finest ingredients in small batches and using no preservatives or artificial additives. This remains her guiding philosophy today and is one of the key reasons for the growth and success of her company.

As her business evolved, Fran continually created new products through endless experimentation. Her product line grew to include cakes, bars, sauces, baking products, and ice cream. Fran's repeat customers especially liked her truffles and she began to create her own centers and signature methods of hand dipping. Fran's passionate focus is on the quality and flavor of every piece of chocolate that leaves her laboratory. She has

Fran Bigelow, Fran's Chocolates, Seattle

been named the best Chocolatier in America by some of the most venerated food publications in the USA, including *The Book of Chocolate.*

I find that the only issue I have with Fran's and Joel's chocolates is that I can never quite get enough and I am forced to discipline myself to resist, which is not easy. Boxes of Fran's truffles or Joel's alphabet treats disappear far too quickly. I am certain you will be just as addicted as I am once you have tasted the chocolate delights that either of these chocolate artisans produce. There is one pleasant danger, however; you may never again be satisfied by lesser, more ordinary alternatives.

Crème Brûlée

Most crème brûlée recipes call for cooking this dessert in an oven, however, this recipe does not. It was included in Michel's original Ten Easy Classic French Recipes that You Can Make at Home *cookbook. It has the advantage of being a dessert that you can make several hours or even a day ahead of time. Serves 6.*

1	pint (480 ml) heavy cream
8	egg yolks
1	tablespoon (25 g) granulated sugar
	Pinch of salt
½	cup (100g) brown sugar

Note *that this dessert makes investing in a kitchen blowtorch worthwhile, although it will have a number of other uses. A kitchen blowtorch can be very helpful in opening stubborn jar lids. You can also use it as a weapon to threaten guests who come into your kitchen work area and get in the way of your cooking.*

Whisk together the cream, egg yolks, sugar and salt until well blended. Transfer the mixture to a saucepan and cook over medium heat, stirring continuously with a wooden spoon, until it thickens to a heavy consistency and clings to the spoon. Note that it is important not to boil the brûlée mixture. If it begins to boil, remove it briefly from the burner and reduce heat to low.

When thickened, pour the mixture into small, shallow, straight-sided bowls or ramekins and place them in the refrigerator to chill, at least 2 hours, after which time you will have thick, rich custard.

Before serving, sprinkle the brown sugar liberally over the custard and, using a kitchen blowtorch, caramelize the brown sugar until it melts and bubbles. Although, with baked crème brûlée, you can caramelize the brown sugar under an oven top broiler, we do not recommend doing that for this recipe, as it may also melt the custard, making it runny. To dress up your crème brûlée, garnish it with a sprig of mint, a slice or two of kiwi fruit or a few berries.

Variations

To make Cappuccino Brûlée, put a small amount (2 tablespoons) of dark chocolate sauce and a teaspoon of strong coffee or espresso, mixed together, at the bottom of each dish, before you pour in the custard. For this variation, be sure to pour the custard on top of the chocolate and coffee mixture slowly, so the chocolate remains at the bottom of the dish and is a surprise when your guests discover it.

Banana & Pecan Flambé

*This is a dessert that Michel served at The Mirabeau and at his own restaurants in
Seattle and London. Like some of the other dessert recipes we have included,
it contains fresh fruit, ice cream and liqueur. Serves 8.*

1	cup (150 g) pecans
6	tablespoons (90 g) unsalted butter
½	cup (120 ml) fresh orange juice
¼	cup (60 ml) Orange Curaçao liqueur
¾	cup (150 g) packed brown sugar
6	ripe bananas, peeled and cut into ¾-inch slices
2	teaspoons cinnamon powder
¼	cup (60 ml) dark rum
8	scoops vanilla ice cream
½	cup (50 g) shredded coconut
8	sprigs fresh mint, for garnish

Variations

*Walnuts or almonds
can substitute for
pecans. Grand
Marnier liqueur is
a substitute for the
Orange Curaçao
liqueur.*

Toast the pecans in a shallow baking pan under the oven broiler, being very careful that they do not burn, and then remove them from the oven and set aside.

Melt the butter in a sauté pan over medium-high heat, until it bubbles and stir in the orange juice, Curaçao liqueur and brown sugar, stirring continuously until the sugar is completely dissolved and the mixture begins to caramelize (thicken and take on a golden-brown color). Add the bananas, pecans and cinnamon, turning them gently until the liquid coats the bananas and pecans. Carefully pour the rum into the pan, let it heat slightly and then ignite. If you are using a gas stove, simply tilting the pan so that the rum is at the edge without spilling should ignite the rum. On an electric stove, you will need to use matches. Fireplace matches are best since they are long and reduce the chance of burning your hand. Once the flames have died, remove the pan from the heat.

Place one scoop of ice cream in each dessert dish and arrange the banana slices and pecans around it. Drizzle the syrup over the banana slices and ice cream. Sprinkle with shredded coconut and garnish with mint. Serve immediately before the ice cream melts.

A Visit with the Bishop

JOHN BISHOP

Since 1985, John Bishop has presided over what has become a Vancouver institution. Bishop's is known and celebrated across Canada and up and down the west coast as one of North America's premier fine dining establishments.

The menu at Bishop's offers fresh seasonal treats from local waters and fields, farms and forests. There are always wild game selections, beautifully prepared and creatively displayed. The wines are excellent, often selected personally by John and sourced from the great wine making regions of the world. The restaurant has a very warm and hospitable feel, owing to both the friendliness of the staff and the décor.

John's love for cooking began when he was a child growing up in Newton Powys, Wales. Starting out by helping in his mother's kitchen, he later learned the formal require-ments of traditional French food preparation as a young man at hotel school.

After working as a chef in Britain and Ireland, John moved to Vancouver in 1973 and continued his career there with local restaurateur Umberto Menghi, first as head chef then eventually becoming Maître d'. At the urging of friends and investors during the recession of 1985, John opened Bishop's. Since then, Bishop's has consistently been one of the city's top restaurants. The restaurant receives top grades from food and wine publications near and far, every year.

Executive Chef Dennis Green credits his passion for using local, fresh and seasonal ingredients to his extensive travels as a child. He joined the team at Bishop's in 1993 and became Chef in 1997. Dennis is continually inspired by the vast amount of ingredients found within the rich northwestern region. His palette draws from the organic produce supplied by local farmers or from fishmongers bringing in their daily

catch. Because of his expertise, John asked to contribute to *Bishop's: The Cookbook* and then, more recently, to co-author *Simply Bishop's,* John's latest cookbook.

At Bishop's, booking a table well in advance is advised. The restaurant is always full and often booked solid for up to two or three weeks at a time. Bishop's popularity and reputation is well deserved. Tim Pawsey, in *Northwest Palate Magazine,* wrote of John, "Thoughtful, sincere and unassuming yet an unswerving perfectionist, John is a consummate host who has placed his brand of understated west coast cuisine firmly on the map." For us, no visit to Vancouver is complete without a dinner at Bishop's. In addition to a magnificent feast, the highlight of the evening is always a chat with John, one of the most gracious and interesting hosts we know, anywhere in the world.

Death by Chocolate
John Bishop, Bishop's Restaurant, Vancouver, British Columbia

This dessert is one that is a delight to the eye as well as the taste. Generous droplets of blood-red raspberry sauce surround the rich, dark chocolate torte, beckoning all chocoholics and anyone else with even a bit of a sweet tooth. Prepare this dessert the day before you plan to serve it. Serves 16.

25	ounces (750 g) semi-sweet chocolate, broken into pieces
6	ounces (170 g) unsalted butter
1¼	cups (300 ml) whipping cream
6	large egg yolks
¾	cup (75 g) powdered sugar, sifted
¼	cup (60 ml) coffee liqueur
2	cups (320 g) fresh raspberries

Melt the chocolate with the butter and whipping cream, in a double boiler over medium heat, stirring continuously until the mixture is completely smooth. Set the chocolate mixture aside in a bowl and keep warm in a 140° F (60° C) oven.

Wash the top of your double boiler and return it to its base over medium heat. Add the egg yolks, powdered sugar and coffee liqueur, whisking continuously until the mixture is pale and thick, and forms 'ribbon' patterns when poured back into the mixture from a spoon. Slowly add the warm chocolate mixture into the yolk mixture, a little at a time, whisking gently and continuously until completely blended.

Line a 9 x 5 x 3 inch (2-liter) terrine or loaf pan with plastic wrap, making sure that the plastic is pushed into all the corners. Pour the batter into the pan and let cool. Cover and refrigerate overnight.

About 30 minutes before serving, take the chocolate mold from the refrigerator, turn it upside down on a cutting board, discard the plastic wrap, and let stand until warmed to room temperature. Purée the raspberries in a food processor and strain through a sieve to remove the seeds. Sweeten to taste with powdered sugar.

When you are ready to serve, use a warm, thin knife to cut the chocolate terrine into ½-inch (1 cm) slices. To serve, place a slice on a plate and splash the raspberry purée over both the chocolate and the plate, to create the death effect.

Mint Chocolate Delight
Vanilla Ice Cream with Crème de Menthe and Chocolate Sauce

This dessert goes really well after fairly spicy main dishes, like a curry or a pasta dish with a spicy tomato sauce. The crème de menthe liqueur is refreshing and complements the chocolate and vanilla ice cream, creating a very nice blend of flavors. Serves 6.

½	cup (120 ml) heavy whipping cream
1	tablespoon (15 g) granulated sugar
6	scoops vanilla ice cream
¼	cup (60 ml) crème de menthe liqueur
½	cup (120 ml) dark chocolate sauce
6	fresh red berries, for garnish
6	sprigs fresh mint, for garnish

For an added touch, *try serving this dessert with light elegant cookies, like chocolate-laced Pirouettes.*

Whip the cream, with the sugar, until it stands in stiff peaks and refrigerate.

Put a scoop of ice cream into chilled dessert bowls. Drizzle a tablespoon of crème de menthe liqueur over the ice cream and then carefully spoon on the chocolate sauce on top of the ice cream. Using a pastry bag, squeeze a dollop of whipped cream on the top, garnish with a red berry and a sprig of mint, and serve immediately.

Variations

You can try other liqueurs and ice cream flavors. Some ice cream and liqueur combinations that work well include: coffee ice cream with coffee liqueur; almond ice cream with Amaretto liqueur; hazelnut ice cream with Frangelico liqueur; and orange sorbet with Grand Marnier liqueur. Pistachio ice cream with a few drops of Chartreuse liqueur is another combination that is a little unusual and is always a hit with guests.

Millefeuilles aux Framboises
Raspberries with Puff Pastry and Crème Anglaise

This is one of the simplest desserts to make and provides a lighter finish to any meal. With the puff pastry baked to a crisp golden brown and the red raspberry filling, this dessert is also quite pleasing to the eye. You can bake the puff pastry a few hours before serving. Serves 6.

2	sheets puff pastry, about 10x16 inches each
½	cup (170 g) raspberry jam
2	cups (320 g) fresh raspberries
2	eggs
1	tablespoon milk
1	cup (120 ml) Crème Anglaise (page 165)
6	sprigs of mint, for garnish
	Berries or grapes, for garnish

Preheat the oven to 375° F (180° C). Dust a cutting board lightly with flour and lay the puff pastry sheets out flat on it. Cut the pastry into 3½-inch diameter circles. Note that 10" x 16" puff pastry sheets will each yield approximately six 3½-inch circles.

In a small bowl, beat the eggs together with the milk. Cover a large baking sheet with foil and lightly oil the foil. Arrange the puff pastry circles on the baking sheet, brush the egg and milk mixture lightly over the top surfaces and bake for approximately 15 minutes, until the pastry puffs up and turns golden brown. Remove from the oven.

Place one pastry circle on a dessert plate and lightly apply raspberry jam to the surface. Arrange raspberries on top, to cover the pastry circle. Place a second pastry circle on top of the raspberries, with another three raspberries and a sprig of mint.

To serve, carefully pour 1 tablespoon of Crème Anglaise onto the edge of each dessert plate, put a few drops of raspberry sauce on the Crème Anglaise, as shown. Place a puff pastry and raspberry stack in the center of each plate and garnish with a few berries or grapes.

Berries Napoleon

This is one of my all-time favorite desserts. It is one I often serve at home when I am short of time, since it takes only a few minutes to make. It always gets rave reviews from guests and they always finish all of the fruit and the sauce, as well. Serves 8.

6	cups (960 g) fresh berries
½	cup (120 ml) cognac, Armagnac or other brandy
½	cup (100 g) packed brown sugar
2	cups (480 ml) heavy whipping cream or crème fraîche
8	sprigs fresh mint, for garnish

The berries

you choose should depend on seasonal availability. Blackberries, strawberries and raspberries are all good options and I have also used fresh peaches, nectarines and papayas, with equal success.

Place the berries in individual dessert bowls. In a blender, whip the cognac and brown sugar, until the sugar dissolves. Pour in the cream and whip until thick and fluffy. Pour over the berries, garnish with a sprig of fresh mint and serve immediately.

Variations

You can alter the flavor by using a different liquor or liqueur. Alternatives that work well include dark rum, Drambuie or B&B liqueur. With the liqueurs, you should eliminate most or all of the sugar, as the liqueurs are very sweet themselves.

Tarte Tatin
Upside-down Apple Tart

This is a classic French dessert that you will find served in restaurants all across France, from Brittany to Nice. It is included on menus throughout most of the year and especially from late fall to early spring. Typically served with vanilla ice cream, it is always popular with restaurant patrons. Serves 8.

½ cup (120 g) unsalted butter
6 tablespoons (30 ml) water
1¼ cups (250 g) granulated sugar
8 tart cooking apples, peeled,
     cored and cut into thick slices
1 puff pastry sheet (10x16 inches)

Melt the butter in a large skillet over medium-high heat and stir in the water. Sprinkle in the sugar, stirring continuously until the sugar is dissolved and comes to a good boil. Continue stirring until the mixture caramelizes to a rich, medium-brown color.

Arrange the apple slices tightly together in the skillet, on top of the caramelized mixture, and cook uncovered until the apples are just cooked through (about 15 minutes). Remove from heat and let stand until cooled to room temperature.

Preheat the oven to 375° F (190° C). Spoon the cooled caramelized apples into a buttered 10-inch-round baking dish. Lay the puff pastry dough out flat over the apples, making sure that the dough touches all the sides of the baking dish. Trim off any overhanging pastry dough.

Bake the tart until the puff pastry turns a rich golden brown (about 10 to 12 minutes). To serve, turn the baking dish upside-down on a serving plate and cut the tart into wedges.

Variations

Tarte Tatin can also be made with other fruits, such as pears, figs, peaches or apricots. Adding ½ teaspoon of cinnamon powder, when cooking the apples, is another popular variation.

Avez Vous des Crêpes, Monsieur?

Dessert crêpes are always a treat and a special way to end any dinner. Crêpes are very thin pancakes that originated in Brittany in northwestern France, where they were first cooked on flat stones.

There are two common types of crêpes: sweet crêpes, which are made with all-purpose flour, and savory crêpes or galettes, which are made with buckwheat flour. The simplest crêpes are sweet crêpes, served only with butter and sugar, as either a dessert or breakfast. Main dish crêpes, at lunch or for an evening meal, may be filled with seafood, chicken, meats or vegetables and are usually served with a sauce. One personal favorite, Crêpes Florentine, are crêpes filled with cooked spinach and melted cheese. Sautéed shellfish or chicken, mushrooms and sweet onions in béchamel sauce mixed with dry white wine, make a nice filling for crêpes, for either lunch or a lighter dinner with a side salad.

The number of different crêpe dishes and desserts you can make is almost unlimited. I have served crêpes with bananas, ice cream and chocolate sauce; melon slices, whipped cream, and liqueur sauces, as well as almost every variety of berry. Let your imagination take over and create your own special crêpes recipes.

Crêpes Suzette is probably the best known of all crêpes dessert recipes. It is very easy to make and can be prepared and flambéed at the table for great effect. Once in a while at home, for a small dinner party, I will serve dessert crêpes or a flambéed dessert such as Banana & Pecan Flambé (page 173) at the table. It is always a hit with guests and will be with yours. However, if you are going to try it, I would suggest that you practice your technique away from the table, first, before trying any flaming tableside presentation for your guests. Some people can be very narrow-minded about having their eyebrows singed.

Crêpes

1¹/₃	cups (315 ml) milk
4	large eggs, lightly beaten
1	cup (120 g) all-purpose flour
2	tablespoons (30 g) unsalted butter, melted
2	tablespoons (25 g) granulated sugar
½	teaspoon salt
	Unsalted butter or vegetable oil for frying

Beat or whisk the milk, eggs, flour, melted butter, sugar and salt together in a large bowl, until smooth. In a crêpe pan or non-stick skillet, over medium heat, add a small amount of butter or oil, lightly coating the bottom of the pan. Pour about 3 to 4 tablespoons of batter into the pan and tilt to cover the entire bottom surface. Cook until the bottom of the crêpe is nicely browned and then turn and cook on the second side. Try the first crêpe. If it is too thick (crêpes should be very thin and still moist), add a bit more milk to the batter. Discard the first crêpe, or eat it, and continue making additional crêpes until you have 12.

Crêpes Alana

This is a dessert I named for my daughter, Alana, who as a child loved crêpes and now still does but as an adult can also enjoy the dessert version with liqueur. This crêpes dessert, with its many easy variations, is always a delightful way to finish a fine meal and our guests have never been disappointed. Serves 6.

4	large nectarines or peaches
1½	cups (360 ml) whipping cream
1	tablespoon of granulated sugar
2	tablespoons (30 ml) Chambord liqueur
1	cup (160 g) blackberries or raspberries
¼	cup (30 g) sliced almonds
2	tablespoons (25 g) powdered sugar
12	crêpes (page 180)

THE SYRUP

2	tablespoons (30 g) unsalted butter
¼	cup (60 ml) cognac, Armagnac or brandy
2	tablespoons (30 ml) freshly squeezed orange juice
2	tablespoon (25 g) brown sugar

For the syrup, melt the butter in a sauté pan, over medium-high heat, until it bubbles, add the cognac, orange juice, and brown sugar, stirring continuously, until the liquids are fully combined and reduced by half, to a medium-thick syrup. Keep hot over low heat, stirring frequently.

Slice the nectarines or peel and slice the peaches. Whip the cream with the sugar until it stands in stiff peaks. Arrange 2 crêpes, side-by-side, on large plates, place slices of nectarines or peaches on each crêpe, and fold the edges over. Pour the hot syrup over the crêpes. Drizzle Chambord over the crêpes and, using a pastry funnel, put a dollop of whipped cream on top. Garnish with a few blackberries or raspberries, sliced almonds and a light sprinkling of powdered sugar, and serve immediately.

Variations

You can experiment with different fruits, liqueurs, sauces and creams or ice creams. Vanilla or coffee ice cream is an easy substitute for the whipped cream.

Fromage, s'il vous plaît!

In addition to being an important ingredient in many recipes, cheese can also be an excellent choice for pre-dinner appetizers, an alternative dessert or as a final, post-dessert course. There is a vast selection of wonderful cheeses made all over the world.

My favorite cheese shop in Seattle carries English, Swiss, French, and Italian cheeses, as well as Cashel Blue from Ireland and Feta from Greece. A bit of English Stilton with bread or crackers, a few grapes, and a glass of port makes for a wonderful final touch to an evening meal.

France may be the world capital of cheese, with more than 1,000 different cheeses made in virtually every region of the country. There are hundreds of small cheese producers, as well as commercial cheese making enterprises that are part of large food producer companies and brands, like Danon and President. Familiar French cheeses include Beaufort, Brie, Camembert, Charolais, chèvre, Emmenthal, Port Salut, and Roquefort. I have a particular fondness for French cheeses made with goat's milk. These range from soft white to more solid varieties like Tomme de Savoie from the French Alps.

No one makes better use of cheese in cooking than the Italians. From pizza to pasta and Veal Parmigiana (page 94), Italian chefs and home cooks use cheese in hundreds of recipes. Well known Italian cheeses include Cambozola, fontina, Gorgonzola, mozzarella, provolone, Romano, and perhaps the most famous of all, Parmigiano Reggiano. It is used to top salads, soups, and omelettes, and as an ingredient in pasta dishes like lasagna and tortellinis. Quatro Formaggi is a four-cheese blend of Gorgonzola, Emmenthal, Taleggio, and fontina, which is used in dozens of pasta dishes and as a topping for pizza.

English cheeses are also well known. The original cheddar cheese comes from Somerset, in the midlands of England. Local legend has it that cheese was discovered accidentally when a village milkmaid left a pail of milk, for safety, in the nearby Cheddar Gorge caves. Later the milkmaid returned to find that the milk had returned to a new tasty substance and cheddar cheese was born. Nothing was ever done to protect or copyright the name, which has allowed it to be used and sometimes abused by producers worldwide. Other popular English cheeses are Cheshire, Derby, Double Gloucester, Leicester, and Shropshire Blue, as well as Stilton, one of the world's best-known blue cheeses.

Mexico, with its Spanish heritage, is another cheese making Mecca. Although before the Conquistadors brought dairy cattle and sheep, cheese was not a part of the native diet. Today in the northern Mexican state of Chihuahua, cheese production is a very important cottage industry still frequently carried out in the homes of small ranchers. Mexican producers make ricotta-like requeson, smooth, moist panela, and pale yellow queso chihuahua. I must confess, however, that for most of my own Mexican cooking I use a medium cheddar made in Oregon by producers of the Tillamook County Creamery Association, which I find perfect for enchiladas, quesadillas, tamales, tacos, and tortilla soup (page 65).

In recent years, there has been an incredible renaissance in cheese making, with small producers using historic methods to create amazing new cheeses

Famous English cheddar at Neil's Yard Dairy

and to bring back traditional cheeses. Today, cheese is made in places that only 20 or 30 years ago had almost no local cheese industry. Ireland has always had quality dairy products but, historically, cheese simply was never a feature of the Irish diet. However, in the last 20 years, Irish cheeses have become known and highly regarded worldwide.

The cheese renaissance is also booming in North America, with great cheeses being produced from New England and the Maritime Provinces of Canada, to California and Washington State. The dairy farmers of Cabot, Vermont founded the Cabot Creamery Cooperative in 1919. Their naturally aged sharp cheddar has won numerous awards, including World Best Cheddar at the World Championship Cheese Contest. Cheese makers in Wisconsin, which calls itself "America's Dairyland," are producing domestic varieties of old country cheeses that easily rival the originals, including authentically made Gruyere and Beaufort-style cheeses.

California cheeses are also winning worldwide recognition. A California-made brie won first place in its category at the World Cheese Awards, held annually in London, a feat that no non-European producer had ever before achieved.

I love blue cheeses and one of the best I have ever tasted is called Original Blue, made at Point Reyes, on the northern California coast by the Giacomini family's Farmstead Cheese Company. It is made within

Point Reyes Original Blue

hours of milking and then aged for at least six months, which definitely qualifies as 'slow food'. The family's dairy heritage from the mountains of Italy dates back more than 100 years.

Chef's Tip. *Most cheese is best when served at room temperature so be sure to rescue it from the refrigerator an hour or so before serving it.*

Menu Suggestions

Following are suggestions for complete three and four course seasonal menus with courses chosen to complement each other. The seasonal references are simply an indication of the times of year when ingredients will most likely be available. Please refer to the specific recipe pages for accompanying wine suggestions.

Three Course Dinners

Spring and Summer Italian Dinner
CAESAR SALAD (PAGE 37)

—

PORC RÔTI BELLAGIO (PAGE 93)
CLASSIC MASHED POTATOES (PAGE 145)
FAVA BEANS IN MINT SAUCE (PAGE 152)

—

MOUSSE AU CHOCOLAT (PAGE 169)

All Seasons Far Eastern Dinner
SEARED AHI TUNA WITH SOY AND
SESAME SAUCE (PAGE 77)

—

THAI GREEN CREAM SHELLFISH CURRY (PAGE 127)
PLAIN BASMATI RICE

—

MOUSSE AU CHOCOLAT (PAGE 169)

Spring and Summer Sea Bass à la Plancha Dinner
LEEK AND POTATO SOUP WITH BACON (PAGE 62)

—

SEA BASS À LA PLANCHA (PAGE 123)
FRIED POTATOES WITH PROVENCE HERBS (PAGE 146)
MIXED VEGETABLES WITH WHITE WINE
AND HERBS (PAGE 160)

—

MILLEFEUILLES AUX FRAMBOISES (PAGE 177)

Fall and Winter Roast Hen Dinner
SOUPE AU PISTOU (PAGE 59)

—

ROAST HEN WITH WILD RICE
AND MUSHROOM STUFFING (PAGE 106)
CURRIED ROAST POTATOES WITH PARSLEY (PAGE 147)
BUTTERNUT SQUASH WITH NUTMEG
AND THYME (PAGE 155)

—

ANANAS VÉRONIQUE (PAGE 167)

All Seasons Italian Dinner
DUNGENESS CRAB CAKES (PAGE 79)

—

VEAL PARMIGIANA (PAGE 94)
LINGUINI WITH PRAWNS IN A SUN-DRIED
TOMATO SAUCE (PAGE 136)
STUFFED ZUCCHINI WITH RICE AND HERBS (PAGE 161)

—

BERRIES NAPOLEON (PAGE 178)

Winter Roast Sirloin Dinner
CHICKEN, RICE AND BUTTERNUT
SQUASH SOUP (PAGE 54)

—

ROAST SIRLOIN ENCRUSTED IN ENGLISH
MUSTARD (PAGE 92)
ASPARAGUS AND MUSHROOM RISOTTO (PAGE 132)
TOMATES GRATINÉES (PAGE 163)

—

CRÈME BRÛLÉE (PAGE 172)

All Seasons Dinner with Sautéed Chicken Breasts
AVOCADO, CUCUMBER & CHÈVRE SALAD (PAGE 44)

—

SAUTÉED CHICKEN BREASTS IN WHITE WINE
AND CREAM SAUCE (PAGE 102)
SHREDDED POTATOES WITH SHALLOTS
AND GARLIC (PAGE 147)
GREEN BEANS WITH ALMONDS (PAGE 153)

—

MINT CHOCOLATE DELIGHT (PAGE 176)

Four Course Dinners

Fall and Winter Asian Dinner

MULLIGATAWNEY SOUP (PAGE 61)

—

POULET ROUGE (PAGE 109)

PLAIN OR SAFFRON BASMATI RICE

BUTTERNUT SQUASH WITH NUTMEG
AND HERBS (PAGE 155)

—

SMALL PENANG SALAD (PAGE 47)

—

DEATH BY CHOCOLATE (PAGE 175)

All Seasons Provençal Dinner

SALMON AND ASPARAGUS TERRINE (PAGE 80)

BŒUF EN DAUBE À LA PROVENÇALE (PAGE 89)

POMMES DE TERRE AU GRATIN (PAGE 142)

MIXED VEGETABLES WITH WHITE WINE
AND HERBS (PAGE 160)

—

SALADE PROVENÇALE (PAGE 43)

—

GÂTEAU AU CHOCOLAT JEAN BANCHET (PAGE 168)

Summer and Fall Seafood Dinner

NORTHWEST CORN AND CRAB CHOWDER (PAGE 63)

—

SOLE AMANDINE (PAGE 118)

WILD RICE WITH MUSHROOMS AND HERBS (PAGE 138)

GREEN BEANS WITH ALMONDS (PAGE 153)

—

HEARTS OF ROMAINE WITH AVOCADO
DRESSING (PAGE 41)

—

CRÈME BRÛLÉE (PAGE 172)

All Seasons Seafood Dinner

COQUILLES ST. JACQUES AU BASILIC (PAGE 75)

—

SALMON IN PUFF PASTRY (PAGE 119)

CROQUETTES DE POMME DE TERRE, (PAGE 143)

GREEN BEANS WITH ALMONDS (PAGE 153)

—

AVOCADO, CUCUMBER AND CHÈVRE SALAD (PAGE 44)

—

TARTE TATIN (PAGE 179)

All Seasons Italian Dinner

AVOCADO MOUSSE WITH SHRIMP, CUCUMBER
AND LEMON (PAGE 72)

—

VEAL MARSALA (PAGE 95)

ASPARAGUS & MUSHROOM RISOTTO (PAGE 132)

TOMATES GRATINÉES (PAGE 163)

—

TRI COLORE SALAD (PAGE 45)

—

MINT CHOCOLATE DELIGHT (PAGE 176)

All Seasons Dinner à la Française

COQUILLES ST. JACQUES AU BASILIC (PAGE 75)

—

FILET AU POIVRE (PAGE 87)

SHREDDED POTATOES WITH SHALLOTS
AND GARLIC (PAGE 147)

TOMATES GRATINÉES (PAGE 163)

—

SPINACH SALAD WITH WARM BACON
DRESSING (PAGE 40)

—

CRÊPES ALANA (PAGE 181)

Fall and Winter Collage
of Cuisines Dinner

NEW ORLEANS STYLE GUMBO (PAGE 67)

—

LAMB CANNONS IN RED CURRANT SAUCE (PAGE x91)

POMMES DE TERRE AU GRATIN (PAGE 142)

STEAMED CABBAGE WITH BACON
AND SHALLOTS (PAGE 157)

—

CAESAR SALAD (PAGE 37)

—

BANANA & PECAN FLAMBÉ (PAGE 173)

Professional Recognition

Michel's many awards and diplomas are a further testimony to his culinary accomplishments. He is a member of the Chaîne des Rôtisseurs, an international gastronomic society founded in Paris in 1950. It is devoted to promoting fine dining and the pleasures of the table through the social interaction, hospitality and expertise of its members.

The Order of the Knights of the Vine, another professional culinary society, was founded to recognize sommeliers and chefs who, in addition to cooking or wine expertise, have demonstrated exceptional knowledge of the pairing of wines with particular foods. In 1980, they designated Michel a Master Knight of the Vine, the society's highest honor.

The *Cercle Epicurien Mondial* (International Epicurean Circle), headquartered in London, is an international society open only to chefs who have demonstrated the highest levels of culinary excellence for many years. Members of the Grand Council of the Circle are renowned chefs from around the world. In 1989, they awarded Michel their highest diploma, *Grand Officier Épicurien et de Maître de Cuisine* (World Master Chef).

The Chefs' Special Menus

Following are four different sample menus, without specific wine pairings, two from special occasion dinners at home and two from La Table de Michel restaurant. Please note that all of the recipes in these menus are included earlier in the book but are shown in these menus with French names.

Menu Provençal
A TRADITIONAL PROVENCE DINNER

SOUPE AU PISTOU
Bean and Vegetable Soup with Garlic and Basil

—

SALADE PROVENÇALE
Mixed Greens, Roast Peppers, Tomatoes and Onions

—

VOLAILLE RÔTIE FARCIE AU RIZ SAUVAGE ET CHAMPIGNON
Roast Hen with Wild Rice and Mushroom Stuffing

POMMES DE TERRE AVEC HERBES DE PROVENCE
Fried Potatoes with Provence Herbs

HARICOTS VERTS AVEC AMANDES
Green Beans with Almonds

—

TARTE TATIN
Upside-down Apple Tart

—

CAFÉ ET THÉ
Coffee and Tea

Menu Français à l'Orientale
MENU OF DISHES INSPIRED BY FAR EASTERN CUISINES

THON AUX FERS AVEC SAUCE ORIENTALE
Seared Ahi Tuna with Soy and Sesame Sauces

—

SALADE DE MALAISIE
Penang Salad with Sesame Soy Dressing

—

POULET CHINOIS AVEC CHAMPIGNONS ET CURRY
Su-Su Chicken Curry

RIZ DE BASMATI AVEC POIVRONS ET AIL
Basmati Rice with Bell Peppers, Garlic and Shallots

LÉGUMES ASSORTIS DE SAISON
Mixed Seasonal Vegetables

—

ANANAS VÉRONIQUE
Caramelized Pineapple with Brandy Sauce and Ice Cream

—

CAFÉ ET THÉ
Coffee and Tea

Lunch is a serious undertaking in the South of France as well as in Italy and Spain. Most businesses, other than restaurants and cafés, close for at least two full hours so that people can take time and enjoy their mid-day meal. The typical midday meal consists of just two or three courses, with dessert becoming increasingly optional. Meals are not to be rushed. It is a time for leisurely enjoyment of a meal in the company of friends and colleagues. A glass of wine and a strong espresso at the end fortifies everyone for their return to work This menu is typical of the fixed price, mid-day Menu du Jour found in many Provence restaurants.

La Table de Michel

MENU MIDI
Luncheon Menu

TERRINE DE SAUMON ET ASPERGE
Salmon and Asparagus Terrine

—

BOEUF EN DAUBE À LA PROVENÇALE
Provence Style Beef Stew in Red Wine

PAIN PAYSAN
Coarse Grain Bread

—

MILLEFEUILLES AUX FRAMBOISES
Raspberries and Puff Pastry with Crème Anglaise

—

CAFÉ ET THÉ
Coffee and Tea

This menu would typically be for a more formal or special occasion. With five courses, coffee or tea and after dinner drinks, portion sizes are relatively smaller and the meal would be very leisurely, with time between courses to enjoy each accompanying wine.

La Table de Michel

MENU FRANÇAIS TRADITIONNEL
Degustation Tasting Menu

COQUILLES ST. JACQUES AU BASILIC
Sautéed Sea Scallops with Basil, Garlic and Pine Nuts

—

SALADE MARA
Fresh Summer Salad with Bay Shrimp

—

FILET D'AGNEAU EN CROÛTE
Lamb Loin with Mushroom Duxelles in Puff Pastry

PURÉE DE POMME DE TERRE
Classic Mashed Potatoes

LÉGUMES ASSORTIS DE SAISON
Mixed Seasonal Vegetables

—

GÂTEAU AU CHOCOLAT AVEC NOISETTES
Dark Chocolate Torte with Hazelnuts and Grand Marnier

—

FROMAGES ASSORTIS AVEC PORTO
Assorted Cheeses with Vintage Port

—

CAFÉ ET THÉ
Coffee and Tea

—

LIQUEURS ET ARMAGNAC ANCIENS
After Dinner Drinks and Vintage Armagnac

Special Restaurants and Restaurateurs

With Michel's profession and my business travels, we have each had the opportunity to dine in many hundreds of restaurants all over the world. Most of the time, we have nice or even very good meals but occasionally, we encounter something really special. All of the restaurants and restaurateurs mentioned elsewhere in this book, like those whose guest recipes are included, are definitely in the 'very special' category. There are others in that same category, some of which are operating today, and some that can only be fondly remembered, as they no longer exist.

A memorable restaurant for both Michel and me is one where the food is unique and delicious; the service is prompt, friendly and courteous; and the atmosphere is conducive to enjoying the food, company, and conversation. Our favorite restaurants are located in the places we have lived and worked, so America, Canada, England, France, and Ireland are well represented. Memorable restaurants do not have to be expensive, although some are, and in our opinion, worth every penny.

On the "Still Going Strong" List

Favorites in North America

Canlis' Dining Room

Canlis opened in Seattle, in 1950, and has been a perennial award winner since that time. Founder Peter Canlis, who first gained fame with his restaurant in Hawaii, offered fine dining and elegant service and attracted the most discerning clientele. Instead of waiters in tuxedos, he chose the grace, charm and beauty of kimono-clad waitresses. Canlis is now owned by Peter's son, Chris, and his wife, Alice. Their sons, Mark and Brian, are carrying on the family's tradition of fine dining and manage the day-to-day operation. The kimonos are gone now but the menu still emphasizes naturally raised meats and fresh seasonal seafood, with fresh, locally sourced produce, all impeccably prepared and served. Canlis is also famous for its spectacular views, looking out across lakes Union and Washington, all the way to the Cascade Mountains. Of course, every guest always wants a window table.

Tom Douglas

At Tom Douglas' **Dahlia Lounge** in Seattle, owner-chef, Tom, and his wife and business partner, Jackie Cross, have delighted customers from across the country and around the world. Tom and Jackie have three other restaurants but the Dahlia remains our first choice. Tom has also authored two best-selling cookbooks with another just released that is dedicated to crab cakes, one of his signature dishes at the Dahlia.

I particularly like Tom since, like me, he never attended culinary school, although he has accomplished far more as a bootstrapped chef than I might dare to dream. Tom's culinary talents were recognized by the James Beard Foundation, who named him "Best Northwest Chef, 1994" and recently named the Dahlia one of America's Best Restaurants.

190

A recent discovery, thanks to friend and recipe tester, Patrick Kane, has been **The Harvest Vine**, with owner-chef Joseba Jiménez de Jiménez and his partner and wife, Carolin. An inspired chef from the Basque Country, in northern Spain, Joseba also studied classical French cooking in Paris and has created a magnificent tapas restaurant in Seattle. Joseba's commitment to authenticity is apparent in every plate. He constantly searches for genuine Basque ingredients imported from Spain and France or grown here to his particular specifications. I have not found a Spanish restaurant anywhere in Spain that I like more. Joseba's dishes are as original as they are delicious, with each one crafted to tease the palate and leave you anxiously waiting for the next.

Joseba Jimenez

Michel and I both love Japanese food and our mutual first choice for Japanese cuisine, in North America, is **Shiro's**, another of Seattle's highly rated dining establishments. A two-time James Beard nominee, Master Chef Shiro Kashiba has been profiled in every major cuisine periodical including *Bon Appetit*, *The New York Times*, and *USA Today*. In 1997, he and his wife, Ricky, opened Shiro's, in the Belltown area of Downtown Seattle. Shiro's blending of classical Japanese technique with the Pacific Northwest's wealth of local seafood and ingredients has, as Zagat says, "set the bar that others aspire to." Jerry Shriver, writing in USA Today, said, "To get a sense of what it must have been like to watch Picasso at work, grab a seat at the sushi bar at Shiro's and watch Chef/Owner Shiro Kashiba."

Shiro Kashiba

Tommy Toy's Cuisine Chinoise in San Francisco is, without a doubt, my favorite Chinese restaurant in America. It has beautifully decorated dining rooms and the dishes are a spectacular fusion of Chinese and French cuisine. Tommy's Special Signature Dinner is just delicious and each dish is a visual masterpiece that neither Michel nor I has ever been able to resist.

Tra Vigne at St Helena in the Napa Valley is our favorite restaurant in the California wine country. You will not taste more delicious Italian dishes anywhere else. A recent review by *The Artisan* said, "On beautiful summer days, the setting is probably the best in the Napa Valley. On beautiful summer evenings, the place to eat is the balcony of the restaurant. At times we have spent four nights in the Napa Valley and have eaten at Tra Vigne four times."

Tommy Toy's Dining Room

A favorite in Chicago is **Charlie Trotter's Restaurant**, which is widely regarded as one of the finest dining establishments anywhere in the world. Charlie Trotter's offers three daily dégustation menus, all of which are created using the freshest available natural ingredients. The award winning wine list features hundreds of selections from the great wine producing countries of the world. The restaurant has received eight awards from the James Beard Foundation and Chef Trotter is the author of 11 cookbooks.

Le Français Restaurant in Wheeling, Illinois, outside Chicago, was established by Chef Jean Banchet in 1972 and won universal acclaim, as "the Best Restaurant in America," according to *Gourmet Magazine*. Chef Jean retired but the Moran family currently owns the restaurant with their partner, Chef Roland Liccioni, previous Executive Chef at Le Français from 1989 to 1999, who returned in 2005 to take over the kitchen. Since Chef Liccioni has returned, the

Chef Roland Liccioni

tradition of fine dining continues unabated, allowing Le Français to achieve four stars from the *Chicago Tribune*. As you would expect, the wine list at Le Francais is also superb, with a wide selection from all over the world and an expert sommelier to assist with your selections.

The Pump Room

For both of us, another very special restaurant is the **Pump Room**, which is located in the Ambassador East Hotel, on Chicago's Gold Coast. Opened in 1938, the Pump Room was regarded for years as one of America's top dining and entertainment venues. Its diners were the stars of the day; John Barrymore roared for champagne, Bette Davis could be found perched on the piano bench, and Humphrey Bogart and Lauren Bacall celebrated their wedding in the famous Booth One. Judy Garland immortalized the restaurant in the lyrics to Chicago, with the words "we'll eat at the Pump Room/Ambassador East, to say the least."

Michel and I each found the Pump Room in our 20s, he while working as a chef at the Playboy Mansion, and I, on a business trip to Chicago in 1975. The food was and is uniquely American Cuisine but with a continental flair and superb quality. The jazz music is captivating, without drowning out conversations, and the service is flawless.

Favorites in Europe

The Conservatory Dining Room

In London, the absolutely stunning **Conservatory Dining Room**, at the Lanesborough Hotel on Hyde Park Corner is where Chef Paul Gayler and his incredible service team have delighted guests from the far corners of the earth. The dining room is spectacular with a 30-foot ceiling and a vaulted glass roof reminiscent of the Regency Pavilion in Brighton. And, for our money, the Library Bar is simply one of, if not the most enjoyable cocktail venues on earth. With George, Mateo and Stefan overseeing the service and Brian at the piano, the atmosphere is perfect and the service is flawless. It is our 'local' in London, anytime we are there. Managing Director, Geoffrey Gelardi, who comes from a long line of famous hoteliers, has created an oasis in central London that is almost always rated as one of the ten best hotels in the world.

Michel Roux, Jr.

Le Gavroche on Brook Street in London's West End is, in our view, one of the best restaurants anywhere on earth. We are certainly not alone in that opinion as the restaurant's three Michelin stars and countless other awards and accolades attest. Brothers Michel and Albert Roux established Le Gavroche in 1967 and it is been the toast of visitors and local patrons alike, ever since. The kitchen is now in the very able hands of Albert's son, Michel, Jr., and the restaurant continues to delight guests. Its popularity is confirmed by the fact that making reservations at least two weeks in advance is usually required, unless you are just extremely lucky or have an 'in' with the proprietors. We have both had many memorable evenings at Le Gavroche and always look forward, with anticipation, to our next visit.

l'Oustau de Baumanière in Les Baux de Provence, just 10 km from Saint-Rémy, may be the single most celebrated restaurant in Europe. Founded 60 years ago by the late Raymond Thuilier, a noted chef and artist, Baumanière is now owned and operated by Jean-André Charial, grandson of the original chef, and his wife, Geneviève. The setting is spectacular with its beautiful rocky backdrop and the food is even more so. It is also a wine lover's idea of heaven with an incredible list and cellars. Restaurant Manager, Sergio Meloni is a most gracious and welcoming host and even after 25 years at Baumanière, never forgets a returning guest.

l'Oustau de Baumanière

Also in Provence is **Auberge de Noves** in Noves. The kitchen is presided over by a brilliant young chef, Robert Lalleman, the son of one of the original eight founders of Relais & Châteaux. He is the third generation at Auberge and clearly has the family's flair for fine dining and hospitality. The restaurant, which is located in a beautiful country house, is as enticing as the excellent dishes prepared with creativity and an unswerving eye for detail.

At **Le Pont de Brent**, in Brent, Switzerland, Chef Gérard Rabaey has created a magnificent restaurant in this beautiful village in the hills above Montreux and Lake Geneva. The food is just delightful and the service impeccable, with a selection of amazing local Swiss wines as well as many others. The last time Ani and I dined there with friends, we enjoyed a most memorable evening.

The Palace Restaurant in the Four Seasons Hotel, on the Limassol beachfront on the island nation of Cyprus, is another very special restaurant. The hotel itself, recently renovated to a world class standard, is truly a Mediterranean paradise. Every aspect of service throughout the hotel is just excellent but it is the food, of course, that gets our notice. The Palace, featuring gourmet international cuisine, is a special treat. Under the direction of Executive Chef, Panicos Hadjitofi, every dish is prepared to perfection and beautifully presented. Cyprus may be a bit off the beaten track for many North Americans but, since my company has an office there, I have been lucky enough to be a regular visitor.

Panicos Hadjitofi

Villa d'Este on the west shore of Lake Como, in northern Italy, is a special treat. It is a spectacular property on the lakeshore, with vast lawns and gardens, and a terrace where guests can enjoy a dance before or after their dinner. It is one of the most magnificent resort settings anywhere in the world. The menu is traditional Italian haute cuisine and the wine list features many of the most sought-after and rare Italian wines and vintages, as well as many other choices.

An aerial view of Villa d'Este, from above Lake Como

Restaurants on our "Only to be Fondly Remembered" list

Ernie's was a San Francisco institution and "the place to dine." It was owned and operated by Roland and Victor Gotti, brothers whose family had owned Ernie's since 1934. The restaurant was decorated in rich wood and plush red velvet. The menu and wine list were both expansive and we never knew anyone who came away dissatisfied. Stan Berde, long-time business partner, close friend and cooking compatriot first introduced me to Ernie's in 1984. Stan was a personal friend of the Gottis and knew all of the staff by name. The food was exquisitely continental with chefs who knew the meaning of excellence. Michel dined there several times as well and we both agree it was always a delightful experience.

For more than 30 years, Victor Rosellini's **Four-10** was Seattle's most noted Italian restaurant and the cocktail headquarters for Seattle's downtown executive set. Victor, a vibrant and gracious gentleman, was the acknowledged dean of Seattle restaurateurs. The food at Four-10 was simply excellent and service was always of the highest standard. Victor, himself, was a role model for many aspiring restaurateurs.

Robert Rosellini's **Other Place** was a truly special restaurant that is much missed in Seattle. It was called the Other Place because the Rosellini family had two other longer established restaurants; Four-10 and Six-10, that were award-winning establishments before the Other Place opened. It was no time at all before Robert was winning wide acclaim and a plethora of his own awards. It featuring locally sourced foods and wild game, and a superb wine list combined with Robert's expertise always assured that diners would enjoy both their meal and the wines.

Lutèce in Manhattan, where chef and owner, André Soltner, defined elegant cooking in New York and earned three Michelin stars, was one of America's most highly regarded restaurants for more than 30 years.

Another special restaurant in Manhattan, was **Maxwell's Plum**, where I often dined with friends whenever I visited New York. The atmosphere was vibrant and I will always remember their steak tartare and veal medallions with morel sauce.

Victor's

One of my personal favorites was **Victor's**, atop the St. Francis Hotel in San Francisco, which is now still used for catered events. Riding up to the 32nd floor in the exterior glass elevators is still a thrill that not everyone appreciates but, for me, always brings back memories of the many special evenings I spent at Victor's. The view was spectacular and the food and service were even more so. Some nights, the fog would roll in during our meal and envelope the restaurant in its grasp, completely obscuring the view and casting a beautiful pale glow across the room. The effect was magic.

There are many other very special restaurants in the world but those we have mentioned here, whether still in existence or gone but certainly never forgotten, are ones we will always think of most fondly. We also believe that our discoveries will continue and this list will grow as we dine in newly found restaurants around the world. The world of food and wine never stands still. It evolves every day with new chefs and regional fusion cuisines. We hope that you will have as many memorable dining experiences as we have had and, if you have the chance to visit some of our favorites, we hope that you will be just as thrilled as we always are.

APPENDICES

Wine Information

Following is a brief bit of information about wine terminology, wine, grapes and related topics. It is included for reference and we hope you may find it useful.

Wine Bottles & Sizes

In Europe, different wine growing regions tend to use particular bottle shapes. In a majority of cases, the shape of a European wine bottle will tell you where the wine is from. In America, winemakers may use any shape of their choosing and, as a result, the shape of wine bottles in America does not provide any clear indication of where the wine is made. A standard wine bottle usually contains 75 centiliters (750 milliliters) of wine, approximately equivalent to 4/5 of a quart. A half bottle, is usually 37.5 centiliters (375 milliliters), approximately 2/5 of a quart or 4/5 of a pint.

There are also large format bottles, the most common of which are Magnums, equal in volume to two standard bottles, and Double Magnums, equal to four standard bottles. In Burgundy and Champagne, a Double Magnum is called a Jeroboam and in Bordeaux, a Jeroboam is equal to six standard bottles. The largest Champagne bottle is called a Nebuchadnezzar and holds 15 liters, the equivalent of 20 standard bottles.

Canlis Restaurant Wine Cellar

Wine Glasses

The choice of wine glasses, like the choice of wines, is mostly a matter of personal preferences. For me, the feel of a glass in my hand is the most important consideration, after the shape and weight of the glass. I like glasses that are lighter in weight without being so fragile that they easily break. Although I own many different types of wine glasses, I seem to use those pictured most often. From left to right: Burgundy glasses, for either reds or whites; bubble or Claret glasses, for more robust red wines; flutes, for champagne; and taller, gently sloping glasses for white wines.

Wine Varieties & Wines

Wine varieties may take their names from the grapes from which the wine is made or may, in many other cases, have a name that is primarily related to where the wine is made. Most American wine names are based on the principal grape from which the wine is made. French wine names are based more on the area where they are made.

White grapes actually range in color from pale yellow to pale green. Red grapes can be a soft dark pink or a dark purple color. Although you might think that, logically, white wines are made from white grapes and red wines from red grapes, that is often but not always the case. Some white wines are made from red grapes. The determining factor in the color of red wine, which is always made primarily from red grapes, is how long the grape skins are left in the early part of the wine making process, before fermentation. If red grape skins are removed very early in the process, a white wine can result.

Following are descriptions of grape and wine varieties that you may encounter most often.

White Grapes & Wines

Chardonnay (Shar-doan-ay) wines are a highly complex and aromatic white grape. Chardonnays are dry, fruity wines with a pleasant mix of delicate flavors and aromas. It is used extensively in both America and Australia and is the principal white grape grown in Burgundy.

Chenin Blanc (Shen-in Blonk) is grown primarily in the Loire Valley region of France and California. Chenin Blanc is used to make Vouvray and makes dry, crisp, well-balanced fruity wines that age well.

Gewürztraminer (ga-VERTZ-trah-Mee-ner) wines originated in Germany but are also made in the Alsace region of France. Although there are some dry Gewürztraminers, it is primarily known as a sweet wine with a spicy floral bouquet.

Muscadelle (Mus-ka-del) is a white grape variety often used with Sauvignon and Semillon in Graves wines and in Sauternes. Muscadelle matures very fast and has a very pronounced taste.

Pinot Gris (PEE-noh GREE) is an Alsatian grape variety, also called Tokay d'Alsace. Pinot Gris is used for the intense white wines of this region. Pinot Gris grape is a very exacting variety with small bluish grapes. Its character varies depending on good or bad season. It might be light and fruity or robust and typically makes dry and very crisp, acidic white wines.

Riesling (REEZ-ling) is a late ripening grape, which has been cultivated in Germany since the 14th century. Riesling is generally thought of as a sweet wine but Rieslings grown in Germany tend to be slightly tart when compared to those grown in America. There are also specific 'dry' Rieslings produced.

Sauvignon Blanc (so-VEEN-yon Blonk) is often sold in America under the name Fumé Blanc. Sauvignon Blancs are very aromatic and flavorful wines that are available in numerous varieties, from light and dry to full and very slightly sweet.

Semillon Blanc (sem-EEE-yon Blonk) was, at one time, a very popular grape, in France, but no longer receives the attention it once enjoyed. In France, Semillon is primarily used as a blending grape in Bordeaux wines like Sauternes and Sauvignon Blanc. It's more popular in America, where it is used to make slightly dry, crisp fruity white wines.

Viognier (vee-YOH-nyay) is a highly perfumed wine of medium to full body and spicy fruit flavor that is growing in popularity. However, Viognier is difficult to grow and is best served young, as its fruity, floral bouquets tend to fade with time. Viogniers can be an excellent compliment to spicy foods.

Red Grapes & Wines

Cabernet Franc (Ka-bear NAY FRONK) is lighter and fruitier than Cabernet Sauvignon and it is often blended with Sauvignon in making red Bordeaux and many Provence red wines. Cabernet Franc wines may be consumed young or stored for 10 to 15 years. Some American wine makers also use this variety in their wines, often under the Meritage name.

Cabernet Sauvignon (Ka-bear NAY so-VEEN-yon) is a medium to full-bodied wine of deep color that blends well with other wines. French red Bordeaux wines contain Cabernet Sauvignon grapes along with Cabernet Franc. Cabernet Sauvignon wine is aged in oak barrels to enhance its flavor. The wines develop slowly, so the aging process is critical. The grapes themselves are quite durable and are grown in many parts of the world.

Gamay is the primary grape of the Beaujolais region of France. Gamay produces a fast maturing wine with a fresh, fruity, light-bodied taste, using a process called *macération carbonique,* used to retain it fruitiness.

Grenache (Gren-OSH). These sweet grapes produce wines rich in alcohol. Grenache is often used with Syrah and Mourvèdre and is essential in the excellent sweet wines of the Languedoc-Roussillon. It's used in making other French wines, such as Châteauneuf-du-Pape, Côtes-du-Rhône, Coteaux du Languedoc and Côtes de Provence. You may also find Grenache rosé in America.

Merlot (Mare-LO) was, at one time, primarily used as a blending wine because its complex but mellow taste takes the edge off of harsher wines. Many Cabernet Sauvignons contain a percentage of merlot, which makes them ready to drink younger. Today, merlots are very popular, in their own right. Excellent merlots are made from

Northern California to Washington with characteristics similar to medium-bodied Bordeaux. Saint-Émilion, in France, also produces wonderful merlots.

Mourvèdre (Moo-ve-DRA) grapes are prominent in the Rhône Valley. It is one of the older grape variety present in France, which probably originated in Provence. Mourvèdre produces a bluish juicy berry and is used to make full-bodied red wines, as well as rosés. Mourvèdre is found in French wines from Bandol, Gigondas, Châteauneuf-du-Pape and Coteaux du Languedoc. A few American wine makers are now growing this variety.

Petite Sirah (Pet-EET Seer-AH) is the American name for the French Duriff grape but Petite Sirah grapes are actually quite large and purple. Petite Sirah is used primarily as a blending wine and can have a strong tannic taste that benefits from aging. In California, a few wine makers produce Petite Sirah wines that are excellent and we have often had guests think they were drinking expensive Clarets or California reserve Cabernets.

Pinot Noir (PEE-noh NWAR) is the main red grape of the Burgundy region and is the grape used in making the red Sancerre wine. Pinot Noir grapes are difficult to grow and cultivate, tending to prefer cooler climates, which is one reason that Oregon's Willamette Valley and the Carneros region, in California, have become centers for these wines. Pinot Noir is usually medium to deep ruby red in color, full-bodied, quite aromatic and possesses a wide variety of flavors.

Syrah (Seer-AH) is a heavy red wine with a spicy fruit flavor. Syrah is originally a Persian varietal grape, best known for its use in the Rhône area of France. In Australia Syrah is known as Shiraz.

Zinfandel is a full-bodied, dry wine with a deep red hue. Zinfandels are known for their intense fruit flavor. Primarily grown in California, Zinfandels have proven to be popular with growers because of their great versatility and their ease of cultivation. Typically drunk as young wines, most also age well.

Wine Terminology

One of the things that contribute to uncertainty about matching wines to particular foods or dishes is that wine terminology can be a bit complicated. And, sometimes, it's just localized jargon, compounded by the fact that different 'experts' will use the same term to mean different things or different terms to mean the same thing.

When we talk about styles of wine, we're referring primarily to the strength of the flavor of a wine, whether red, white or rosé and sparkling or fortified. Wine terms do not have the same meanings as the colloquial understanding of the words that are used.

A 'dry' wine isn't, in fact, dry at all, if we apply the dictionary definition of the word, *"Free from liquid or moisture."* In wine terminology, 'dry' is essentially the opposite of 'sweet' as opposed to being the opposite of 'wet.' Here are very brief explanations of some of the terms that we've used to describe wines in this book.

TASTING TALK AND TERMS

Acidity	A wine's acidity should be detectable as sharpness in the mouth, particularly around the front sides of the tongue. It should be neither too obvious nor absent. It provides a refreshing sensation in white wines, and grip and balance in reds. Its absence makes a wine dull and 'flabby,' a defect in any wine but a disaster in sweet wines which to me become undrinkable without it. Too much acidity makes the wine difficult to drink.
Aftertaste	The taste left on the palate after the wine has been swallowed. The persistence of aftertaste, also described as the 'length,' is used by some as an indication of the quality of the wine.
Austere	A term used to describe a wine that is not yet ready to drink. This term is often used to describe young, tannic wines. Such wines may simply be immature and often will improve with age.
Balance	The taste of a wine is influenced primarily by four factors: tannin, acidity, texture and flavor. A 'balanced' wine is one that has a complementary combination of these factors.
Blind tasting	If you are ever poured a wine without knowing what it is, this is a blind tasting. The advantage of a blind tasting, usually achieved by simply covering the label - is that it removes all prejudices about the wine, and you have to judge it entirely on its merits.
Body	A wine with plenty of flavor, alcohol, extract and tannin may be described as full-bodied. It is a less specific term than 'texture.'
Closed	A wine where there is no, or very little, aroma ('nose') or flavor. Many young wines are described as 'closed' before they 'open' again as they age and become mature or ready to drink.
Corked	Wines that have spoiled. A corked wine is not one with bits of cork floating in it. Technically, a corked wine has been contaminated by trichloroanisole. This chemical compound is the product of mould infection in the cork. It may result in a wine that simply lacks fruit and can be difficult to detect, even when tasting. It may also be very obvious, with cardboard or mushroom tastes and musty, dank aromas and flavors. These corked wines are usually completely undrinkable.
Dry	Essentially this is the opposite of sweet, although a wine that tastes dry still contains sugar, perhaps just a few grams per bottle. The term 'dry' can also be used to describe the tannins or mouth feel, when it refers to the dry, puckering sensation the wine imparts.

Entry	Describing the wine on entry is to describe your impression of the wine as it lands in your mouth. Followed by 'mid-palate', 'finish' and 'length'.
Finish	The finish is how the wine tastes at the point of, and just after, swallowing. After finish comes the 'length.'
Forward	This denotes a wine which the taster feels is developing quickly, and is ready to drink before it might otherwise be expected. Forward is the opposite of 'backward.'
Hollow	A wine that lacks flavor and texture, often through the mid-palate, would be described as hollow.
Integrated	When the components of wine, such as tannin, oak and acidity, fade as the wine develops, they are said to have integrated. This refers to wines that are past their prime for drinking and are said to be 'fading' or 'going downhill.'
Legs	This refers to the tear-like tracks that a wine makes down the side of a glass after it has been swirled. In France, these are called *larmes*, which means tears.
Length	Describes how long the flavor of the wine persists on the palate after it has been swallowed. A lengthy persistence of flavor may be taken as a sign of quality, but timing it, as some people do, is in our opinion an affectation.
Mid-palate	When describing how the wine develops in the mouth, you are describing the mid-palate. After taking a mouthful of wine, hold it in the mouth, and see what you get from the wine. Does it have enough flavor and texture? What are the tannins and acidity like?
Mousse	A description of the *mousse* refers to how fizzy a sparkling wine seems in the mouth. A soft *mousse* is not too fizzy. A harsh *mousse* is too fizzy, like a very carbonated mineral water or soft drink.
Nose	The nose of a wine simply describes how a wine smells.
Oakey (also Oaken)	A term that describes the taste that a wine that has been stored in oak casks or barrels derives from the oak. The longer a wine is aged in oak, the more the wine will take on an oakey flavor.
Structure	When a wine is described as having structure, the taster is referring to the tannin and acidity levels. These elements give the wine a presence in the mouth; without them wine would tend towards a flabby, fruit flavored drink.
Texture	The texture of a wine describes how the wine feels in the mouth. Is it silky, velvety, rounded, or smooth? It is a more specific term than 'body', which describes the general impact of the wine.
Toasty	Toasty literally means just that, smelling or tasting of toast. It may reflect toasting of the barrels, when they may be placed around a fire (sometimes as they are made), the flames altering the physical and chemical composition of the surface of the wood, and subsequently this will have a significant effect on the flavor of the wine.

Conversion Tables for Cooking

Many cooks struggle with recipes based on either metric or American and English (Imperial) measures, when they are familiar with only one and not the other. A further complication is that some American dry weight measures have different metric equivalents, depending on the density of the ingredients. These tables give you an instant conversion for varying measures, as well as the formulae for conversion.

Oven Cooking Temperatures (also for deep frying)

Fahrenheit	Celsius	Gas Mark		Fahrenheit	Celsius	Gas Mark
225 F	110 C	¼		375 F	190 C	5
250 F	120 C	½		400 F	200 C	6
275 F	140 C	1		425 F	220 C	7
300 F	150 C	2		450 F	230 C	8
325 F	160 C	3		475 F	240 C	9
350 F	180 C	4		500 F	260 C	10

Note that 'Gas Marks' are found on some European ovens, instead of temperatures.

Fluid Measures

American	Fluid Ounces	Metric		American	Fluid Ounces	Metric
2 Tbsp	1 fl oz	30 ml		1¾ cups	14 fl oz	420 ml
¼ cup	2 fl oz	60 ml		2 cups	16 fl oz	480 ml
⅓ cup	2½ fl oz	75 ml		1 pint	16 fl oz	480 ml
½ cup	4 fl oz	120 ml		3 cups	24 fl oz	720 ml
⅔ cup	5 fl oz	150 ml		4 cups	32 fl oz	960 ml
¾ cup	6 fl oz	180 ml		2 pints	32 fl oz	0.96 litres
1 cup	8 fl oz	240 ml		1 quart	32 fl oz	0.96 litres
1¼ cups	10 fl oz	300 ml		2 quarts	64 fl oz	1.9 litres
1½ cups	12 fl oz	360 ml		3 quarts	96 fl oz	2.9 litres
1⅔ cups	13 fl oz	375 ml		4 quarts	128 fl oz	3.8 litres

Note that: 1 teaspoon (tsp) = 5 ml; and 1 tablespoon (Tbsp) = 3 tsp = 15 ml.

Standard measure conversions for cooking temperatures and fluids are always the same for all purposes. Fluid measures, whether American or metric, always indicate volumes, and temperature equivalents always indicate relative levels of heat or cold.

Dry Measures

American	Metric	American	Metric	American	Metric
1 oz	30 g	¾ lb	360 g	3½ lbs	1.6 kg
2 oz	60 g	1 lb	450 g	4 lbs	1.8 kg
3 oz	90 g	1¼ lb	570 g	4½ lbs	2 kg
4 oz	120 g	1½ lb	690 g	5 lbs	2.25 kg
¼ lb	120 g	1¾ lb	810 g	5½ lbs	2.5 kg
⅓ lb	150 g	2 lbs	900 g	6 lbs	2.7 kg
½ lb	230 g	2½ lbs	1.15 kg	7 lbs	3.2 kg
⅔ lb	300 g	3 lbs	1.4 kg	8 lbs	3.6 kg

American Measurement Equivalents

Fluid Measure Equivalents

1 quart = 2 pints = 4 cups = 32 fl oz
1 pint = 2 cups = 16 fluid ounces
1 cup = 8 fl ounce
1 fluid ounce = 2 tablespoons

Dry Measure Equivalents

1 pound (lb) = 16 ounces
1 cup = 8 ounces
1 ounce = 2 tablespoons
1 tablespoon = 3 teaspoons (Fluid or Dry)

Specific Dry Ingredient Equivalents

The dry measure tables shown above are adequate for almost all cooking purposes. There is, however, a complication in converting from standard American to metric measures and that is because different dry ingredients have varying densities. Standard American dry measures are a combination of volumes and weights. A tablespoon (Tbsp) or a cup measures volume whereas dry ounces and pounds (lbs) measure weight. Metric dry measures, expressed in grams (g) and kilograms (kg) always are measures of weight. The table below provides examples.

Flour		Sugar		Butter	
American	Metric	American	Metric	American	Metric
2 Tbsp	15 g	2 Tbsp	25 g	2 Tbsp	30 g
¼ cup	30 g	¼ cup	50 g	¼ cup	60 g
½ cup	60 g	½ cup	100 g	½ cup	120 g
¾ cup	90 g	¾ cup	150 g	¾ cup	180 g
1 cup	120 g	1 cup	200 g	1 cup	240 g

The equivalent measures for flour are the same as the standards but a given volume of sugar or butter is heavier than the same volume of flour. This only matters if you are converting from a Canadian or European recipe giving metric weights. Simply remember that heavier, more dense dry ingredients weigh more and translate to relatively smaller American volume measures.

Acknowledgements

This book and our culinary lives are products of the many individuals who influenced our early interests in food and wine, as well as colleagues and friends, with whom we have collaborated, in home and restaurant kitchens, over the years.

For Michel, Chef Denis Gayte, in Avignon, and Chef Monsieur La Planche, at the Savoy, started him on a 40-year culinary journey that still continues. Michel Cippola, Executive Chef at the Playboy Club and Resort, who first brought Michel to America, with Chefs Jean Banchet and Gérard Parrat. Jean Banchet, the owner-chef at Le Français. Michel's colleagues at The Mirabeau: Owner-Managers, André Mercier and Gilbert Barthe; Sous-chefs Serge Clerc and Jacques Jarriault; and Captain, Phillip Gayte, Denis' son, were key members of the team that made the restaurant a success.

Long-time friend, Anton Mossiman, the famous London chef, restaurant owner and cookbook author, who Michel first met when they were members of the Braniff Airways International Board of Chefs. Gérard Parrat, fellow chef and émigré to Seattle, who's own classic French restaurant, Gérard's Relais de Lyon, was located in the Seattle suburb of Woodinville. Otto Denkinger, Executive Chef at the Seattle Yacht Club, who became a sort of Seattle 'Godfather' to Michel and introduced him into the local chefs' community and social network. Stella Richman, owner of the White Elephant Club, in London, who ruled the club with a velvet glove covering an iron hand and, underneath it all, a good heart.

And last, but not least, Anne Marie and Bruno Donche-Gay, Denis Gayte's daughter and grandson, and Bruno's immensely talented Brazilian wife, Cynthia. It was Anne Marie and Bruno who enticed Michel back to Provence, after nearly 40 years, to the Hôtel du Palais des Papes. And Cynthia, who helped Michel and me establish La Table de Michel; organizing the initial property investment and financial planning, interior decoration and even waiting tables in the first few months of operation.

For me, Bill Murphy and Egon Shultz, Chef and Manager, respectively, at Seattle's Casa Villa Restaurant, gave me my first experience and lessons in a restaurant kitchen. Bruno Patassini, Maître d'Hôtel at Victor's, atop the St Francis Hotel in San Francisco, showed me the art of tableside preparation and service. David O'Connor, the Master Sommelier, at Victor's, provided me with my earliest exposure to and lessons about fine wines. The late John Louie, chef and owner of the Golden Coin Restaurant, in Seattle, gave me my first lessons in Cantonese cooking.

Noted Seattle restaurateur, Victor Rosellini, who provided inspiration for early forays into gourmet Italian cooking and his restaurateur son and my schoolmate, Robert, contributed immeasurably to my knowledge of wines. Stan Berde, a business partner and dear friend in San Francisco, and an inspired cook in his own right, exposed me to the best of California wines and his many Napa and Sonoma winemaker friends. Collaborating in a kitchen with Stan, who was a 'naked' chef, in the traditional meaning of the word, long before Jamie Oliver, was an adventure, every time.

This book would not have been possible without the help and support of enthusiastic home cooking friends and family, who devoted the time and energy to testing all of the recipes. They are: my current work colleagues, Anthony Major, Roisin McCool, Adam Todd and Josh Rogers; daughter, Alana, long-time friend, Dhiren Fonseca, an Expedia executive and avid cook; Patrick Kane, from Northern Ireland, now living in Seattle; dear friends and former work colleagues, Cathy Allen and Nicola (Walsh) Hampton, who was my 'head coach' on living and working in Ireland; personal friend in London, Jerome O'Mara, a former banking executive and graduate of the New School Culinary Institute in New York, where Julia Child taught; Kim Piotrowski, a current bank executive at Columbia Bank in Tacoma; Linda Jensen, another Seattle cooking enthusiast friend and former cooking teacher; and Stan Berde, himself, whose testing comments provided key refinements and lots of humor.

Also deserving our heartfelt thanks are our professional chef reviewers, Bill Morris, Executive Chef, at Seattle's exclusive Rainier Club; Paul Gayler, Executive Chef at the Lanesborough Hotel in London; and Robert Mancuso, Executive Chef, at The Country Club, outside Boston, all of whom took their time to critique the manuscript and make many very useful observations.

Master Sommelier, David O'Connor, from San Francisco, reviewed all of our wine suggestions and pairings, providing many refinements. Long-time friend and former work colleague, Paul Jaenicke, who went to culinary school when he retired, reviewed recipes and provided a consistency check on the draft manuscript.

The Behnke family and Carl and Renée Behnke, co-owners of Sur La Table, also have our sincere thanks, both for their wonderful gourmet kitchen stores and for generously providing equipment for our photography sessions. Established in 1972 in Seattle's Pike Place Market, today Sur La Table operates more than 50 stores nationwide, with new stores opening every year.

Commercial restaurant supplier, Bargreen-Ellingson, in Seattle, provided glasses, dishes, flatware and other table accessories for our photography sessions. John Sheard and his colleague Jan, of Cookin', a wonderful independent gourmet kitchen store, in Seattle,

provided advice, encouragement and equipment.

Friend, neighbor, professional chef and cookbook author, Heidi Rabel, reviewed our drafts and provided invaluable insights. Professional food writer and editor, Cynthia Nims' literary, cooking and cookbook expertise made certain that the entire book was technically correct and that all of the content contributed to meeting our goals. Long-time friend, writer and editor, Pat Corning, edited our stories and information content to assure that they read properly and conveyed our messages effectively. And finally, my daughter Alana, proofed the final text, and my bi-lingual wife, Ani, corrected my atrocious French spellings and grammar.

Michel Deville & Brendan O'Farrell

View of Seattle Center and Lake Union

Photography and Credits

Since I had never even owned a camera until a few years ago, I had absolutely no idea of what an incredible combination of art and science goes into taking really professional photographs, of any kind, let alone images of food. Fortunately, in our research, we managed to find Christopher Conrad and his team at Conrad & Company, right in Seattle. They have a fully equipped studio, with a commercial kitchen and all of the most up-to-date digital photography equipment and technology.

Christopher and his team, former chef, food stylist and now Conrad & Company's Marketing Manager, Charmaine Nicole, and Studio Manager, technology wizard and Second Shooter, Toni Dysert, made all of our dishes come alive, in print. Christopher's knowledge of sets and lighting, and his artistic talents were priceless. Charmaine helped us to understand how to plate dishes, in the best way for the camera. And Toni's work, assisting Christopher on the set and using the computer to polish the images was quite amazing. Christopher shot all of our food photos and the cover portrait and Toni took impromptu shots of the team to preserve a record of our time together in the studio.

Christopher collaborated closely with Ani, as the designer, selecting the plates and background pieces for each photo, and making sure that everything was ready for the dishes. But, most of all, they were a joy to work with, never failing to explain the why of what should be done, and keeping us focused on the tasks at hand, with lots of laughter and good cheer.

Other photographs, listed below, came from other professional photographers and a few friends, who are experienced amateur photographers. In particular, long-time friends, Christopher Todd and Dhiren Fonseca, took dozens of photos, 'on location', when they visited us in Provence.

All other photos contained in this book are either from our own private archives or, in the cases of chefs, restaurants and restaurateurs, were provided by the individuals and organizations mentioned.

Baldwin, Kate: Page 171
Borrelli, Joe (StockFood): Page 110
Burton, Susan: Page 38
Canlis Restaurant: Pages 190, 196
Conrad, Christopher: Recipe photography and pages 24, 183, 197, 207
Corbis: Pages 106, 125
Dysert, Toni: Pages 16, 134
Fonseca, Dhiren: Pages 6, 96, 166
Lamont, Dan (Tom Douglas): Page 190
Merrion Hotel, Dublin: Page 122
Murray, Neil: Page 8
Nickell, Diana (Klutina Salmon Charters): Page 124
O'Farrell, Ani: Pages 4, 5, 17, 25, 38, 46, 68, 74, 78, 83, 186, 205
O'Farrell, Brendan: Pages 19, 20, 21, 22
Randy (Lucky Lady Charters): Page 114
Rapp, Melissa (Original Impulses): Spices, page 154
Todd, Christopher: Pages 3, 12, 18, 23, 38, 42, 56, 58, 82, 83, 116, 144, 162, 181
Wafik, Amar (Al-Sultan restaurant): Page 100
Winkellmann, Bernhard (StockFood): Page 26
Zimmerman, Ron (The Herbfarm): Page 158

Photograph by Christopher Conrad

Food & Wine Resources

Throughout this book, we have referred to kitchen tools and equipment, wines and styles of wine, and food ingredients. Here are some of the resources I returned to again and again while writing this book, as well as website links for food producers, and food organizations.

KITCHEN TOOLS AND EQUIPMENT

- Gourmet Kitchen Store, at **www.gourmetkitchenstore.com**
- Sur La Table, at **www.surlatable.com**
- Williams Sonoma, at **www.williams-sonoma.com**
- The 'Kitchen and Housewares' section at **www.amazon.com**

WINE INFORMATION

The Internet is also a great place to start, if you want information about wines. The wine sites I have found most useful, include:

- The Wine Doctor, at **www.thewinedoctor.com**, a UK-based site from Chris Kissack, who provides lots of general and technical information, as well as lots of advice and opinions;
- The Wine Spectator, at **www.winespectator.com**, perhaps the most complete source of wine information, including tasting notes and hundreds of articles on any wine topic that may be of interest;
- Steve Tanzer's site, at **www.wineaccess.com**, also a terrific reference for finding out about particular wines and commentaries;
- The French Wine Guide, at **www.terroir-france.com**, which is the official site of the French wine industry;
- Kermit Lynch Wine Merchant, at **www.kermitlynch.com**, a site with lots of information resources by the man that Wine Critic, Robert Parker, described as "One of our country's most important, influential and, dare I say, historically significant importers of wine."
- Nat Decants Free Wine E-Newsletter: Award-winning journalist, Natalie MacLean, publishes a by-weekly newsletter that contains a wealth of information about wines, food matching, serving and cellaring tips, and related topics. Sign up to receive it at **www.nataliemaclean.com**.

Another excellent reference on this subject is *Matching Food & Wine - Classic and Not So Classic Combinations* by Michel Roux, Jr., Chef at London's Le Gavroche Restaurant. His knowledge of wine and food pairings is extraordinary and the book is filled with wonderful tips, as well as delicious recipes.

If you want a tool to keep track of your own cellar and have access to information on tens of thousands of wines, Eric Levine, a former Microsoft manager and wine lover, has created a Wine Community website that is free to individuals. The functionality is extremely robust. You can register at **www.cellartracker.com**.

To find out about current retail prices for specific wines, go to **www.wine-searcher.com**.

Beef Information Resources

The National Cattlemen's Beef Association at **www.beef.org**

Cheese Information Resources

California Cheese producers' website at **www.realcaliforniacheese.com**
Farmstead Cheese Company, Point Reyes, California at **www.pointreyescheese.com**
Cabot Creamery Cooperative, Vermont, at **www.cabotcheese.com**
Wisconsin cheese information at **www.wisdairy.com**

Gourmet Chocolates

If it is gourmet chocolates or chocolate sauces that you are after visit either:
Fran's Chocolates at **www.franschocolates.com** or
Joel Durand, Chocolatier at **www.chocolat-durand.com**.

Lamb Information

American lamb Board at **www.americanlamb.com**
Farmer Sharp - Herdwick Lamb from Cumbria at **www.farmersharp.co.uk**

Produce Tips

For a wonderful reference on choosing quality produce, Carol Ann Kates' *Secret Recipes from the Corner Market*, by Penny Lane Press, provides a wealth of information and detailed tips on choosing more than 90 different fruits and vegetables. **www.secretrecipesfromthecornermarket.com**.

Slow Food

The slow food movement is a worldwide effort to promote healthier eating, use naturally grown and produced foodstuffs and the pleasures of cooking and dining. There are slow food organizations in many countries, which provide a wealth of information, and an international organization with more than 80,000 members. Visit:
www.slowfood.com and **www.slowfoodusa.org**

Spices

Get spice information and purchase quality spices on-line:
Spice Islands Trading Company at **www.spiceislands.com**
Vann's Spices at **www.vannsspices.com**

INDEX